THE HIDDEN COSTS OF REWARD:

New Perspectives on the Psychology of Human Motivation

List of Contributors

James Chambers
Cornell University
Ithaca, New York
John C. Condry
Cornell University
Ithaca, New York
Mihaly Csikszentmihalyi
Committee on Human Development
Chicago, Illinois
Edward L. Deci
University of Rochester
Rochester, New York
David Greene
SRI International
Menlo Park, California

Arie W. Kruglanski
Tel-Aviv University
Tel-Aviv, Israel
Mark R. Lepper
Stanford University
Stanford, California
John C. McCullers
Oklahoma State University
Stillwater, Oklahoma
Kenneth O. McGraw
University of Mississippi
University, Mississippi
Joseph Porac
University of Rochester
Rochester, New York

THE HIDDEN COSTS OF REWARD:

New Perspectives on the Psychology of Human Motivation

EDITED BY

MARK R. LEPPER
Stanford University

DAVID GREENE
SRI International

 LAWRENCE ERLBAUM ASSOCIATES, PUBLISHERS

1978　　Hillsdale, New Jersey

DISTRIBUTED BY THE HALSTED PRESS DIVISION OF

JOHN WILEY & SONS

New York　　Toronto　　London　　Sydney

Copyright ©1978 by Lawrence Erlbaum Associates, Inc.
   All rights reserved. No part of this book may be reproduced in any
form, by photostat, microform, retrieval system, or any other means,
without the prior written permission of the publisher.

Lawrence Erlbaum Associates, Inc., Publishers
62 Maria Drive
Hillsdale, New Jersey 07642

Distributed solely by Halsted Press Division
John Wiley & Sons, Inc., New York

Library of Congress Cataloging in Publication Data
Main entry under title:

The Hidden costs of reward.

   Includes bibliographical references.
   1.   Reward (Psychology)—Addresses, essays, lectures.
2.   Motivation (Psychology)—Addresses, essays, lectures.
I.   Lepper, Mark R.   II.   Greene, David, 1945–
BF319.5.R48H5   152.5   78-15279
ISBN 0-470-26487-X

Printed in the United States of America

Contents

Preface

In recent years, the most prevalent approach to the study of rewards and reinforcement processes has been an empirical, functional analysis. In this tradition, reinforcers are defined by their positive effects on task performance and the subsequent frequency of the responses on which they are contingent. The scientific and practical benefits of this approach have been numerous and highly publicized. Systematic reinforcement programs derived from this model have proved successful, time and again, in helping to change maladaptive behavior patterns, even with individuals for whom other treatment programs had consistently failed.

By contrast, the common theme among the contributors to this volume is that there are potential costs involved in the indiscriminate use of explicit reward systems and that these costs have received little scrutiny. In support of this contention, the contributors provide considerable evidence that tangible rewards may have negative as well as positive effects on both task performance and subsequent choice behavior. In presenting these data, our fundamental aim is to expand the scope of inquiry relevant to the study of human motivation. Most generally, the book constitutes an appeal for closer consideration of "contextual" and "intrinsic" determinants of behavior—factors that appear to have received disproportionately little attention within the reinforcement Zeitgeist that has prevailed in recent years.

There is no denying that the data in this book have been controversial; in fact, much more controversial than they need have been. One need not discard the Law of Effect to recognize that there are questions concerning the consequences of the use of rewards that are not addressed by this analysis. Nor do data suggesting that the inappropriate use of rewards can have detrimental consequences, under some circumstances, imply that systematic incentive programs cannot be used, under other conditions, to produce significant benefits. The question is not whether reward programs are good or bad, but how they can be used most effectively and how their effectiveness should be evaluated.

This volume provides no final answers to these questions. The papers presented here are intended to acquaint the reader with the most recent research and theory concerning the conditions under which rewards may have detrimental, as well as beneficial effects, and the processes that may underlie such effects. This work is new, and our formulations necessarily tentative. If the presentations serve to alert the reader to the complexity of the study of rewards in their social context, the book will have served its purpose.

This volume is divided into three parts. The first section encompasses two introductory chapters that provide an overview of the principal historical contexts from which the work in this volume has derived. McCullers (Chapter 1) reviews early accounts of detrimental effects of rewards on performance and learning in the experimental laboratory and contrasts these early approaches with the more influential current models in which reinforcers, by definition, have only positive effects on behavior. Kruglanski (Chapter 2) approaches the issue from a social-psychological perspective and considers the history of findings that suggest an inverse relationship between the salience of extrinsic incentives employed to produce a given response and the subsequent likelihood of, and attitudes toward, that response.

The second section comprises five original, integrative essays in which the contributors summarize their own research programs and related work and present their current theoretical perspectives on this field. Although it is the convergence of empirical findings across these historically independent research programs that provided the stimulus to this volume, the differences in approach and theoretical orientation appearing in these chapters provide the reader with a variety of unsolved problems and questions for further research. The opening essay by McGraw (Chapter 3) reviews evidence concerning the effects of reward on performance in common experimental learning tasks and seeks to specify when increments and decrements in performance are likely to occur. Condry and Chambers (Chapter 4) focus on the process of learning and the manner in which this process is affected by the motivational context in which an activity is presented. Kruglanski (Chapter 5) considers the effects of rewards on task performance and subsequent behavior in terms of the attributions individuals make concerning their reasons for engaging in activities. Lepper and Greene (Chapter 6) examine the consequences of undertaking activities as means or as ends in terms of the attributional and the attentional processes by which rewards may produce detrimental effects on task performance and subsequent interest in the activity. Finally, Deci and Porac (Chapter 7) consider the effects of rewards on behavior from the perspective of cognitive evaluation theory, in terms of the different functions served by the information rewards convey.

In the final section of the book, several of the contributors examine some of the implications and limitations of the data presented in the preceding chapters. Condry (Chapter 8) discusses the implications of the hidden costs of rewards for the socialization of children. Deci (Chapter 9) examines the dependence of prescriptive judgments on one's goals and values in evaluating reward programs. Csikszentmihalyi (Chapter 10) considers the implications for society of the fact that many activities can be either onerous or enjoyable as a function of the social context and the skills and frame of mind of the actor. Finally, Lepper and Greene (Chapter 11) discuss the goals, procedures, and presuppositions that underlie the research reported in this volume and compare and contrast them with those that underlie traditional applications of reinforcement procedures to solve social problems. Understanding the benefits and costs likely to result from the use of reward programs in applied settings, they argue, requires attention to these issues and the different parameters embraced by each of these approaches.

Although somewhat obscured by differences in terminology, emphasis, and interpretation, there are a few central themes that run through the research reported in this volume. It is clear that contingent extrinsic rewards generally increase the probability of the rewarded behavior in similar situations; however, their use also has other, less visible, and potentially detrimental, consequences. In this volume, these consequences are viewed as the result of several collateral processes simultaneously affected by the use of salient extrinsic rewards.

For example, the promise of extrinsic incentives often serves to focus an individual's attention on aspects of performance directly relevant to the attainment of those rewards. This focusing of attention on instrumentally-relevant response parameters may improve performance along those selected dimensions. At the same time, it may also result in performance decrements along other dimensions not seen as relevant to the attainment of reward. Thus, the availability of extrinsic rewards can affect the criteria a person employs in deciding whether to approach, how to engage in, and when to terminate engagement in activities for which rewards are offered.

Similarly, contingent extrinsic rewards often provide significant information about an individual's competence. In many contexts, rewards serve to define or signal success or failure at a task, or to provide explicit evidence concerning the adequacy of a person's performance relative to others. Such information can affect one's feelings of effectance or perceptions of competence, and thereby influence his or her subsequent approach to, or enjoyment of, the activity in question.

Finally, the explicit use of extrinsic rewards to modify a person's behavior may also make issues of volition and compulsion salient to that person. In that case, their presence could affect the individual's perceptions of control and/or attributions concerning the intrinsic value of the previously rewarded activity. These processes can result in a redefinition of the conditions under which the individual would expect to enjoy or would choose to engage in this same activity in the future, in the absence of further extrinsic rewards.

Through the study of these collateral processes, the authors of this volume aspire to a better understanding of the "hidden costs" (as well as the more obvious benefits) of the use of extrinsic rewards to control behavior. The shared goal that unites the contributors is the search for appropriate conceptual analyses of these processes, their empirical manifestations, and their social consequences.

That there is substantially more commonality to our various efforts than may be superficially apparent became obvious when the editors attempted to construct the subject index for this volume. Because this field of study is, as yet, embryonic and lacks a clear consensus on fundamental terms and concepts, the design of a subject index that would both do justice to the formulations of individual authors and guide the reader to points of common argument and discussion proved a considerable challenge. As a consequence, the index to this volume evolved into a significantly more intricate construction than might be expected for a volume of this sort. We hope that it will serve as a useful supplement to direct the reader to the major themes that recur, in slightly different guises, across the chapters of the book.

The idea to assemble this volume arose at a symposium organized by John McCullers and presented to the 1975 meeting of the American Psychological Association in Chicago, Illinois. This symposium brought together investigators independently pursuing closely related research programs in laboratories literally continents apart, and made evident the common themes among their separate lines of evidence relating to the hidden costs of rewards. An edited collection, in which each of the contributors could present a coherent theoretical summary and account of his findings, seemed a sensible way to go beyond tantalizing, but truncated, convention papers.

In the two years between convention commitments and the completion of a final manuscript, much has happened. New research has been completed, theoretical formulations have been sharpened, and numerous revisions have been made in our initial plans. The result is an up-to-date report on the current state of research and theory concerning the potential, and generally unrecognized, costs that may result from the inappropriate use of rewards and constraints.

One decision emanating from our initial discussions—that each of the contributors would provide comments on the first drafts of the others' chapters— aided us substantially in our task of editing this volume. Although not all of the advice generated by this process (or that contained in our own sage editorial comments) found its way into subsequent revisions, the exchange of ideas stimulated by this cross-editing process clarified for all of us some of the important points of agreement and disagreement among the contributors. The present volume also benefited greatly from the assistance of other colleagues. Teresa Amabile, Janet Dafoe, and Jerry Sagotsky all read substantial portions of this book and shared their reactions with us. Though their facility in pointing out significant theoretical shortcomings and obtuse passages was alarming, their wise counsel and insightful critiques were of great assistance. Likewise, the excellent editorial assistance of Phyllis Amabile, Gail Hampton, and Susan Lyte helped to turn some of the more ponderous prose into intelligible English. Finally, Ruth Prehn, Patricia Hallenbeck, and Suzanne Taylor provided indispensible assistance in turning muddled manuscripts into clean and seemingly cogent chapters.

Preparation of this volume was also facilitated by financial support from several sources. Our own research described in this volume, as well as the compilation of the collection, was supported, in part, by Research Grants MH-24134 from the National Institute of Mental Health and HD-MH-09814 from the National Institute of Child Health and Human Development. Additional financial support was provided by the Department of Psychology at Carnegie-Mellon University during David Greene's tenure there. Nor would much of our research have been possible without the continual encouragement and assistance of Edith M. Dowley, Director, and the staff of the Bing Nursery School at Stanford University. Development of a number of the theoretical formulations presented in this volume was also aided by a fellowship to the senior editor from the Andrew W. Mellon Foundation.

Equally significant support of a different sort came from family and friends. Jeanne Wallace Lepper provided significant insights and assistance on many levels throughout this venture; Geoffrey Lepper a model of enthusiasm and intrinsic motivation. Their continuous encouragement is gratefully acknowledged. John Carroll's equanimity is widely appreciated, and its contribution to this project also deserves acknowledgment. The intangible rewards of our interactions with them helped to sustain our intrinsic interest in this project.

Mark R. Lepper
David Greene

THE HIDDEN COSTS OF REWARD:

New Perspectives on the Psychology of Human Motivation

BACKGROUND

There are many histories that might be written concerning the study of the "hidden costs" of reward. Social philosophers from Locke to Dewey have concerned themselves with the manner in which rewards and punishments may be used most effectively to motivate performance and shape behavior. Likewise, much of modern-day experimental psychology had its roots in early laboratory investigations of the effects of rewards and punishments on learning and performance.

The two papers in this introductory section, however, focus in some detail on the two experimental traditions that have most directly shaped the thoughts and research of the contributors to this volume.

McCullers (Chapter 1) traces the history of the study of detrimental effects of rewards on measures of performance and learning from its roots in the study of motivational processes in animals, and he describes the theoretical models offered to deal with evidence of detrimental effects of reinforcement procedures observed in that context. These early theoretical models are then contrasted with an operant approach in which reinforcers are defined empirically and hence, by definition, have positive effects on behavior. This approach, McCullers maintains, has helped to blind us to the possibility that there may be "hidden costs" to the use of rewards.

Kruglanski (Chapter 2) examines a quite different tradition concerned with the social–psychological distinction between compliance and internalization or intrinsic and extrinsic motivation. The significance and interpretation of detrimental effects of rewards or other extrinsic constraints are traced from their roots in the experimental social psychology tradition begun by Lewin and his students to their current incarnation in the area of attribution theory and related theoretical formulations.

1 Issues in Learning and Motivation

John C. McCullers
Oklahoma State University

Given the title and general theme of this volume, it is clear that the reader is being asked to consider the perhaps surprising notion that reward can have adverse effects on intrinsic motivation and objective task performance. Some evidence and argument in support of that idea is presented in the following chapters. In this chapter, we raise the question of whether and to what extent the idea that reward can have detrimental effects on motivation and performance is in conflict with existing theory.

We shall begin with a discussion of theoretical principles that might account for the detrimental effects of reward. From available alternatives, we have selected three possibilities: The Yerkes–Dodson law, the Hull–Spence theory, and reinforcement contrast phenomena. All three reflect different perspectives and involve different explanatory mechanisms. These three theoretical viewpoints have been around in psychology for years and are rather widely known. If traditional theories of learning and motivation contain the necessary mechanisms to account for some of the adverse effects of rewards, as we believe they do, we then are left with another question: In what sense should the idea that rewards can have adverse effects be considered at all surprising? The remainder of the chapter, following the discussion of theoretical mechanisms, is devoted to this second question.

DO CLASSICAL THEORIES OF LEARNING AND MOTIVATION PROVIDE FOR A DETRIMENTAL EFFECT OF REWARD?

As we review our three classic theoretical positions and how they might account for reward's detrimental effects, it may be helpful to consider also reward's general relation to motivation and behavior for each theory. This may help us to identify the boundary conditions of any detrimental effects of reward and clarify the circumstances under which reward would be expected to have an enhancing effect.

The Yerkes–Dodson Law

One of the earliest expressions of the relationship between motivation and performance is contained in the curvilinear or U-shaped function first observed by Yerkes and Dodson (1908), since known as the Yerkes–Dodson law. According to this "law," increasing the intensity or level of motivation will enhance performance up to a point; after that, further motivation will result in poorer performance. This relationship was found to hold for difficult tasks. With easy tasks, however, performance generally continues to improve with increasing motivation.

Most of the empirical support for the Yerkes–Dodson law has come from studies with animals where the experimental tasks, both easy and difficult, have been mainly discrimination-learning problems. Motivational level in these situations has been manipulated typically through variations in the amount of noxious stimulation (e.g., intensity of electric shock, seconds of air deprivation, and the like). The Yerkes–Dodson law tells us, for example, that rats should make fewer errors in learning a difficult discrimination under an intermediate level of aversive stimulation than under a low or high level.

The conceptual leap from rats to humans and from an induced aversive drive state to reward (particularly from drives that seem to threaten the organism's survival to the paltry sort of rewards that are typically dispensed in human research) may be more than many readers would care to make. Beyond that, there is the added problem that the research evidence, even with rats, does not lend itself to a clear-cut and unambiguous interpretation because of some methodological complications that need not concern us here.

If the Yerkes–Dodson principle had found no wider acceptance than in the animal-laboratory context in which it was formulated, we would hesitate to offer it here in connection with the present problem. That has not been the case, however. The notion that motivation should facilitate learning and performance only up to some optimal level (neither too low nor too high) has an intuitively logical and common-sense appeal about it. Perhaps for that reason, this concept has been employed widely in human social and developmental theories. Virtually all of the grand-scale, developmental theorists such as Freud, Piaget, Werner, and Lewin have incorporated this principle into their theories. Further, these theorists have not seemed particularly troubled about making the leap from animals to humans or from drives to incentives. For example, Lewin (1946) tells us that "increasing incentives favor the solution of detour and other intellectual problems only up to a certain intensity level. Above this level, however, increasing the forces to the goal makes the necessary restructurization more difficult [p. 815].'' Not only has this principle been used widely, it continues to do service in current theoretical efforts. For example, one of our present contributors, Edward L. Deci, in his recent volume on intrinsic motivation (Deci, 1975), suggests that ''intrinsic motivation increases as the goal difficulty increases, up to some optimal level [p. 117].''

Taken in its most general sense, the Yerkes–Dodson law suggests that there is an optimal level of motivation for any task or activity and that the more complex or difficult the task, the lower the optimal level. The critical assumption seems to be that an activity that can be performed efficiently at an optimal level of motivation will become disintegrated under excessive motivation. Just why this should be the case is not clear, other than the rather vague implication that the answer lies somewhere in the organization and function of the nervous system. At a phenomenological level, the literature of animal psychology and human psychopathology provides many examples of the fact that ongoing normal activity can be dramatically disrupted under the stress of excessive motivation. The reader may wonder if such disruption could be explained more economically another way or whether rewards can produce this type of disruption. Nevertheless, so long as rewards can be considered to provide a source of motivation, it is difficult to escape the conclusion that rewards should have an influence on motivational level relative to the optimum.

If incentives are considered to influence behavior independently of other sources of motivation, then the Yerkes–Dodson principle would predict that an intermediate level of incentive should enhance performance on a complex task but that a high level should interfere with performance. On the other hand, if incentives merely provide one source of motivation that combines with other sources, then the addition of even a low level of incentive in a complex task might be enough to put total motivation beyond the optimal level. Either way, it seems clear that the Yerkes–Dodson law could predict a detrimental effect of reward in some situations.

Hull–Spence Theory

Clark L. Hull and his colleagues, notably Kenneth W. Spence, formulated some of the most elegant and sophisticated statements in psychology on the relationship of reward to behavior. Hull-Spence theory has relied upon simple, stimulus–response (S–R) mechanisms to explain behavior, with a careful distinction being maintained between learning and performance. Learning is seen as the elaboration and extension of innate, reflexive responses through the associative principles of classical conditioning. Performance, on the other hand, occurs as the joint result of learning and several nonassociative factors, chiefly motivation.

There are some important differences between Hull's statement of the theory in his *Principles of Behavior* (Hull, 1943) and his later revisions (Hull, 1951,

1952)—as well as between Hull and Spence (e.g., 1956)—concerning the theoretical conceptualization of the role of reward. Most of these differences are ignored for the present purpose. In later versions of the theory, reward performed several important functions. For example, reward may serve as reinforcement and thus influence learning directly through the development of habit strength $(_SH_R)$. In the form of incentive motivation (K), the effects of rewards may combine with available habit strength to determine reaction potential $(_SE_R)$ and thereby influence performance. Rewards play a part in the development of secondary motivation and secondary reinforcement. Also, reward as incentive motivation plays an important role in the formation of the fractional anticipatory goal response (r_g), the S-R equivalent of the concept of expectancy that serves to guide instrumental behavior. For present purposes, we need consider only the relationship between E, H, and K.

The equation, $E = H \times K$, indicates that reaction potential results in part from the multiplicative combination of habit and incentive motivation. Given that performance is determined by the strength of E, any increase in either H or K will increase the value of E and thereby increase the likelihood of occurrence of a particular response. Learning or habit formation involves the strengthening of the associative bond between "S" and "R" in the S-R relationship. Habit strength develops as a positive growth function of the number of reinforced trials. Within the theory, learning (H) cannot occur without reinforcement, and reinforcement provides the only systematic influence in the development of habit strength. Similarly, incentive motivation (K) increases as a negatively accelerated function of the amount of reward. Up to some asymptotic maximum value, the greater the amount of reward, the greater the value of K.

Given these considerations, it may appear to readers unfamiliar with this line of theorizing that reward's only effect upon performance should be to enhance it. That is not the case, however. Similar to the Yerkes–Dodson principle, the Hull–Spence theory predicts an enhancing effect of reward (K) on performance in simple tasks but a detrimental effect in complex tasks. The reason is that K multiplies indiscriminately with all available habits or response tendencies of the organism. In simple situations, the desired or correct response tendencies would be dominant or most likely to occur. Indeed, simple or easy tasks may be defined as those in which correct responses have a ready availability and high probability of occurrence. Given that the subject is likely to make correct responses anyway, any increase in K serves merely to increase the strength of E for correct responses (E_c), thereby enhancing performance. With complex tasks, on the other hand, the desired responses are not as dominant initially as error tendencies. A predisposition to make more errors than correct responses is perhaps the defining characteristic of a complex or difficult task. In this situation, increasing K serves to increase the tendency to make errors (E_e) and thus lower the quality of performance. It is true that K combines with the H for correct response tendencies in complex tasks also and thereby increases the value of E_c. However, because of the multiplicative relationship between H and K, an increase in K would function to magnify the differences between E_e and E_c. This provides the basis for improved performance in simple tasks, where the desired responses are dominant, but for poorer performance in complex tasks where the dominant responses are incorrect.

The Hull–Spence theory thus makes the same empirical predictions as the Yerkes–Dodson law with respect to a detrimental effect of reward in complex tasks, but for different reasons. The Yerkes–Dodson law implied that detrimental effects were due to a disruption of behavior beyond some optimal level of motivation. From the Hull–Spence perspective, the value of E for any given correct response tendency cannot decline so long as K or H increase in value. A greater amount of reward means a higher value of K, and a greater number of reinforced trials means a higher value of H. The detrimental effect of reward in Hull–Spence theory comes from the differential influence of K, as a multiplier of H, on error tendencies relative to correct response tendencies.

As with the Yerkes–Dodson law, the empirical foundation for the concept of K came out of the animal laboratory. For that reason, K has been defined as a function of "the weight (w) of food or quantity of other incentive (K') given as reinforcement" (Postulate VII, Hull, 1952, p. 7). Because the Hull–Spence theory has been actively extended to a wide range of human learning and social phenomena during the past 25 years, it clearly qualifies for consideration in the present discussion. Nevertheless, it is perhaps worth noting that the bulk of the evidence upon which the theoretical model rests came from a systematic study of white rats in simple learning situations. In such a context, reward was considered to facilitate performance whenever the same (and desired) response occurred more quickly, more vigorously, more frequently, and the like and showed greater resistance to extinction in the face of nonreinforcement. This same trend in most complex human performance situations would be viewed as an unfortunate one toward mechanization and rigidification of behavior. We shall return to this point a bit later in this chapter.

Reinforcement Contrast Effects

Another possible mechanism to account for reward's detrimental effects comes from research on contrasted conditions of reinforcement. The classic investigation in this area was conducted by Crespi (1942) with rats in a runway. Crespi found that animals trained to different magnitudes of reinforcement (amount of food in the goalbox) reached asymptote at about the same point in training and that asymptotic running speeds were directly related to incentive magnitude. Following asymptote to a given level of incentive, an upshift or downshift in amount of incentive resulted in a corresponding sharp increase or decrease in running speed. Further, the postshift speeds were faster (or slower) than would have been predicted on the basis of the absolute postshift incentive level. Crespi referred to this phenomenon whereby postshift speeds exceeded expectations as *elation* and *depression effects;* other investigators referred to it for some time as the *Crespi effect.*

Crespi's findings, and similar ones by Zeaman (1949), had an important influence in shaping the concept of incentive motivation in the Hull–Spence model. The theoretical role of K and its influence in the fractional anticipatory goal response (r_g–s_g mechanism) were based heavily on the data of these early incentive-contrast studies. Because of the theoretical importance attached to this line of inquiry, there has been an active and continuing interest in contrast phenomena up to the present time. In recent years, the term *Crespi effect* has given way to *contrast effect,* and *elation* and *depression effects* have been replaced by the more neutral *positive contrast effect* (PCE) and *negative contrast effect* (NCE) respectively.

Some major methodological differences in the study of contrast phenomena have led to a distinction that is currently maintained between two broad categories of research (for a general review of research on contrast effects, see Dunham, 1968). The term *incentive contrast* has been used to refer to discrete-trial studies with between-subjects designs. These studies typically have involved rats in runways under appetitive learning conditions. In this situation, the critical measure of performance is running speed to food reward. The term *behavioral contrast* has been used to refer to within-subject, free-responding, operant studies. In these studies, the subjects typically have been pigeons and rats trained under multiple schedules of reinforcement, where response rate provides the critical measure of performance. For a recent review of incentive contrast studies, see Cox (1975); for a review of the behavioral contrast work, see Freeman (1971).

The importance of research on contrast effects for the present discussion rests in the prediction that a downshift in incentive magnitude should produce an NCE. Strictly speaking, a downshift in incentive should result in a depression in *speed* and/or *rate* of responding below the levels expected on the basis of the absolute postshift incentive magnitude. However, it might be possible to extend the NCE concept to cover a lowered quality of performance as well. If so, reducing the amount of incentive should not only cause correct responses to be made more slowly or less often but should also increase error responding in situations where that is possible.

Of the three mechanisms we have discussed, reinforcement contrast offers perhaps the poorest account of the detrimental effects of reward for several reasons. First, the NCE assumes asymptotic performance to the higher preshift incentive magnitude prior to the downshift. This assumption is a difficult one to meet in most human experimentation, particularly the research discussed in this volume. Second, in the relatively few instances of contrast research with human subjects, "incentive" shifts often have amounted to shifts in feedback information, or points, or the like, which do not seem conceptually equivalent to the sort of incentives used in animal research. Third, where the shift has involved reward vs. no reward (rather than large vs. small reward), contrast effects sometimes disappear altogether. Finally, the PCE typically has not been obtained in incentive contrast studies, and there has been some tendency to obtain "reversed PCE" with both humans and animals. That is, upshifted subjects "have been found to respond *slower* to a large reward than large-reward control subjects" (Cox, 1975, p. 374). Similarly, reversed NCEs have been obtained, also. Nevertheless, in spite of these demurrers, reinforcement contrast makes some predictions that are pertinent to our central theme, and we include the contrast concept here for that reason.

WHY SHOULD IT BE SURPRISING TO FIND DETRIMENTAL EFFECTS OF REWARD?

Given that we have found three theoretical mechanisms to account for some of the detrimental effects of reward, why should the idea that rewards can have "hidden costs" come as any surprise? All three models were developed, of course, in the animal laboratory; whereas most of the evidence on the detrimental effects of reward presented in the following chapters has come from work with humans. However, each of the three models has been extended to a variety of tasks and situations involving human subjects. Also, because these models are among the most widely known ones in psychology, it is unlikely that their implications concerning the detrimental effects of reward should have escaped notice. The reason that much of psychology and the culture at large have come to regard rewards as universally beneficial must be sought elsewhere.

The Large Shadow of B. F. Skinner

Although the Yerkes–Dodson law and the Hull–Spence theory carry implications of an adverse effect of reward (at least in complex tasks), both were developed to account for the relationship of motivation (drive) to learning and performance. Only in the work of B. F. Skinner do we find a system that puts reinforcement at the very center of research and theorizing. Skinner (e.g., 1938) indeed argued that the prediction and control of behavior rests entirely on reinforcement and the ways and means by which it is delivered. This view led to the development of a special technology for the behavioral analysis of many scientific and practical problems. The operant model has been extended into the field of education (programmed instruction) and psychotherapy (behavior modification) (e.g., Skinner, 1953) and to society in the broad sense (Skinner, 1948, 1971). The potential that Skinner's model offers for resolving important scientific and practical problems has generated enormous interest both in and out of psychology. This extensive interest has resulted in the formation of a separate division of the

American Psychological Association, the launching of a number of basic and applied technical journals in psychology and elsewhere, and the amassing of an army of enthusiastic followers. All of this has caused many psychologists and other people to look to operant conditioning principles for an understanding of the role of reward in behavior and motivation.

The Skinnerian concept of reinforcement. Skinner's system, with its philosophical roots in logical positivism, offers an objective, natural science approach to the study of behavioral phenomena. His discussion of the relationship between reward and reinforcement, however, has generated some systematic inconsistencies. These conceptual difficulties have not attracted much attention to date, partly because we have understood in a general way what Skinner means. The confusion arises, it would seem, from Skinner's remarkable ability to function both as scientist and litterateur.

In the general view of the layman, the terms *reward* and *punishment* refer to pleasures and pains, respectively, that normally are delivered in recognition of and payment for desired and undesired activities. Skinner began with this conception and these terms and at one level of discourse continues to use them. Early in his scientific career, however, he came to prefer the term *reinforcer* to *reward*. Herrnstein's (1970) comment on this point may help to explain why:

> The use of "reinforcement" in the vocabulary of instrumental conditioning was promoted in the mid-1930's, particularly by Skinner and primarily as a substitute for the traditional term "reward," whose very age tainted it with the suspicion of mentalism. Mentalism notwithstanding, "reward" was more neutral than "reinforce," for while reward simply names a class of events that have some effect on the organism, "reinforcement" implies what the effect is, namely a strengthening [pp. 379–380].

Although the term *reward* was generally avoided in Skinner's more technical works, the term *punishment,* interestingly, was not. Both punishment and negative reinforcers continued to be defined solely in terms of aversive stimulation (e.g., Ferster & Skinner, 1957).

On the other hand, Skinner has defined reinforcers in three ways: in terms of (a) what they are; (b) how they are administered; and (c) what effects they have. By the first of these definitions, reinforcers (positive reinforcers) are simply rewards. This definition appears to be Skinner's favorite for more literary purposes. Some examples: "Some of these changes are what the layman calls reward, or what are now generally referred to technically as reinforcers:..." (Ferster & Skinner, 1957, p. 1). "This serves as a reward or—to use a term which is less likely to be misunderstood—a 'reinforcement' for the desired behavior" (Skinner, 1959, p. 413). "Good things are positive reinforcers.... The things we call bad... are all negative reinforcers, and we are reinforced when we escape from or avoid them" (Skinner, 1971, pp. 102–103).

By the second definition, reinforcers are rewards that are delivered contingent upon the occurrence of some desired response. The first and second definitions are mutually compatible and consistent with the layman's view of rewards: Rewards are good things that can be obtained as a result of good behavior.

By Skinner's third definition, reinforcers must reinforce or strengthen behavior. This definition is Skinner's favorite for scientific purposes. A reinforcer is any stimulus event that follows an operant response and thereby increases the strength (or probability of occurrence) of that response. Response rate provides the usual performance measure of increased response probability.

Skinner (1953) identifies two main classes of reinforcers—positive and negative. *Positive reinforcers* increase response probability by being added to the situation; *negative reinforcers* increase response probability by being removed. Positive reinforcers are those desired, sought-after stimuli such as food, sex, praise, and money that we ordinarily call rewards. Negative reinforcers are also sought after but have their effect through the termination of noxious stimulation, or what we ordinarily would call the removal of punishment.

By equating positive reinforcement with a strengthening process, Skinner has ensured that rewards—by definition—can have only one effect, and that is to enhance behavior. The more frequently a reward is dispensed, the greater the response probability (as reflected in rate of responding), and consequently, the better will be the performance. The idea that more reward should lead to better performance and less reward to poorer performance was central to the reinforcement contrast phenomena discussed above. Behavioral contrast effects are obtained, of course, by means of operant research methods.

The notion that reward can have only one consistent effect on behavior has the systematic appeal of providing a clear-cut, operational definition of a difficult concept. It seems inevitable, however, that such a viewpoint might lead to some confusion in our understanding of rewards as we commonly think of them, and as Skinner often speaks of them.

There are many stimulus events that both scientists and plainer folk have come to regard as "good things," worth striving for regardless of their possible adverse effect on behavior and motivation. Money provides a good example. To the layman, money is a fine, general-purpose reward; similarly, to Skinner (e.g., 1968) it is a "universal, generalized reinforcer [p. 62]." If research should reveal that money does not always facilitate performance and at times even hinders it, we would find ourselves in the strange position of having to declare that by Skinner's definition money suddenly was no longer a good thing (reward) or that it was no longer a "universal, generalized reinforcer." Such a peculiar view of money would be required empirically at whatever point in a task performance took a downward turn. A redefinition of money as nonreward would seem even more perplexing if subjects continued to regard money as a reward, strived no less vigorously to obtain it, and acted as though it produced a pleasing and satisfying state of affairs when they got it.

In his second letter to Timothy, Saint Paul warned that the love of money was the root of all evils. It seems reasonable to believe that at least since Biblical times, thinking people have recognized that attractive rewards can indeed have some rather significant "hidden costs." Skinner's conception of reinforcement, as reflected in the third definition, may have helped to blind us to this simple fact in recent decades, particularly since the work of Skinner and his followers in that time has dominated our thinking about rewards.

WHAT DOES IT MEAN TO SAY THAT REWARDS ENHANCE BEHAVIOR?

Most of the theoretical work concerning the influence of rewards on behavior is a product of the animal laboratory. This work not only made use of simple subjects but employed even simpler tasks and dependent measures of performance. When a rat traverses a straight runway to a food reward, there is little sense in which the animal can do anything other than make a "correct" response. The same may be said of a rat pressing a bar in a Skinner box or a pigeon pecking at a lighted disk. Reward in these situations increases the speed and/or frequency of responding. It is in this sense that reward is said to facilitate performance. As rewarded behavior occurs at faster speeds and more frequent rates, it becomes less variable, more smooth running, and thus more efficient. Unnecessary movements become eliminated. This is a trend toward greater mechanization and rigidity of behavior; it is also a trend toward greater proficiency in reward retrieval.

Another interesting feature of reward is that it stabilizes behavior and preserves it against change. This can be seen in the great resistance to extinction that a previously rewarded behavior exhibits when reward is withdrawn. It can be seen in acquisition as well. One of the clearest examples comes from Skinner's work on the development of "superstitious" behavior. Skinner (1953) found that a single, noncontingent reward is often enough to capture and "freeze" whatever behavior may be ongoing at the time the reward is delivered.

Whenever the demand characteristics of the task require simple, routine, unchanging responses and when circumstances favor the making of such responses quickly, frequently, and vigorously, rewards typically enhance performance. Rewards generally enhance performance also in those situations that require a resistance to behavioral change or the maintenance of routine behavior that otherwise would be discontinued. On these points, the research evidence is powerful and convincing, and none of the present authors wishes to dispute it.

It also may be the case that rewards can be used to enhance performance in situations that depend heavily upon flexibility, intrinsic motivation, conceptual and perceptual openness, creativity, and the like. The research evidence in support of such a contention is much harder to find. Reward programs have been applied, of course, to a wide variety of human problems and situations. Such programs appear to have had their greatest success in the case of very young children and institutionalized adults. In these situations, the principal use of reward has been to initiate and maintain rather simple, routine behaviors, albeit important ones to the welfare of the individuals concerned. As the reader examines the evidence being presented in this volume, he or she may notice a striking difference in the task requirements and dependent measures from those traditionally employed to study the effects of reward on behavior. To argue a detrimental effect of reward in some situations by some measures is not to deny an enhancing effect of reward in other circumstances.

At this point, a thoroughgoing behaviorist of the Skinnerian persuasion may object that it isn't fair to examine any aspect of performance other than the target behavior that has been reinforced. After all, it isn't cricket to reinforce Behavior A and then look for the effects of that reinforcement on Behavior B. The traditional Skinnerian argument is that we must specify the behavior that we wish to obtain and then selectively reinforce that behavior, or successive approximations to it, until we finally achieve the desired behavioral end product. This orientation to reinforcement seems to rest on the assumption that reinforcement will enhance target behavior and that all other measurable aspects of the organism will either remain constant or also be enhanced.

The present authors raise the possibility for consideration that reward may enhance a given target behavior and at the same time adversely affect other concomitant behaviors, attitudes, and interests. The authors also raise the question of whether every aspect of human performance can be ''shaped'' toward a desired end through the application of external rewards. Specifically, they ask whether intrinsic motivation can be undermined through the use of extrinsic incentives. These questions imply that rewards may in some contexts produce a net detrimental effect where any gain in one area of behavior may be more than offset by losses in other areas.

A FINAL WORD

We have reviewed three theoretical mechanisms that might be used to account for a detrimental effect of reward. Whether or not any of them will prove to be entirely satisfactory will depend on how well they handle the data. We leave a precise assessment in that regard for later parts of the book. However, it may be well to remember that for a model to be satisfactory, it must not only predict appropriately the detrimental effects of reward; it must also predict accurately the conditions of an enhancing effect of reward. The Yerkes–Dodson law, the Hull–Spence theory, and the reinforcement contrast work all make predictions about when reward should have a beneficial effect. As products of the animal laboratory in the S–R tradition, however, none of these models has been used to any extent to account for the sort of data presented in this volume. Whether or not they could be modified to adequately handle data on complex human problem solving, intrinsic motivation, interest, and the like or to account for the effects of reward on attitudes and behavior after such rewards are no longer available is questionable.

During the last 20 years, there has been a growing interest in more cognitively based explanations of learning and motivational phenomena. This interest is reflected in such diverse areas as Piagetian theory, symbolic and linguistic processes, planning functions, competence and affectance, exploration, and self-reinforcement as well as in liberalized extensions of S–R theory to include attentional and mediational processes. The data and orientation of the present volume are generally compatible with these current interests in cognitive explanatory mechanisms.

In the final analysis, we may wonder if existing theories of learning and motivation are adequate to the task. Several new theoretical points of view are presented in later chapters. Beyond these, there are other options. For example, we might seek to understand reward's detrimental effects in terms of the distraction of attention (e.g., J. Spence, 1970) or perhaps in terms of a biological model. The task of finding a satisfactory theoretical explanation for reward's adverse effects on performance and motivation will be an important and exciting one, if reward can be shown convincingly to have adverse effects. And that is what we hope to do.

ACKNOWLEDGMENTS

Preparation of this chapter as well as the chapter by Kenneth O. McGraw and the research activities of McCullers and McGraw were supported by PHS/DHEW grants MH22041-01A1 and MH 26359-01, -02 from NIMH to the University of Oklahoma and MH 30570-01 to Oklahoma State University, John C. McCullers, Principal Investigator. McCullers and McGraw were colleagues as faculty and doctoral student respectively in the Department of Psychology, University of Oklahoma, where they began their work on the detrimental effects of reward. McCullers's present address: Department of Family Relations and Child Development, Oklahoma State University, Stillwater, Oklahoma 74074.

REFERENCES

Cox, W. M. A review of recent incentive contrast studies involving discrete-trial procedures. *Psychological Record,* 1975, *25,* 373–393.
Crespi, L. P. Quantitative variation of incentive and performance in the white rat. *American Journal of Psychology,* 1942, *55,* 467–517.
Deci, E. L. *Intrinsic motivation.* New York: Plenum, 1975.
Dunham, P. J. Contrasted conditions of reinforcement: A selective critique. *Psychological Bulletin,* 1968, *69,* 295–315.
Ferster, C. B., & Skinner, B. F. *Schedules of reinforcement.* New York: Appleton-Century-Crofts, 1957.

Freeman, B. J. Behavioral contrast: Reinforcement frequency or response suppression? *Psychological Bulletin,* 1971, *75,* 347–356.

Herrnstein, R. J. On the law of effect. In P. B. Dews (Ed.), *Festschrift for B. F. Skinner.* New York: Appleton–Century–Crofts, 1970.

Hull, C. L. *Principles of behavior.* New York: Appleton–Century–Crofts, 1943.

Hull, C. L. *Essentials of behavior.* New Haven: Yale University Press, 1951.

Hull, C. L. *A behavior system.* New Haven: Yale University Press, 1952.

Lewin, K. Behavior and development as a function of the total situation. In L. Carmichael (Ed.), *Manual of child psychology.* New York: Wiley, 1946.

Skinner, B. F. *The behavior of organisms: An experimental analysis.* New York: Appleton-Century-Crofts, 1938.

Skinner, B. F. *Walden two.* New York: Macmillan, 1948.

Skinner, B. F. *Science and human behavior.* New York: Macmillan, 1953.

Skinner, B. F. *Cumulative record.* New York: Appleton-Century-Crofts, 1959.

Skinner, B. F. *The technology of teaching.* New York: Appleton-Century-Crofts, 1968.

Skinner, B. F. *Beyond freedom and dignity.* New York: Knopf, 1971.

Spence, J. T. The distracting effects of material reinforcers in the discrimination learning of lower- and middle-class children. *Child Development,* 1970, *41,* 103–111.

Spence, K. W. *Behavior theory and conditioning.* New Haven: Yale University Press, 1956.

Yerkes, R. M., & Dodson, J. D. The relation of strength of stimulus to rapidity of habit-formation. *Journal of Comparative Neurology and Psychology,* 1908, *18,* 459–482.

Zeaman, D. Response latency as a function of the amount of reinforcement. *Journal of Experimental Psychology,* 1949, *39,* 466–483.

2 Issues in Cognitive Social Psychology

Arie W. Kruglanski
Tel-Aviv University

The problem of motivating persons to their tasks has been of perennial importance in human affairs. Pervasively, individuals have vested interests in the activities of others. Parents and educators are concerned about the appropriate channeling of children's behaviors. Employers have a stake in keeping the employees at their jobs. Lovers desire to attract to themselves their partners' attention, etc. Not surprisingly, the problem of task motivation has received attention from diverse psychological perspectives, e.g., in the domains of industrial psychology (cf. Herzberg, 1966; Vroom, 1969), developmental psychology (Hunt, 1965), social psychology (cf. Deci, 1975; Kruglanski, Riter, Amitai, Margolin, Shabtai, & Zaksh, 1975; Lepper, Greene, & Nisbett, 1973), personality theory (Allport, 1961), learning theory (Spence, 1970), and motivation theory (cf. Day, Berlyne, & Hunt, 1971). Within social psychology, a recent upsurge of interest in task motivation dates to the late 1960s (e.g., de Charms, 1968) and the early 1970s (e.g., Deci, 1971; Kruglanski, Friedman, & Zeevi, 1971). My purpose in this chapter is to outline the conceptual background of this trend.

The articles in this volume examine task motivation as it may be affected by contingent rewards. The learning-theory approach (see, e.g., Chapter 1 by McCullers and Chapter 3 by McGraw in this volume) has focused on the characteristics of behavior under different degrees of reward-induced motivation and on the interaction of behaviors and tasks as it affects the quality of performance. The learning theorists' primary motivational concern has been with *ambient* factors that affect the organism's intensity of motivation to perform the activity, e.g., the several parameters of reinforcement for the activity: the magnitude of reinforcement, the reinforcement schedules, etc.

By contrast to the learning-theory perspective, the social psychological sense of task motivation has not implied the intensity of motivation to perform a task

19

for a circumstantial reward; rather it has referred to the motivating properties of *the task's content*. This approach has derived from social psychologists' traditional interest in attitudes. In other words, "task motivation" has meant "attitude toward the task," and the relation between rewards and motivation (to the task) has been considered a special case of the relation between rewards and attitudes toward an object. Let me mention now several social psychological notions relevant to the effects of rewards on attitudes. First, I list briefly some theoretical mechanisms whereby rewards have a positive effect on subsequent attitudes. Following this I outline in greater detail the historical development of theoretical mechanisms that suggest a negative effect of rewards on attitudes.

REWARDS AND ATTITUDES I: THE POSITIVE RELATION

A.   Social-Learning Approaches

The label "social learning" generally denotes the application of behavioristic principles toward the explanation of processes whereby socially pertinent behaviors, beliefs, or attitudes are acquired by the individual. The relevance of social learning to the effects of rewards on attitudes is now made explicit via discussion of the two basic mechanisms of conditioning: classical and instrumental.

   1.   Classical conditioning.   Within the classical-conditioning paradigm, an initially neutral stimulus, paired repeatedly with another stimulus capable of evoking an affective response, will eventually acquire the capacity to evoke a similar response. By now there exists evidence (cf. Staats, 1969; Zanna, Kiesler, & Pilkonis, 1970) that attitudes toward objects may be appropriately modified via the classical-conditioning procedure. Pertinent to the present concern, "reward" is a positively valued stimulus. Its repeated association with a (less positive, or neutral) task should, therefore, enhance the task's positive valence.

   2.   Instrumental conditioning.   In the instrumental-conditioning framework, "reward" is a positive reinforcer, i.e., a stimulus that enhances the frequency of the preceding response. Accordingly, reward contingent on the performance of a task should strengthen the tendency to perform the task on future occasions. Does this mean that reward should render more positive the attitude toward the task? Only to the extent that positive attitude is necessary for overt behavior (task performance) to occur. However, there are good reasons to distinguish between private attitudes and public actions (cf. Collins, 1968; Fishbein & Ajzen, 1975). After all, a person could be strongly motivated to perform actions for circumstantial reasons unrelated to the actions' content. To state this differently, the effects of reward on task performance might be *situation specific,* i.e., confined to circumstances in which recurrent delivery of the rewards may be expected. (For a detailed discussion of this point see Lepper and Greene, Chapter 6.)

B. Other Approaches

3. Cognitive balance.   According to Heider's (1958) balance formulation, if P likes X and X is associated with Y, the P-X-Y triad will be balanced to the extent that P likes Y as well. Substituting "reward" for X and "activity" (or task) for Y, it follows that tasks associated with rewards will come to be liked as a consequence of strivings for cognitive balance.

4. Functional autonomy.   Several prominent theoreticians (e.g., Allport, 1961; Brentano, 1902; Tolman, 1951) have argued that activities performed first as means to something else come to be desired for their own sake. This tendency has been labeled the "functional autonomy" of motives (cf. Allport, 1961, pp. 227–257) and has been proposed as a major principle whereby complex, adult motivation evolves from the simpler motivational schemes of the infant. In connection with the present issues, the notion of functional autonomy suggests that at least for initially neutral or unpleasant activities, the introduction of contingent rewards will occasion a positive attitude change.

REWARDS AND ATTITUDES II: THE NEGATIVE RELATION

The convergence of major theoretical views in psychology on the prediction of a positive relation between rewards and attitudes renders particularly unobvious the implication of dissonance theory (Festinger, 1957)—that the relation will be negative for counterattitudinal tasks. According to dissonance theory, a counterattitudinal act will arouse the state of dissonance to the extent that the act is not otherwise justified. Thus, a counterattitudinal act performed for a barely sufficient reward will result in a higher degree of dissonance than the same act performed for an amply sufficient reward. The aversive properties of a dissonant state should motivate its reduction, and one way of reducing dissonance occasioned by a counterattitudinal act would be by adopting a more positive attitude toward the act in question. All of which implies that final attitude toward an initially unpleasant act would be negatively related to the magnitude of contingent reward.

Early support for the above prediction was obtained in the "forced-compliance" experiment by Festinger and Carlsmith (1959). The subject in this study performed a series of dull tasks and then received either a $1 or a $20 inducement for reporting to another, prospective subject that the activities in question were, in fact, exciting and enjoyable. In accordance with the dissonance-theory prediction, subjects in the $1 condition expressed subsequently more positive attitudes towards the experimental tasks than did subjects in the $20 condition. The negative relation between rewards and attitudes has been replicated since in several contexts (e.g., by Carlsmith, Collins & Helmreich, 1966; Cohen, 1962; Collins & Hoyt, 1972; Linder, Cooper, & Jones, 1967; Nel, Helmreich, & Aronson, 1969).

The dissonance-theory account of attitude change in "forced-compliance" situations was contrasted with the cognitive-contact theory (cf. Janis & King, 1954; King & Janis, 1956). According to the latter interpretation, persons induced to perform a counterattitudinal role publicly will try to elaborate supporting arguments for the role; and as a consequence of their new familiarity with such arguments, these persons will adopt a less negative attitude toward the role in question. Furthermore, the motivation to convincingly enact the required role should increase as a function of contingent rewards. Thus, the cognitive-contact theory predicts a positive relation between rewards and attitudes. It is noteworthy that cognitive contact is more restricted in scope than the previously mentioned mechanisms of positive relation, i.e., conditioning, balance, or functional autonomy. The latter explanations refer to the general case in which rewards are contingent on *any* act or utterance. By contrast, cognitive-contact theory applies to the very special situation in which rewards are contingent on the *production* of *favorable arguments* for an act or an utterance (on this point also see Rosenberg, 1968).

THE DISSONANCE VS. REINFORCEMENT CONTROVERSY ABOUT THE REWARDS–ATTITUDES RELATION

In the 1960s a veritable "paradigm clash" occurred between proponents of the positive vs. the negative relation between rewards and attitudes toward an initially antagonistic behavior (for a review of the relevant literature see, e.g., Collins & Hoyt, 1972). Each side in this controversy confronted empirical evidence supporting the opposing view. Cognitive-contact (or reinforcement) theorists had yet to account for the negative relation documented in several "forced-compliance" studies (e.g., Carlsmith, Collins, & Helmreich, 1966; Cohen, 1962; Festinger & Carlsmith, 1959; Linder, Cooper, & Jones, 1967). Dissonance theorists faced an equally compelling array of findings suggesting a positive relation between rewards and attitudes toward counterpositional acts (cf. Carlsmith, Collins, & Helmreich, 1966; Elms & Janis, 1965; Linder, Cooper, & Jones, 1967; Rosenberg, 1965).

The reinforcement vs. dissonance controversy generated a considerable body of research. In the early stages of this work, the reinforcement theorists specified the nature of the task required for cognitive contact to take effect (cf. Rosenberg, 1968) and treated instances of the negative relation between rewards and attitudes as possible artifacts of "evaluation apprehension" (cf. Rosenberg, 1965) or "discombobulation" (cf. Elms & Janis, 1965; Janis & Gilmore, 1965). Dissonance theorists succeeded in producing several experimental reversals of the relation between rewards and attitudes. They proceeded to delineate the boundary conditions of the negative relation, implicating—in this connection—variables like choice (cf. Linder, Cooper, & Jones, 1967), commitment (cf. Aronson, 1966, 1968), personal responsibility, and consequences (cf. Collins, 1969; Collins & Hoyt, 1972).

THE SELF-PERCEPTION VS. DISSONANCE CONTROVERSY REGARDING THE NEGATIVE RELATION

In the late 1960s the debate between dissonance and reinforcement views lost some of its poignancy. In part, this might have been because the negative relation between rewards and attitudes had by then become the center of a new controversy in social psychology: the dispute between dissonance vs. self-perception accounts of forced-compliance experiments. The self-perception framework had originated with the provocative work of Daryl Bem (e.g., 1965, 1967, 1972). Bem interpreted the negative relation between rewards and attitudes within a cognitive framework that did not require reference to an aversive motivational state like dissonance. According to Bem, an individual does not "know" his (her) attitudes in any immediate sense; rather, he (she) infers them from his (her) behavior and from the circumstances in which the behavior was enacted. Thus, a person who commits a "counterattitudinal" act and receives only a minimal reward for doing so may infer that the act was not so counterattitudinal after all. By contrast, a person who commits the same act for a considerable reward need not infer a positive attitude, as the reward provides a perfectly plausible explanation of the behavior's occurrence. A critical feature of the self-perception analysis is its information-processing emphasis that does not posit the individual's motivational involvement in the behavior and/or the attitude in question. This suggested to Bem a crucial test of the self-perception vs. the dissonance hypothesis. In the relevant experimental paradigm known thereafter as the "interpersonal replication," the subject does not personally commit an act under a high or a low reward but merely receives information about another person who did perform the act. The results of Bem's experiments (1965, 1967) lent support to the self-perception position. "Interpersonal replicators" informed about an actor who received a low (vs. a high) reward exhibited a stronger tendency to infer this person's positive attitude toward his (her) act. Contrary to the dissonance implication, then, the negative relation between rewards and attitudes need not presuppose a person's motivational involvement.

The role of motivational involvement has been only one of the issues that separated the dissonance and the self-perception accounts of "forced-compliance" experiments. Another major issue, particularly pertinent to the concerns of this volume, has been that unlike the dissonance analysis, the self-perception view does not restrict the negative relation between rewards and attitudes to counterpositional (hence, dissonant) behaviors. More specifically, the self-perception analysis implies that the inference of a positive attitude to any behavior would be inversely related to evidence that (in a given instance) the behavior occurred because of extrinsic rewards. By now, the existence of a negative relation between rewards and attitudes to consonant activities has been demonstrated in several experiments (e.g., Kruglanski, Alon, & Lewis, 1972; Kruglanski, Riter, Amitai, Margolin, Shabtai, & Zaksh, 1975; Weick, 1964).

The debate between proponents of the dissonance and the self-perception interpretations of forced-compliance studies has engendered some exciting research (e.g., Bem, 1968; Jones, Linder, Kiesler, Zanna, & Brehm, 1968; Snyder & Ebbesen, 1972). Though neither the dissonance nor the self-perception account has clearly gained an upper hand in the controversy, popularity of the latter approach was enhanced by its close correspondence with the tenets of attribution theory, a novel theoretical paradigm in social psychology whose advent in the late 1960s has gradually replaced the heretofore predominant perspective of cognitive consistency theories (Abelson, Aronson, McGuire, Newcomb, Rosenberg, & Tannenbaum, 1968).

Self-Perception, Attribution, and Intrinsic Motivation

Bem's self-perception theory suggests that one's attitude toward an activity may be understood as an inference that an actor draws from his (her) behavior and the surrounding circumstances. This renders the self-perception framework compatible with attribution theory (Jones & Davis, 1965; Jones, Kanouse, Kelley, Nisbett, Valins & Weiner, 1971, 1972; Jones & McGillis, 1976; Kelley, 1967, 1971, 1972, 1973) on two counts:

1. The main concern of attribution theory is with the *process* whereby any inference (including the attitude inference) is reached.
2. The attribution-theoretic approach shares with the self-perception framework the assumption that variables traditionally classified as affective or motivational may be fruitfully reconceptualized as kinds of knowledge or inference (see, e.g., Schachter & Singer, 1962; Nisbett & Schachter, 1966; Nisbett & Valins, 1971; Valins & Nisbett, 1971).

It is of interest to note that Bem's initial analyses employed Skinnerian terminology and were considered instances of radical behaviorism (a point of view diametrically opposed to the cognitive flavor of attribution theory). But Bem's subsequent statements closely corresponded with Kelley's attributional exegesis of the self-perception hypothesis. Le me review these developments in some detail.

Bem's early interpretation of forced-compliance research stressed Skinner's (1957) distinction between "tact" and "mand." *Tact* has been defined as a verbal response "under the discriminative control of some portion of the environment," and *mand* as a verbal response "under the control of specific reinforcing contingencies" (Bem, 1965, p. 200). When the magnitude of inducement is high, the reward contingency is clear; hence, a mand inference may be made, which implies the possibility that a statement (verbal response) has not reflected the subjectively true properties of the entity about which it was spoken. But with a low inducement, a tact inference is more likely; and it should imply that the statement is relatively more sincere.

Kelley's (1967, 1971) attributional interpretations of forced-compliance research preserved the basic notion of self-perception but (1) replaced the distinction between *tacts* and *mands* by a distinction between *internal* and *external* attributions; and (2) introduced the principle of *discounting* as the vehicle whereby an attitude inference may be reached. The discounting rule states that the attributor's confidence in the role of a given cause in producing an effect is inversely related to the number of causes that seem plausible. In a high-reward condition of a forced-compliance study there seem to exist *two* plausible causes of the actor's behavior: (1) the external reward and (2) the actor's internal favorability toward the behavior. In a low-reward condition, there seems to exist only *one* plausible cause—the *internal* favorability—as the *external* reward seems too low to be a plausible explanation of the actor's behavior. According to the discounting principle, the inference of a favorable attitude should be stronger in the low-reward (one-cause) condition than in the high-reward (two-cause) condition, precisely the finding obtained.

INTERNAL ATTRIBUTIONS OR ENDOGENOUS ATTRIBUTIONS?

Recently some questions were raised about the suitability of the internal–external dimension with respect to the explanation of actions, or voluntary behaviors (see, e.g., Kruglanski, 1975; Kruglanski, Riter, Amitai, Margolin, Shabtai, & Zaksh, 1975). Briefly, any action is commonly assumed to be prompted by a motive, i.e., by an *internal* desire to attain some *external* goal. In a sense, then, any action has *both* an internal and an external reason that are actually the very same reason expressed in different terms. For example, a person who does work for money may be said to act because of an internal pecuniary motive or because of the external monetary object. But it should be obvious that these two seemingly different explanations are quite redundant. All of which suggests that the internal–external partition may be an illusive basis for classifying the reasons of different voluntary actions. The internal–external partition may be less problematic in the domain of occurrences, i.e., events (like success or failure at some task) that unlike *actions* contain a considerable nonvoluntary component. (For a further consideration of the distinction between actions and occurrences see Kruglanski, 1975.)

Because of conceptual difficulties with the distinction between internal and external attribution of actions, I recently proposed (Kruglanski, 1975; Chapter 5, this volume) that the inference of intrinsic motivation is coordinable, instead, to the partition between endogenous and exogenous attributions. By an endogenous attribution is meant that the action is perceived as an *end* in itself; and by an exogenous attribution, that the action is perceived as *means* to a further end. For example, in a low-reward condition of a forced-compliance study, the actor may be led to attribute his (her) action endogenously, and in the high-reward condition, exogenously. This would explain why greater liking (or intrinsic motivation) for the activity is expressed in the low- (vs. high-) reward conditions of forced-compliance research. For a detailed discussion of the relation between endogenous attribution and intrinsic motivation see Chapter 5.

CONCLUSIONS

In this chapter I attempted to adumbrate the conceptual background for the social psychologists' current interest in the problem of intrinsic motivation. By the way of summary, the following points may be made:

1. Social psychologists arrived at the topic of intrinsic motivation via their fundamental interest in attitudes. Typically, "social-psychological" studies of intrinsic motivation (reviewed in subsequent chapters of this volume) employ attitude measures (verbal or behavioral) as their major dependent variables. At the same time, the immense practical significance of task motivation has rendered this area of research considerably more than a testing ground for attitude theories. Consequently, we see attempts by social psychologists to encompass within their analyses such nonattitudinal variables as, e.g., the quality of task performance, (cf. Kruglanski, et al., 1971; Lepper & Greene, 1975, Chapter 5; Kruglanski, Chapter 6).

2. Early social-psychological conceptions (functional autonomy, conditioning, balance) converged on the prediction of positive relation between rewards and attitudes and stressed in this connection the role of motivational constructs (e.g., the role of motivation intensity in the "cognitive-contact" theory, or the role of inconsistency strain in balance theory).

3. More recently there has been a shift of emphasis in social psychology from

the positive to the negative relation and from the motivational to the cognitive theoretical mode.

4. As often is the case in science, the shifts mentioned reflect more the excitement about novel, promising paradigms than full resolution of problems posed by the old paradigms. Thus, while current social-psychological interest revolves about the negative relation (between rewards and attitudes), the conditions for the reversal of relationship are not yet clearly understood. Similarly, contemporary emphasis on cognition does not negate the possibility that motivational constructs may still furnish significant insight into the phenomena at stake. Ultimately, the paramount pragmatic significance of task motivation may imply the questions that need to be answered regardless of the paradigmatic origin of potential answers.

ACKNOWLEDGMENT

This chapter was prepared while the author was on a leave from Tel-Aviv University at Vanderbilt University, Nashville, Tennessee.

REFERENCES

Abelson, R., Aronson, E., McGuire, W., Newcomb, T., Rosenberg, M., & Tannenbaum, P. (Eds.), *Theories of cognitive consistency: A sourcebook*. Chicago: Rand McNally, 1968.

Allport, G. W. *Pattern and growth in personality*. New York: Holt, Rinehart & Winston, 1961.

Aronson, E. The psychology of insufficient justification: An analysis of some conflicting data. In S. Feldman (Ed.), *Cognitive consistency*. New York: Academic Press, 1966.

Aronson, E. Dissonance theory: Progress and problems. In R. Abelson, E. Aronson, W. McGuire, T. Newcomb, M. Rosenberg, & P. Tannenbaum (Eds.), *Theories of cognitive consistency: A sourcebook*. Chicago: Rand McNally, 1968.

Bem, D. J. An experimental analysis of self-persuasion. *Journal of Experimental Social Psychology*, 1965, *1*, 199–218.

Bem, D. J. Self-perception: An alternative interpretation of cognitive dissonance phenomena. *Psychological Review*, 1967, *74*, 183–200.

Bem, D. J. The epistemological status of interpersonal simulations: A reply to Jones, Linder, Kiesler, Zanna and Brehm. *Journal of Experimental Social Psychology*, 1968, *4*, 270–274.

Bem, D. J. Self-perception theory. In L. Berkowitz (Ed.), *Advances in experimental social psychology* (Vol. 6). New York: Academic Press, 1972.

Brentano, P. *The origin of the knowledge of right and wrong*. London: Constable, 1902.

Carlsmith, J. M., Collins, B. E., & Helmreich, R. L. Studies in forced compliance: I. The effect of pressure for compliance on attitude change produced by face-to-face role playing and anonymous essay writing. *Journal of Personality and Social Psychology*, 1966, *4*, 1–13.

Cohen, A. R. An experiment on small rewards for discrepant compliance and attitude change. In J. W. Brehm & A. R. Cohen (Eds.), *Explorations in cognitive dissonance*. New York: Wiley, 1962.

Collins, B. E. Counterattitudinal behavior. In R. Abelson, E. Aronson, W. McGuire, T. Newcomb, M. Rosenberg, & P. Tannenbaum (Eds.), *Theories of cognitive consistency: A sourcebook*. Chicago: Rand McNally, 1968.

Collins, B. E. The effect of monetary inducement on the amount of attitude change produced by forced compliance. In A. C. Elms (Ed.), *Role-playing, reward, and attitude change*. New York: Van Nostrand, 1969.

Collins, B. E., & Hoyt, M. F. Personal responsibility-for-consequences: An integration and extension of the "forced-compliance" literature. *Journal of Experimental Social Psychology*, 1972, *8*, 588–593.

Day, H. E., Berlyne, D. E., & Hunt, D. E. (Eds.), *Intrinsic motivation: A new direction in education*. Holt, Rinehart and Winston of Canada, 1971.

de Charms, R. *Personal causation: The internal affective determinants of behavior*. New York: Academic Press, 1968.

Deci, E. L. Effects of externally mediated rewards on intrinsic motivation. *Journal of Personality and Social Psychology*, 1971, *18*, 105–115.

Deci, E. L. *Intrinsic motivation*. New York: Plenum Publishing Corp., 1975.

Elms, A. C., & Janis, I. L. Counter-norm attitudes induced by consonant versus dissonant conditions of role-playing. *Journal of Experimental Research in Personality*, 1965, *1*, 50–60.

Festinger, L. *A theory of cognitive dissonance*. Evanston, Illinois: Row, Peterson, 1957.

Festinger, L., & Carlsmith, J. M. Cognitive consequences of forced-compliance. *Journal of Abnormal and Social Psychology*, 1959, *58*, 203–210.

Fishbein, M., & Ajzen, I. *Belief, attitude, intention and behavior: An introduction to theory and research*. Reading, Mass.: Addison–Wesley, 1975.

Heider, F. *The psychology of interpersonal relations*. New York: Wiley, 1958.

Herzberg, P. *Work and the nature of man*. New York: World, 1966.

Hunt, J. McV. Intrinsic motivation and its role in psychological development. *Nebraska Symposium on Motivation*, 1965, *13*, 189–282.

Janis, I. L., & Gilmore, J. B. The influence of incentive conditions on the success of role-playing in modifying attitudes. *Journal of Personality and Social Psychology*, 1965, *1*, 17–27.

Janis, I. L., & King, B. T. The influence of role-playing on opinion change. *Journal of Abnormal and Social Psychology*, 1954, *49*, 211–218.

Jones, E. E., Kanouse, D. E., Kelley, H. H., Nisbett, R. E., Valins, S., & Weiner, B. (Eds.), *Attribution: Perceiving the causes of behavior*. Morristown, N. J.: General Learning Press, 1971, 1972.

Jones, E. E. and Davis, K. E. From acts to dispositions: The attribution process in person perception. In L. Berkowitz (Ed.) *Advances in experimental social psychology* (Vol. 2). New York: Academic Press, 1965.

Jones, E. E. and McGillis, D. Correspondent inferences and the attribution cube: A comparative reappraisal. In J. M. Harvey, W. J. Ickes and R. F. Kidd (Eds.), *New directions in attribution research*, Vol. I. Hillsdale, New Jersey, Lawrence Erlbaum Associates: 1976.

Jones, R. A., Linder, D. E., Kiesler, C. A., Zanna, M., & Brehm, J. W. Internal states or external stimuli? Observers' judgments and the dissonance–self-perception controversy. *Journal of Experimental Social Psychology*, 1968, *4*, 247–269.

Kelley, H. H. Attribution theory in social psychology. In D. Levine (Ed.), *Nebraska Symposium on Motivation* (Vol. 15). Lincoln: University of Nebraska Press, 1967.

Kelley, H. H. *Attribution in social interaction*. Morristown, N.J.: General Learning Press, 1971.

Kelley, H. H. *Causal schemata and the attribution process*. Morristown, General Learning Press, 1972.

Kelley, H. H. The processes of causal attribution. *American Psychologist*, 1973, *28*, 107–128.

King, B., & Janis, I. L. Comparison of the effectiveness of improvised vs. non-improvised role-playing in producing opinion changes. *Human Relations*, 1956, *9*, 177–186.

Kruglanski, A. W. The endogenous–exogenous partition in attribution theory. *Psychological Review*, 1975, *82*, 387–406.

Kruglanski, A. W., Alon, S., & Lewis, T. Retrospective misattribution and task enjoyment. *Journal of Experimental Social Psychology*, 1972, *8*, 493–501.

Kruglanski, A. W., Friedman, I., & Zeevi, G. The effects of extrinsic incentives on some qualitative aspects of task performance. *Journal of Personality* 1971, *39*, 606–617.

Kruglanski, A. W., Riter, A., Amitai, A., Margolin, B., Shabtai, L., & Zaksh, D. Can money enhance intrinsic motivation? A test of the content–consequence hypothesis. *Journal of Personality and Social Psychology,* 1975, *31*, 744–750.

Lepper, M. R., & Greene, D. Turning play into work: Effects of adult surveillance and extrinsic rewards on children's intrinsic motivation. *Journal of Personality and Social Psychology,* 1975, *31*, 479–486.

Lepper, M. R., Greene, D., & Nisbett, R. E. Undermining children's intrinsic interest with extrinsic reward: A test of the overjustification hypothesis. *Journal of Personality and Social Psychology,* 1973, *29*, 129–137.

Linder, D. E., Cooper, J., & Jones, E. E. Decision freedom as a determinant of the role of incentive magnitude in attitude change. *Journal of Personality and Social Psychology,* 1967, *6*, 245–254.

Nel, E., Helmreich, R., and Aronson, E. Opinion change in the advocate as a function of the persuasibility of his audience: A clarification of the meaning of dissonance. *Journal of Personality and Social Psychology,* 1969, *12*, 117–125.

Nisbett, R. E., & Schachter, S. Cognitive manipulation of pain. *Journal of Experimental Social Psychology,* 1966, *2*, 227–236.

Nisbett, R. E., & Valins, S. *Perceiving the causes of one's own behavior.* Morristown, N. J.: General Learning Press, 1971.

Rosenberg, M. J. When dissonance fails: On eliminating evaluation apprehension from attitude measurement. *Journal of Personality and Social Psychology,* 1965, *1*, 28–42.

Rosenberg, M. J. Discussion: On reducing the inconsistency between consistency theories. In R. Abelson, E. Aronson, W. McGuire, T. Newcomb, M. Rosenberg, & P. Tannenbaum (Eds.), *Theories of cognitive consistency: A sourcebook.* Chicago: Rand McNally, 1968.

Schachter, S., & Singer, J. E. Cognitive, social, and physiological determinants of emotional state. *Psychological Review,* 1962, *69*, 379–399.

Skinner, B. F. *Verbal behavior.* Englewood Cliffs, N.J.: Prentice–Hall, 1957.

Snyder, M., & Ebbesen, E. B. Dissonance awareness: A test of dissonance theory versus self-perception theory. *Journal of Experimental Social Psychology,* 1972, *8*, 502–517.

Spence, J. T. The distracting effects of material reinforcers in the discrimination learning of lower- and middle-class children. *Child Development,* 1970, *41*, 103–111.

Staats, A. W. Experimental demand characteristics and the classical conditioning of attitudes. *Journal of Personality and Social Psychology,* 1969, *11*, 187–192.

Tolman, E. C. *Collected papers in psychology.* Berkeley, Calif.: University of California Press, 1951.

Valins, S., & Nisbett, R. E. *Attribution and the treatment of emotional disorders.* Morristown, N.J.: General Learning Press, 1971.

Vroom, V. H. Industrial social psychology. In G. Lindzey & E. Aronson (Eds.), *The handbook of social psychology* (Vol. 5). Reading, Mass.: Addison–Wesley, 1969.

Weick, K. E. Reduction of cognitive dissonance through task enhancement and effort expenditure. *Journal of Abnormal and Social Psychology,* 1964, *68*, 533–539.

Zanna, M. P., Kiesler, C. A., & Pilkonis, P. A. Positive and negative attitudinal affect established by classical conditioning. *Journal of Personality and Social Psychology,* 1970, *14*, 321–328.

II
RESEARCH AND THEORY

The history of science is surprisingly replete with examples of independent "multiple discoveries" of new phenomena or new approaches to classic problems. In these cases, novel findings or ideas have appeared nearly simultaneously in laboratories often separated by continents. Different investigators, working independently and often within different theoretical frameworks, happen upon common solutions from different directions.

Much of the research in this volume has this same property. For the most part, the research programs described in this section were undertaken by investigators unaware that other related work was being or had been carried out by their colleagues elsewhere. As a result, the research programs undertaken by the contributors to this volume show a surprising diversity in theoretical approach and research styles within the framework established by the common problem of examining the potential "hidden costs of reward."

In this section, each of the authors provides a presentation focusing primarily on his own program of research and theory, allowing the reader to compare and contrast these different approaches. Though each of the contributors has by now benefited from the insights of others, the similarities and differences in approach suggest a number of avenues for further research in this area.

McGraw (Chapter 3) concentrates on the experimental literature concerned with the effects of rewards on measures of learning and task performance along both qualitative and quantitative task dimensions. His analysis of this literature suggests that the appearance of facilitative and detrimental effects of rewards will depend on both the structure of the task or response involved and the prior relationship between the subjects' interests and abilities and the demands imposed by the task.

Condry and Chambers (Chapter 4) examine the effects of reward on the process of learning and the manner in which subjects approach and disengage themselves from particular activities. The context created by the offer of rewards, they suggest, may have significant effects on behavior at each stage of an individual's engagement with the activity.

Kruglanski (Chapter 5) analyzes the effects of rewards on performance and subsequent behavior in terms of an attributional model. In this account, rewards are viewed as a significant determinant of the individual's attribution of his or her behavior to either endogenous or exogenous factors; and these attributions, in turn, are hypothesized to serve as partial determinants of subjects' performance and subsequent behavior.

Lepper and Greene (Chapter 6) explore several complementary mechanisms by which rewards may affect both the nature of one's engagement in an activity in the immediate presence of salient, extrinsic contingencies and one's subsequent interest in the activity in the later absence of salient, extrinsic contingencies. They suggest that distinct, though partially overlapping, processes must be considered to account for the detrimental effects of reward on both immediate performance and subsequent interest.

Deci and Porac (Chapter 7) present a broad conceptual model of the nature and determinants of intrinsic motivation and an analysis of the effects of rewards on intrinsic motivation in terms of cognitive evaluation theory. To comprehend the detrimental effects of reward, they conclude, requires simultaneous attention to both the informational and the controlling properties of rewards.

3 The Detrimental Effects of Reward on Performance: A Literature Review and a Prediction Model

Kenneth O. McGraw
University of Mississippi

If asked to rate "reward" on a 5-point evaluative scale, psychologists and members at large of the cultures of the Western world would surely give it a healthy 4+. Reward, incentive, bonus—these terms carry positive connotations. This feeling no doubt arises from the scientific and cultural belief that reward[1] is a facilitator. If you want someone to do a better job, for instance, you increase the incentives. To solve a problem, you throw money at it. Given this general orientation in the science and the culture, John McCullers and I were surprised a few years back to discover some evidence that children who were simply asked to cooperate by solving a discrimination problem solved it faster than children who were rewarded for the same task.

Our first reaction to this discrimination learning research that showed reward to have an apparent detrimental effect—and indeed the reaction of the investigators responsible for uncovering the effect—was to see the results as anomalies attributable to either task or procedural variables. Now, however, it is obvious from our own work and that of others we have reviewed that the detrimental effect of reward on children's discrimination learning is but part of a larger picture. We now know that tangible, extrinsic incentives that are offered for performance often produce detrimental effects on performance on a number of standard laboratory tasks, and the aim in the first section of this chapter is to draw together the research that demonstrates this. In the second section we try to make sense of the data by pointing to variables that appear crucial in determining whether incentives will enhance or hinder performance. What emerges from this

---

[1] By *reward* both here and throughout the paper, unless otherwise specified, we mean tangible, extrinsic incentives of the sort that are commonly used to promote performance.

review and analysis is the claim that incentives will have a detrimental effect on performance when two conditions are met: first, when the task is interesting enough for subjects that the offer of incentives is a superfluous source of motivation; second, when the solution to the task is open-ended enough that the steps leading to a solution are not immediately obvious. In terms that are developed later, this reduces to the requirement that the task be inherently attractive and have a heuristic solution.

A.   DETRIMENTAL EFFECTS OF REWARD ON PERFORMANCE

Discrimination Learning

The area that is richest in instances of reward having a detrimental effect on performance is that of children's discrimination learning. A pioneer study by Miller and Estes (1961) is illustrative. Third-grade subjects were given the task of distinguishing between line drawings of "Bill" and "his twin brother." There were two incentive conditions that differed in magnitude of incentive—$.50 and $.01—and a nonreward (knowledge of results) condition. Each child was given 100 trials on which he or she had to say which of the two drawings was of Bill. Although there was no difference between the two incentive groups in numbers of errors, both incentive groups made more errors than did the nonreward subjects. Also, there were more learners in the nonreward condition (15) than in the $.50 (12) and $.01 (10) conditions, but these differences were not significant. Since Miller and Estes's report, a number of other studies have appeared that substantiate the finding that reward can have a detrimental effect on children's discrimination learning. The children in these cases have ranged from preschoolers to seventh graders. Their rewards have been money, candy, or some other tangible object that was delivered trial–by–trial, contingent upon their being correct. The tasks have included Miller and Estes's perceptual discriminations, verbal discriminations (Haddad, McCullers, & Moran, 1976; Spence, 1970), picture discriminations (Schere, 1969; Spence & Dunton, 1967; Spence & Segner, 1967), and a patterned probability task (McGraw & McCullers, 1974).

Concept Attainment

Two concept-discrimination experiments (McCullers & Martin, 1971; Terrell, Durkin, & Wiesley, 1959) that provide evidence of a detrimental effect of reward were procedurally identical to the studies just cited. Subjects and rewards were the same as well. They differed only in the nature of the solution. Pairs of events, each of which was defined by the conjunction of three attributes, were presented trial–by–trial; and the subject's job was to say which of the two was correct. To be consistently correct, the subject had to detect that one of the three attributes (e.g., the size, shape, or color) correlated perfectly with correctness and so provided the means of determining whether an event was or was not correct. As before, all subjects were given knowledge of results following each trial; but in addition, rewarded subjects received some valued object as an incentive for being correct as often as possible.

Other concept-attainment studies that provide evidence of a detrimental effect of reward have differed radically from these. They have used adult subjects and a more demanding type task. Rather than the correct concept being defined uni-dimensionally, it was defined multidimensionally—meaning that correctness of an event was determined not by the presence of a single attribute (e.g., redness) but by the presence of a conjunction of attributes (e.g., redness and squareness). A second feature making these tasks more demanding was that a selection rather than a reception procedure was used to present information to the subjects. A selection procedure requires that subjects request—as in the game of 20 ques-tions—the information they would like to have. The task stimuli, therefore, are not presented to subjects by trials; rather they are all laid before the subject in an array. The experimenter gets the subject started by pointing to one of the events that conforms to the rule he or she has in mind; then the subject must, by asking about other events in the array, determine what the experimenter's rule is.

Tasks of this sort have been used in two studies to compare the performance of incentive and nonincentive subjects. Condry (1975), using high school stu-dents, found that subjects who were promised $.50 for each of six concept-attainment problems solved them less efficiently than did subjects not offered an incentive. This difference in relative efficiency was reflected both in the number of information requests needed to determine the experimenter's rule and the proportion of logical to illogical requests. McGraw and McCullers (1975b) ob-tained similar results. In this study, the time taken to achieve a solution was recorded along with the number of information requests. On each of four prob-lems, reward subjects ($.50 per solution) took longer and asked more questions than did nonreward subjects, but the differences were not statistically reliable.

Weick (1964), from a different theoretical perspective, found volunteer adult subjects to do better on all measures of concept-attainment performance than subjects who participated for experimental credit. It is not clear, though, that experimental credit functioned as an incentive for performance in the same sense as the financial incentives used by Condry (1975) and McGraw and McCullers (1975b). Weick invoked dissonance theory to explain his results.

Tasks Requiring Insight and Creativity

As we turn more toward problems requiring "insight" or "creativity" for their solution, the tasks become harder to classify; but they remain consistent in showing reward to have a detrimental effect on performance. Viesti (1971), for example, describes two experiments he conducted using an "insight learning task." On each page of a 15-page booklet there appeared a set of three computer-generated patterns. Two of the patterns were 2/3 redundant, and the other was completely different. The subject's job was to say which of the three patterns was different. Subjects in Experiment 1 were initially given practice on the problem and then 4 months later were divided into reward ($.50 per problem) and nonreward groups to complete the same task again. It was apparently the case that Phase 1 exposure to the task did not contaminate the results of Phase 2, because the complexity of the task was such that subjects were never explicitly aware of the grounds they were using for making their decision as to which pattern was different. Statistical tests confirm the similarity of the performance curves in Phase 1 with those in Phase 2. A comparison of results in Phase 2 alone, however, showed the nonreward subjects to have been correct more often than the reward subjects. As this finding was contrary to Viesti's hypothesis that reward should facilitate insightful learning, a second experiment was conducted—this time with no Phase 1 practice session. Again nonreward subjects were correct more often than the reward subjects, even though in this second study the reward had been doubled ($1 per problem) over that in Experiment 1.

Viesti's (1971) specific hypothesis was that reward should "shift the point of insight so that fewer trials would be necessary to achieve it [p. 181]." From figures that are presented, however, an opposite effect appears to have resulted. In both studies, the point at which detection of the different pattern jumps to above chance came earliest in the nonreward group.

In a study that more clearly indicates reward to have a detrimental effect on complex problem solving, Glucksberg (1962) gave college students Duncker's (1945) functional fixedness problem involving a candle, a box of thumbtacks, and a book of matches; the subject's job is to mount the candle on a vertical screen. To do so, he or she must empty the tacks from their box and use the box as a platform that can be thumbtacked to the screen. The difficulty in this task is in seeing the box as a platform rather than a container. Nonreward subjects were told that their solution times would be used to establish norms for this type problem. Reward subjects were told that they could win either $5 or $20 by solving the problem quickly. Five dollars was to be paid to each subject in the top 25%, with $20 going to the one subject who was fastest. The results showed that reward subjects took some 3 1/2 minutes longer to solve the problem than nonreward subjects, and this difference was highly significant. Using a different functional fixedness problem—one in which a screwdriver must be used to complete a circuit when the available wires prove to be too short—Glucksberg (1964) replicated this result.

Recently, McGraw and McCullers (1976a) have found reward and nonreward groups to differ in solution time on a complex problem requiring insight. Adult

maybe the
reward made there
more care-
ful solutions

subjects were given a series of water-jar problems, patterned after those of Luchins (1942). All but the last problem in the series (extinction problem) were soluble in a single way by a well-defined rule that involved using all three of the available jars in a precise order. The extinction problem required a more direct, two-jar solution. As in Duncker's functional fixedness problem where the difficulty is in seeing a box full of tacks as a platform rather than a container, the difficulty in solving the extinction problem is in seeing the novel possibility of using just two jars rather than the accustomed three. Reward subjects were told that money was being offered for each correct solution ($.10) in order to motivate them to do their very best and that a bonus ($.50) would be paid if all the problems were correct. At the same time, all subjects had been assured that they would be able to find a correct answer to each problem if they just persisted, and they were promised unlimited time to solve the problems. Thus, although the reward was contingent on performance, performance requirements were lenient enough that subjects should not have felt the pressure that was perhaps present in Glucksberg's studies where subjects competed for rewards of up to $20 or in Viesti's where there was a time limit on each problem. Nevertheless, in three studies, reward subjects consistently took longer to find the correct solution to the final problem and, in addition, made more errors than nonreward subjects even though their reward was contingent upon recording a correct answer.

Two creativity tasks were included by Kruglanski, Friedman, and Zeevi (1971) in a battery of five tests that were administered to fifth-grade, Israeli school children. The first task required subjects to supply as many titles as possible for a literary paragraph. The second involved the composition of a story in which children were to use as many words as they could from a specified list of 50. Both tasks were scored both quantitatively (number of titles and number of specified words employed) and qualitatively (originality of the titles and originality of the story). The reward in this task departed from the "tangible" rewards of previous studies. For their cooperation, reward subjects were promised a trip to the University of Tel Aviv. Correlations for performance on the two creativity tasks were high, so they were collapsed into a single creativity score. The subjects who were promised nothing for their participation did significantly better on these tasks than those subjects who had been promised the trip.

Incidental Learning

A research area that has produced considerable evidence that reward can have a detrimental effect on performance is incidental learning. Reward in these studies is offered for intentional task performance, and then incidental learning is measured as a function of whether or not a subject was rewarded during the intentional learning phase. One convenient separation of studies in this area can be made on the basis of whether the incidental events that subjects are not instructed to attend to are spatially separate or contiguous with the intentional stimuli that subjects are instructed to attend to. There is evidence of a detrimental effect of reward on both types of tasks.

Bahrick, Fitts, and Rankin (1952) provided a clear illustration of the detrimental effect of reward on learning involving spatially separate events. While adult subjects were engaged on a tracking task, for which half had been promised reward and half had not, three of four lights located at the periphery of the visual field were unexpectedly turned on for 5-second durations. Subjects were then scored on whether they had noticed the lights and, if so, whether they recalled the sequence. Subjects who were being rewarded contingent upon their tracking performance not only scored fewer points than nonrewarded subjects but 17 of the 50 reward subjects as compared to only 4 of the 50 nonreward subjects failed to notice any lights at all.

Results from a study by McNamara and Fisch (1964) support those of Bahrick et al. (1952). College students learned a 6-item, serial-order task using verbal materials and the anticipation method. The target words were typed in upper-case letters at the center of stimulus cards. Arranged at varying distances around the center on each card were 4 lower-case words whose purpose the experimenter did not explain. After subjects had reached criterion on the central task, they were asked to recall as many of the 24 incidental words (4 per card × 6 cards) as they could. Subjects not rewarded for their central task performance were superior at this incidental learning and had fewer intrusion errors in their recall lists. Nonreward subjects recalled an average of 21 incidental words and had an average of only 2 intrusions. Comparable figures for the reward group were 13 and 4. A third group that was motivated by fear of shock did least well. They recalled an average of only 7 incidental words and made an average of 9 intrusion errors. A further difference between these groups was reflected in the spatial distributions of those words recalled. The words recalled by the fear group were restricted to an area near the target word at the center of the card. The words recalled by the monetary reward group were more widely spread but not so widely spread as those recalled by the nonreward group. The strength of these data is somewhat dampened by the inadequate statistical analyses. Chi-square tests that did not allow for individual comparisons were used to determine the significance of the incidental recall scores. No analysis was made of the differences in size of the field from which information was sampled.

There is always the problem in incidental learning that subjects may self-instruct themselves to learn the incidental material. To control for this problem, Johnson and Thomson (1962) made the incidental material distracting so that it would interfere with learning the intentional task. To do this, subjects learned a serial list of 10 nonsense syllables while a second subject learned a similar but different list beside them. Anticipations of the upcoming nonsense syllable had to be vocalized, so each subject was exposed to the other's list auditorily while being exposed to his own visually. The incidental and intentional stimuli were thus experienced in different perceptual modes, which would seem to make this study more similar to those by Bahrick et al. and McNamara and Fisch than the studies discussed next, in which the incidental and intentional stimuli were spatially (and modally) coincident. Johnson and Thomson's results add further support to the findings that incidental learning is inferior when reward is offered for intentional performance, because the recognition scores for the nonsense syllables in the partner's list were higher for nonreward than for reward subjects. In fact, the recognition scores for reward subjects were not significantly better than chance, indicating that very little incidental learning had taken place. Unlike the previous two studies where rewarded subjects were given money, Johnson and Thomson's reward subjects were motivated by the chance of improving their borderline grades in psychology.

Johnson and Thomson controlled for self-instruction to learn the incidental material by making the incidental stimuli distracting. In a final study demonstrating incidental learning of spatially separate cues to be less when subjects are rewarded for central-task performance, the danger of self-instruction was controlled by using nonhuman subjects (Davis & Lovelace, 1963). In this study rhesus monkeys were presented with a discrimination problem in the usual way with a Wisconsin General Test Apparatus. Six inches behind the intentional stimuli that covered the food wells were a pair of incidental stimuli. One of these was consistently paired with the correct intentional stimulus. Rewards were either raisins or celery, and raisins were, of course, the preferred reward. Following mastery of the central task, the incidental stimuli replaced the intentional stimuli as covers for the food wells. Had subjects been attentive to peripheral cues during training, it would be reflected in second-problem performance. Using number of errors to second-task mastery as a measure of performance on the second problem, it was shown that second-task learning was significantly better when celery rather than raisins had been the reward for central-task performance.

Evidence that reward can have a detrimental effect on the formation of incidental associations, not only when the incidental stimuli are spatially separate but also when spatially contiguous, comes from two studies. In the first of these (Bahrick, 1954), adult subjects were given a serial list of 14 geometric forms (moons, circles, triangles, etc.), each of which was distinctively colored. The intentional task required only serial learning of the forms, but the subjects were later tested using a recognition procedure for acquisition of form–color associations. On this test, reward subjects, who had been told that they could win up to $1.50 by learning the serial list rapidly, matched fewer colors to forms than did subjects who were not given an incentive set. Staat and McCullers (1974) produced a similar effect using an entirely different procedure. The task in this case was to learn 9 paired associates using the anticipation method. Each correct anticipation won reward subjects $.05. When subjects reached a criterion of 6 consecutive, correct anticipations, training was stopped and an R–S recall test given. R items were listed, and subjects had to supply the S items. Subjects not rewarded during acquisition were able to recall 6.05 of the stimulus items, whereas reward subjects could only recall 3.85 of them.

CONCLUSION

As is obvious from this review, the discrimination learning results that set off our search for detrimental effects of reward are indeed but part of a larger picture. In addition to discrimination learning, evidence of detrimental effects of reward comes from concept attainment, insightful learning, functional fixedness, incidental learning, and creativity tasks as well. In establishing generality for the phenomenon of reward's effect, as important as the variety of tasks is the variety of subject and procedural variables over which the phenomenon appears to hold. Neither the age of the subjects, the method of presenting the reward (trial-by-trial or upon completion of the task), the contingency of the reward on performance, nor the type of extrinsic reward (tangible or intangible such as the trip to Tel Aviv University or the improved grade) appears for the moment to be a critical variable in producing a detrimental effect. This is not to say that none of these is critical. That conclusion could only come from studies in which these variables are manipulated intraexperimentally. The less satisfactory evidence on which the current conclusion is based is principally interexperimental. If these variables are truly not important, then the detrimental effect of reward on performance at these tasks becomes a very general one whose presence cannot be ignored, and the problem becomes one of determining what it is about these tasks that makes performance on them susceptible to a disruptive effect of reward.

B.   WHEN FACILITATION? WHEN DISRUPTION?

The Aversive-Attractive Task Dimension

Acknowledging that the detrimental effect of reward is reliable and widespread produces the problem of reconciling this phenomenon with the more familiar one of reward facilitation. As a first step toward solving that problem, it is important to note that there is little overlap between the sorts of tasks used to produce a detrimental effect and those that are used to produce a facilitating effect. Discrimination learning, concept attainment, insight learning, creativity problems, and incidental recall, as we have seen, are the types of problems used in the research that has produced evidence of reward having a detrimental effect. In contrast, marble dropping, lever pressing, letter canceling, and vigilance are prime examples of tasks that show facilitation. The two sets of tasks differ in many ways. One that we see as important is their attractiveness for subjects.

The tasks used in the literature on the detrimental effects of reward can generally be characterized as attractive. The accuracy of this characterization has not been empirically demonstrated;[2] however, it holds a certain subjective validity for anyone who has administered these problems to school-age and college subjects such as were used in the research cited in Section A. The tasks appear to be tests of intelligence; and subjects, at least those in the student population, are generally motivated to do well regardless of whether they are rewarded. In contrast, the perceptual–motor tasks that predominate in the literature on facilitating effects of reward involve little intelligence. Retarded subjects not suffering a motor dysfunction, for example, would be expected to perform as well on them as normals. When one speaks of facilitation on such tasks, then, what is meant is that there are increases in rote performance measures such as rate, latency, and persistence. Because these latter tasks provide no challenge to intellectual competence and only a minimal challenge to perceptual–motor competence, we judge them to be at least relatively unattractive for subjects.

Why it should be the case that reward should have the effect of improving performance at unattractive tasks such as those that measure only the rate, speed, or persistence of simple–perceptual motor behavior has an intuitively appealing answer—nonreward subjects on these tasks simply do not try as hard as reward subjects. Certainly no one would argue with this explanation if put into the context of performance differences in a behavior modification program. The goal of such a program might be to increase the rate of some socially desirable behavior. All subjects know equally well how to perform the behavior and are equally capable of emitting it at a high rate. Only the reward subjects are motivated to do so, however; hence, the facilitating effect of reward.

In summary, then, the first condition that is relevant to distinguishing the instances of facilitation from instances of disruption involves what we interpret to be the attractiveness of the task for nonreward subjects. Reward subjects will presumably engage wholeheartedly in any task, no matter how odious, if the reward is perceived as equitable. Not so, however, the nonreward subjects: The extent to which they compete against standards set by the experimenter or their own standards will vary with the interest they take in the task set them. Because it

---

[2] We did, however, ask subjects in a recent water-jar study (McGraw & McCullers, 1976a) how likely they would be to work the water-jar problems on their own time. The question was put in this way: "Imagine that the experimenter were suddenly called away and so had to excuse you from the study before you could begin work on the water-jar problems. Before leaving, though, he handed you a list of problems saying, 'Here are some of the problems you would have worked which you might want to look at sometime.' How likely would you be to work these problems?" So that there would be no influence of social desirability, subjects answered this question in private and dropped their answer in a box out of the experimenter's sight. On a 5-point scale running from "Surely wouldn't" to "Surely would" the mean response was 4.1. We feel confident that equally high ratings would be given by school children and adults to discrimination learning, concept attainment, and other problem-solving tasks.

is against the performance of these nonreward subjects that the effect of reward is to be measured, prerequisite to the appearance of a detrimental effect is a task sufficiently attractive to elicit their best effort. Much of the evidence of reward facilitation of performance has been obtained in studies where this was probably not the case; that is, in cases where the comparison—in the extreme—was between subjects who were trying very hard and those who were hardly trying at all. We assume this to be the case on the basis of the noteworthy difference between the types of tasks used to produce a detrimental effect and the types of tasks used to produce facilitating effects. We need now to further define attractiveness.

Although it is true that some tasks are generally more attractive than others, it would be totally inadequate to define task attractiveness solely in terms of task variables. Because we are concerned with the attractiveness of a task for individual subjects at the time of the experiment, between- and within-subject variables also become important in defining attractiveness. Within-subject variables of obvious importance would involve present mental states. No matter how interesting a given task usually is for a subject, it would be decidedly uninteresting if the subject were tired, sick, or in some way preoccupied by "more important" matters. Between-subject variables involve individual preferences. No doubt a host of personal history factors determine preference, but one that concerns us now is past history of success with problems of the sort used in the experiment.

We need to make a special issue of a subject's past history of success, because it provides a way of explaining away the results of three studies that are inconsistent with the findings reported in Section A. These are that Kausler, Laughlin, and Trapp (1963) found rewarded subjects to be superior in incidental learning to those that were not rewarded, that Terrell and Kennedy (1957) found the same to be true on a concept-attainment task, and that Ward, Kogan, and Pankove (1972) found reward superiority on creativity tasks. Examining these studies for a common factor that might account for the aberrant findings reveals that these three studies, unlike the bulk of the studies cited in Section A, used lower-class children as subjects. Social class, therefore, stands out as a likely candidate among factors that might have made these studies different. This is not to say, of course, that social class is a limiting condition on the detrimental effect of reward but rather that there might be some variable associated with lower-class status that is. We assume that variable to be the lower incidence of success at intellectual tasks among lower- than among middle-class school children.

Social class per se does not limit the detrimental effect, because Spence, using conceptual and discrimination—learning tasks (Spence, 1970, 1971; Spence & Dunton, 1967; Spence & Segner, 1967), obtained evidence for a detrimental effect with lower-class children. She attributes her results, however, to the special care she took to assure subjects, through pretraining, of their ability to solve problems of the sort they would be posed. In the absence of such training and assurance, she suspected that the experimental situation and instructions for a conceptual task of the sort she was administering might intimidate a significant portion of her lower-class subjects and cause them to withdraw from the situation. It was to this supposed withdrawal that she attributed the reward facilitation found by Terrell and Kennedy.

If it is the case that the lower-class, nonreward subjects in the three studies in question were inferior to their rewarded counterparts because they withdrew from the task—that is, because the task was unattractive to them—it would be nice to have some evidence of this. At present it is only a likely hypothesis. One helpful bit of evidence would be cross-study comparisons showing the nonreward subject performance for the three studies in question to be abnormally poor. Evidence of this sort does indeed exist for two of the three studies.

The nonreward subjects in the Terrell and Kennedy (1957) study took 35.7 trials to reach criterion. Nonreward middle-class subjects in a later study using the same task (Terrell, 1958) took only 7.35 trials. Intelligence data are not reported for the two samples, but it is almost certain that the performance differences are greater than any ability differences that might have existed. Similarly, in the Kausler et al. (1963) study, there is evidence of subpar performance. After 10 trials, the lower-class subjects, who were of average intelligence (mean IQ = 98.3), had reached only 60% mastery of the 14-item intentional list; whereas previous subjects reached "near perfect mastery [p. 197]" in the same number of trials. Both these comparisons suggest that reward facilitation occurred in the Terrell and Kennedy and Kausler et al. studies, because nonreward subjects were performing at subpar levels. The explanation for reward facilitation here, therefore, may be the same as the explanation for reward facilitation on any unattractive task; that is, reward facilitates because it is a *necessary* source of motivation. In its absence, subjects do not make a serious effort at task mastery. This is in contrast to situations in which reward is a detriment, for in these situations reward is superfluous to producing an interest in good performance.

A rather simple way of conceptualizing the scheme being developed here for predicting reward's effects is a 2 × 2 matrix of activities (tasks) and anticipated outcomes (incentives). Though the attractiveness of tasks (again keeping in mind that this is a variable determined by between- and within-subject factors that interact with the particular task specified for the experiment) is conceived of as a continuous variable, here we make a simple binary distinction between attractive and aversive tasks. Independently of whether one perceives a situation as being attractive or aversive, one can be either rewarded or not for engaging in it. The four cells resulting from this two-way split on orthogonal dimensions are given in Figure 3.1.

There are two possible experimental pairings of the four cells of Figure 3.1. These are indicated by arrows. There are only two pairings, because attractiveness is a measure independent of one's incentive condition. Some might argue that this is insensitive to the dynamics of attitudes. That is, incentives could act to

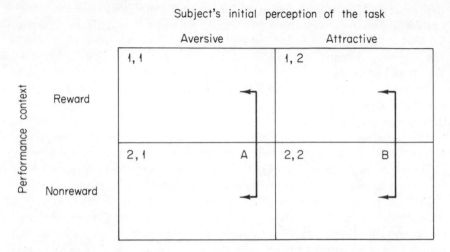

Fig. 3.1. A matrix of activities (tasks) and anticipated outcomes (incentives) for predicting reward's effects. The arrows indicate the two experimental comparisons that can be made using these variables.

make a task more attractive via secondary reinforcement, or nonreward might have the same effect via dissonance reduction. This, however, would be to miss the point. Attractiveness here is a preexperimental determination of the interest a task holds for a subject. That being the case, there are only two pairings, and reward should facilitate in A and be detrimental in B.

The Algorithmic–Heuristic Solution Dimension

Although there is a very large amount of evidence to show that reward has a facilitating effect on the rate, speed, and persistence of performance on unattractive, perceptual–motor tasks and a respectable amount of evidence to show that reward has a detrimental effect on performance on attractive, problem solving tasks of the sort mentioned in Section A, the aversive–attractive dimension alone will not be sufficient to predict when reward will be facilitating and when detrimental. The reason is that many tasks that fall toward the attractive side of the aversive–attractive dimension—examples from serial learning, paired-associate learning, mental multiplication, and perceptual recognition will be given—do not show reward to have a detrimental effect. For this reason, a third dimension will have to be added to the matrix in Figure 3.1.

Mental multiplication.   When college student subjects are asked to mentally multiply three-digit numbers, the task surely has the appearance of a test of intelligence, and so we would assume that the subjects are highly motivated to do well regardless of whether they are rewarded. On the basis of the aversive–

attractive distinction alone, then, we might expect reward to disrupt performance on this task. As it turns out, however, reward appears to facilitate. Weinstein demonstrated this in a number of studies (Weinstein, 1971a, 1971b, 1972) looking at negative and positive contrast effects in human performance. "Upshifts" in incentive brought faster solution times, and "downshifts," longer solution times. More to the point here is that preshift times were reliably differentiated by magnitude of incentive.

It was possible that facilitation in Weinstein's studies was just an artifact of procedure because he failed to control for correctness of response. Any response at all, correct or incorrect, was accepted as a solution and its latency recorded. This meant that subjects who took time to check their answers would appear to do less well than subjects who responded more quickly but with less accuracy. In unpublished work, however, (McGraw & McCullers, 1976b) using a between-groups design in which only correct answers were accepted, mean differences in the same direction as Weinstein's were found. Reward subjects were faster to solve the mental multiplication problems than were nonreward subjects.

Serial learning. The evidence for reward's effect on serial learning is extensive, because serial-learning tasks are so frequently used as the intentional task in incidental-learning studies. In three studies that have used the same serial list of 14 geometric forms (circle, moon, cross, square, etc.), 2 show incentive subjects to have taken fewer trials to learn the list to the criterion of one errorless trial (Dornbush, 1965; Bahrick, 1954). The third (Kausler, Laughlin, & Trapp, 1963) found no difference between incentive and nonincentive subjects. Wray (1966), using a list of 10 geometric forms, likewise found no difference. Both the latter studies used junior high students and limited training to a fixed number of trials. Kausler et al. (1963) argue that this is the reason that incentive subjects were not superior to nonincentive subjects in their study. There are, of course, a welter of variables—exposure rate, subject characteristics, position of the incidental cues, instructions, etc.—that could be used to qualify the above results; but discussing them would not greatly aid us in reaching the goal of determining when reward will facilitate and when it will hinder performance. The general conclusion would stand that reward will either facilitate or have no influence upon serial-learning tasks of the type used in the above studies, despite the fact that this can be an attractive task for some students.

Paired-associate learning. Paired-associate tasks have been much used in research into reward's effect on memory. One standard paradigm is to vary the incentive value of pairs in the list and to cue subjects, most frequently at the time of exposure, as to the value. What one finds in this case is that the high-value pairs are recalled better than low-value pairs (e.g., Harley, 1965a). One finds that same effect in free-recall tasks (Cuvo & Witryol, 1971). These within-subject procedures, however, fail to answer the question of whether a subject performing for no reward will do better or worse than a subject who is working for an extrinsic incentive. To answer this question, between-subject comparisons are necessary.

Using a between-groups design, Goyen and Lyle (1971) are the only investigators to have found a large degree of reward facilitation in paired-associate learning. Their subjects were 6- to 7-year-old children who learned a nine-pair list in which both stimulus and response were familiar pictures. Tests were administered using a multiple-choice procedure. The work of other investigators makes it equally plain, however, that even though paired-associate learning can be attractive, the effect of reward will not invariably be detrimental. Renne (1965), for example, found a tendency for reward to facilitate the paired-associate learning of fourth- and fifth-grade children when the list was constructed so as to be low in interstimulus, interresponse, and stimulus–response similarities. Harley (1965b) found nearly perfect overlap between the learning curves of reward and nonreward adult subjects on a 13-pair list constructed of low-association-value, CVC trigrams.

Perceptual recognition.   There is nothing noxious about participating in a short-term, perceptual-recognition study, yet one frequently finds evidence for reward facilitation on these tasks. Glucksberg (1962), for example, found that rewarded adults had significantly lower recognition thresholds for tachistoscopically presented familiar words (e.g., *painter, market, church*) than did nonreward subjects. Reward in this case was substantial, ranging from $5 for being among the top 25% to $25 for being the subject with the lowest recognition threshold. Shantz, Rubin, and Smock (1962) and Smock and Rubin (1964) used a second type of recognition task with children 9 to 12 years of age. In this task a target form was shown to subjects, and then a slide was presented that included the target form along with three similar forms. The subject's job was to locate the target as rapidly as possible. Promise of a prize (necklace, model airplane, etc.) improved both the speed and accuracy of subjects on this task. A feature of both of these studies was to use stimulus forms of varying complexity, with the most complex being 16-pointed, random figures. Even in this condition, the reward subjects were superior. In a related task, Jeffrey and Skager (1962) found that reward (poker chips that could be used to pay to see a movie the experimenters had brought) resulted in a sharper stimulus-generalization gradient and fewer errors on a task that required subjects to respond to illuminations of a central light but to ignore illuminations of four lights arranged at regular intervals to the right and left of the target light. Subjects were of two ages: 7 and 10 years.

The instances just cited from mental multiplication, serial and paired-associate learning, and perceptual recognition in which reward failed to have a detrimental effect, despite the attractiveness of the tasks, prove to be theoretically very important. Although it is true that these tasks are probably not as intrinsically interesting as more complex problem-solving tasks and thus fall somewhere between lever pressing and creativity tasks on the aversive–attractive dimension, the reason that reward either facilitated or had no effect can have nothing to do with their attractiveness per se. The reason, as we see shortly, is that there is evidence from research using the same type of tasks that indicates reward to have a detrimental effect. We have here, then, cases of within-task facilitation and disruption. By determining in what way the tasks differed when the effects of reward differed, a second crucial dimension for predicting reward's effect can be isolated.

The task feature we propose as responsible for reward facilitation on the mental multiplication, verbal learning, and perceptual-recognition tasks we have reviewed so far is that the solutions to them were algorithmic. By that term we mean that the paths to the solutions were well mapped and straightforward, just as they are on other tasks where reward has been found to facilitate, like lever pressing and signal detection. No time needs to be spent in discovering what to do. For the tasks we are presently considering, this is best illustrated by mental multiplication. Finding the solution 4326 to the problem 721 × 6 may not be easy without the use of paper and pencil; but there is no question about where to begin, because multiplication is such a well-honed skill.

In clear contrast to problems like multiplication, for which one has a solution algorithm prior to beginning the task, are those problems for which one must develop the algorithm. It is these tasks that we label as requiring heuristic solutions. One very clear example of these are the functional-fixedness problems used by Glucksberg (1962, 1964). When confronted with the task of mounting a candle on the wall or completing an electrical circuit, the whole difficulty is in determining what operations would be relevant to a solution. We propose, then, that by adding the algorithmic–heuristic distinction to the attractive–aversive distinction, much better predictions of reward's effect on performance can be made, with the most favorable case for detrimental effect of reward being in the case where attractive tasks requiring heuristic solutions are used.

Figure 3.2 makes this prediction explicit. Reward and nonreward subjects can be compared on tasks that are aversive and algorithmic (Situation A), attractive and algorithmic (Situation B), aversive and heuristic (Situation C), or attractive and heuristic (Situation D). Only in D should reward be detrimental. In other cases it will facilitate.

Situation A has been amply discussed already in connection with Figure 3.1. Situation C deserves some mention, however, because it is a condition we will not see illustrated even though it is easily imagined. It would hold when an otherwise interesting and heuristically solvable task is not presently interesting for reasons of momentary subject factors such as fatigue. Situations B and D have been optimally illustrated as reward–nonreward comparisons on mental multiplication and functional-fixedness problems respectively. Both the conceptual and practical distinctions between them, however, need further explanation.

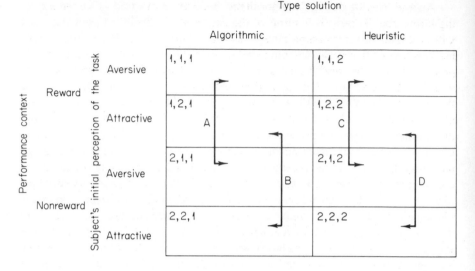

Fig. 3.2.   A matrix for predicting reward's effects that adds the algorithmic-heuristic distinction to the attractive–aversive distinction. Arrows indicate the four experimental comparisons which can be made using these variables.

Application of the Algorithmic-Heuristic Distinction

Though mental multiplication and functional-fixedness problems provide a clear contrast in what we mean by problems requiring either an algorithmic or heuristic solution, it is more difficult to see how the algorithmic–heuristic distinction applies to other tasks that have been an essential part of the discussion to this point. We next try to show how this distinction applies.

Serial and paired-associate learning.   Application of the terms *algorithmic* and *heuristic* to the solutions required in serial- and paired-associate learning tasks is not as straightforward as in the case of mental multiplication. It is not that these tasks tend to be algorithmic in the sense that the subject merely has to memorize the serial order or response item. Rather, these tasks, and other verbal learning tasks as well, are fit to the algorithmic–heuristic solution dimension in terms of the degree to which elaborate coding and mediation are required. In our review of serial and paired-associate tasks we have principally seen tasks in which the importance of coding and mediation were minimal. Consequently, it is no surprise that reward either facilitated or had no effect upon learning. We would predict, however—and some slight evidence is reviewed shortly—that as coding and mediation become more important, that is, as the effective strategy becomes more heuristic, reward will have an increasingly detrimental effect.

Another way of stating the algorithmic–heuristic distinction as we are applying it to verbal learning is in terms of the extent to which subject-produced cues
will be useful in short-cutting purely associative processes. Underwood (1964)
has pointed out that verbal learning studies are not *just* studies of the associative
process. To the contrary, the nature of some verbal learning tasks can be such as
to cause the subject to "call upon all his repertoire of habits and skills to outwit
the investigator [p. 52]." What we are suggesting is that when one is "calling
upon his habits and skills" with no clear plan for how to use them, one is solving
the problem heuristically. Therefore, whether reward will have a detrimental
effect on verbal learning or not is in our view a function of such variables as
meaningfulness and pronounceability of the materials, the amount of interitem
competition, etc. When task mastery is principally dependent upon rote variables
like amount of rehearsal and frequency unit accumulations, reward should either
facilitate or have no effect, depending on whether the nonreward subjects view
the tasks as aversive or attractive. But when the use of heuristically derived codes
and mediators provides a means of forming associations that would otherwise
have to be formed by rote, reward should begin to have a detrimental effect
because of nonreward subjects' superiority at heuristics. There is some slight
evidence for this view.

In the studies cited earlier under the heading "serial learning," the most
frequently used list—and the only one to provide evidence of reward
facilitation—was a list of easily discriminated geometric forms. This was the task
employed by Bahrick (1954), Dornbush (1965); Kausler, Laughlin, and Trapp
(1963); and Wray (1966). An equally simple, meaningful word list was employed by McNamara and Fisch (1964). No differences were apparent on this
task as a function of reward; perhaps because with only six items in the list, very
little variance was created in the trials-to-criterion measure. The failure of two
other tasks to show reward superiority is more relevant to the current hypothesis,
because these studies all used nonsense syllables for stimulus items (Johnson &
Thomson, 1962; Kausler & Trapp, 1962; Mechanic, 1962). There is, then,
within these few studies some evidence for a shift from reward facilitation to
findings of no difference when the stimulus items shift from being easily differentiated and meaningful to still distinguishable but less meaningful. The paired-
associate tasks reviewed provide additional evidence of this sort.

Of the studies previously reviewed under the heading of "paired-associate
learning," the two that indicated reward to have a facilitating effect on performance were ones that employed meaningful and easily differentiated items. In
the case where the reward effect was strongest (Goyen & Lyle, 1971), the task
was to pair pictures of familiar objects. The weaker instance of reward facilitation was found by Renne (1965), using meaningful word pairs that produced
minimal interitem competition. Both of these, then, were straightforward associative tasks in which subjects could not gain any appreciable advantage by

"calling upon their habits and skills to outwit the investigator." Other paired-associate tasks do provide this opportunity, and it is on these that the facilitating effect of reward apparently disappears.

The first piece of evidence of this sort comes from a high-competition-list condition that was included to contrast with the low-competition list in Renne's (1965) study. Whereas Renne found reward facilitation on the latter, he found reward to be detrimental to performance on the former. There was thus an interaction ($p <.$ 10) between incentive and the degree to which mediation and coding were required to master the list, and this tends to support the present claim that reward will facilitate verbal learning only to the extent that brute associative variables determine learning.

Evidence for this claim is available also in the study by Staat and McCullers (1974), which was previously mentioned in the section on incidental learning. Stimulus items for the paired-associate intentional task were bigrams, and response items were two-digit numbers; thus the nine pairs in the list were of the sort *SG-64* and *WP-15*. Because there are no obvious associates to use to code bigrams and numbers and to mediate bigram–number associations, subjects were forced by the Staat and McCullers task to be more creative in their mnemonics. It is thus significant that there was a strong tendency for nonreward subjects to learn the nine-pair list more rapidly than reward subjects ($p <.$ 10). The only other paired-associate study reviewed (Harley, 1965b) found no difference between reward and nonreward subjects when CVC trigrams of low-association value were used, and this is hardly contrary to the hypothesis.

Concept Identification and Concept Attainment   Another set of studies that are somewhat problematic as regards application of the algorithmic–heuristic solution distinction are concept-identification and concept-attainment tasks. The difficulty with these is that objectively, no matter how complex the concept, the way to a solution is straightforward: Identify the dimensions on which the stimuli are contrasted and the stimulus values belonging to those dimensions; then systematically eliminate dimensions by systematically eliminating values. All the necessary stimuli lie right in the task, so there is no need for subject-produced cues as was the case in verbal learning. Nor can conceptual behavior on the part of the subject short-cut the learning process. To reach a solution requires a fixed and inalterable amount of information. Thus, in a sense, there cannot be a "heuristic" solution to a concept-identification or attainment problem any more than there can be a heuristic solution to a multiplication problem.

What the above discussion overlooks, however, is that first discovering the algorithm for adding numbers x number of times was a heuristic process. Likewise, discovering the algorithm to use for concept identification and attainment is a heuristic process. In more familiar terms, discovering this algorithm is the process of learning to learn. Our hypothesis regarding the effects of reward on concept identification and attainment, then, is that reward will facilitate performance (or have no effect depending on the relationship of subjects to the task on the aversive–attractive dimension) when the algorithm is formed preexperimentally but that it will have a detrimental effect when the algorithm is formed in the course of the experiment.

Simple evidence that subjects do not begin complex conceptual tasks with the solution algorithm in mind is that subjects are not as efficient in solving the problems as are computers. One might argue that the computer differs from the human problem solver in more than having a program for solution prior to presentation of the problem: The computer has a perfect memory. This factor alone might account for the inferiority of human subjects to computers. But on examination of the types of problems that are used with children, it becomes obvious that it is the algorithm and not memory that is lacking.

Two-choice, three-dimensional, concept-identification problems are common among those used with school-age children. The dimensions might be shape, color, and position and the respective values—triangle–rectangle, black–white, right–left. To discover which of these values the experimenter is using to determine correctness, even if only one bit of information is gathered on each trial, would require only five trials or five bits of information in all, and the task for memory in this case should be no greater than in a five-item, serial-learning task. Yet subjects are often terribly slow to discover the experimenter's basis for classification.

Recently we conducted a series of investigations using a two-choice, five-dimensional, discrimination problem with fourth- and fifth-grade subjects (McGraw & McCullers, 1975a). After 100 trials, only 24 of the 160 subjects had learned the basis for determining which figure was correct. All 160 subjects should have been able to discover the solution within the allowed number of trials if they had been able to take the first step in an algorithm for solving concept-identification problems which is to break down the stimuli into dimensions and values. The fact that the majority did not solve the problem suggests that they did not know how to go about solving problems of this sort. Rather than performing the required exhaustive feature analysis, the unsuccessful subjects on this task were unsuccessful because they persisted in perceiving the figures as "wholes" or, at best, only in terms of their most salient dimensions.

The point that it is not lack of memory but lack of an algorithm that accounts for human subjects doing so much more poorly on concept-formation problems than a computer can also be made using the data from adult concept-attainment tasks. In our own research with concept attainment (McGraw & McCullers, 1975b), we gave extensive instructions. The dimensions on which the stimuli were distinguished were carefully pointed out, and subjects were given practice in discovering conjunctive concepts of the type that would be required in the task. To ease the memory load, markers were provided that subjects could lay beside each instance of the concept they found. Despite the instructions and practice that would have aided subjects in developing an algorithm and despite the memory aides that should have helped in its application, subjects took an average of 7.5 questions to solve the first of four problems whereas an ideal problem solver would never take more than 3. Interestingly, the number of questions significantly diminished over trials. This suggests that there was considerable learning to learn, or what we would call algorithm discovery. Again it appears, then, that the first step of concept-identification and concept-attainment problems involves a heuristic process in which the subject discovers how to go about solving the problem. Our own data suggested that nonreward subjects were superior to reward subjects in this heuristic stage, because, on each of four problems, the nonreward subjects required fewer questions to discover the concept. The strongest evidence for this, though, was that of Condry (1975), who found a highly significant between-groups difference. We take it to be significant that Condry gave far less practice to his subjects, a procedure that probably had the effect of extending the heuristic stage.

Perceptual recognition. The term *algorithmic* is used for perceptual-recognition studies in the case where subjects know what they are to look for. This was the case in all the studies previously reviewed under the heading of perceptual recognition that showed reward facilitation. Recall that in the Shantz et al. (1962) and Smock and Rubin (1964) studies, for example, the task was to locate a target form. The target forms—figures that ranged in complexity up to 16-pointed, random figures—were shown to subjects who then had to find the target in a display that included the target form along with three similar forms. In this case subjects very clearly knew what they were to look for. In the Jeffrey and Skager (1962) study of stimulus generalization, the same thing was true. Subjects had to discriminate illuminations of the center light from the illuminations of adjacent lights. In a study cited in another context (Rosenkrantz & Van de Riet, 1974) in which subjects had to search for and underline *s*'s that appeared in lists of random words, the same principle is illustrated.[3] The term *algorithmic* would seem to apply to the Glucksberg (1962) study—the last of those cited as providing evidence of reward facilitation—because the words that were recognized when tachistoscopically presented were all common words and therefore of high associative value. Subjects were in effect, then, more prepared to see these words than less familiar words.

If it is true that the familiarity of the to-be-recognized materials and the presence of a set to see some well-defined object provide the crucial characteris-

---

[3] The reason for not citing this study as a perceptual-recognition study was simply that the task materials were such as to make it superficially an uninteresting and therefore aversive task. This feature made it appropriate for discussion under the heading of the aversive-attractive factor. Nonetheless, the algorithmic nature of the solution along with the aversiveness of the task probably contributed to creating the conditions for the reward facilitation that was observed.

tics for determining when reward will facilitate perceptual recognition, then it must be the case that when the materials are not familiar or when the subject is not given a perceptual set, reward will hinder perceptual recognition. This is precisely what one finds.

In the Glucksberg (1962) study just reviewed, familiarity of the stimulus words was factorially varied with incentive. As we have seen, reward facilitated the recognition of familiar words. When the words were unfamiliar ones, however (e.g., *elegies, beatific, vignette*), reward had the opposite effect. There was, then, a significant familiarity × incentive interaction, and both simple main effects were significant as well. This finding, of course, supports the importance of the algorithmic-heuristic distinction if one accepts the argument that when we are asked to recognize a word that is made ambiguous by tachistoscopic presentation, we are less prepared to perceive an unfamiliar word than a familiar one.

A second task that showed reward to have a detrimental effect on perceptual recognition was one used by Pikulski (1970). This task required the heuristic solution of identifying some event *x,* which is in contrast to the algorithmic procedure of looking for a specified *x* and telling the experimenter when you have found it. Pikulski's subjects were kindergarten children, and the task was to recognize printed words after having seen the printed word matched with a picture that identified it. The procedure was to give a study trial (word + picture), followed by a test trial (words only). Immediate feedback was available either in the form of knowledge of results (the picture appeared), social reward ("good" + the picture for correct responses and "no" + the picture for incorrect responses), or material reward (M&M + the picture for correct responses and buzzer + picture for incorrect responses). The detrimental effect of reward in this case occurred relative to the social-reward group, with material-reward subjects making an average of twice as many errors.

Also giving evidence that reward will facilitate perceptual recognition only when one has an algorithm in the form of a strong set for what to see comes from studies cited in other contexts. Recall that reward had a detrimental effect on the perceptual discrimination problem (Miller & Estes, 1961) that required subjects to discriminate line drawings of twins who differed only in the height of their eyebrows. Objectively, this discrimination is no more difficult than distinguishing one 16-pointed figure from three others that are similar; yet reward produced a detrimental effect on discrimination of the twins and a facilitating effect on the discrimination of the 16-pointed figures. The difference was, of course, that in the case of the twins, subjects were not told what to look for, whereas in the case of the 16-pointed figures they were. Also relevant here are the results of the host of incidental-learning studies presented earlier. A final study in which the detrimental effect of reward is explained by the fact that the subjects did not know what to look for is Viesti's (1971) problem that required subjects to determine which one of three computer-generated series was "different." To the extent that this problem was solved perceptually—and Viesti's data argued that subjects had no cognitive appreciation for their basis of selection—the problem has the same characteristic as all the other perceptual-discrimination problems in which subjects lacked a solution algorithm.

Tasks requiring insight and creativity.   The application of the algorithmic–heuristic distinction to types of solutions is probably least obscure in the case of the problems that remain to be discussed, which is that mixed bag of functional fixedness, water-jar, and creativity problems discussed in Section A. The sole difficulty in such problems is in discovering the operations that are relevant to a solution. Once found, the application is obvious. This is to say that nearly the entire problem-solving period is taken up by the heuristic stage. To solve the last problem in McGraw and McCuller's water-jar series, for example, required only the step, $24 - 3 = 21$. The difficult part was in seeing the possibility of using just the two smaller water jars and ignoring the larger one. Likewise, to solve Glucksberg's candle problem, one had only to see the possibility of using the box as a platform rather than as a container. Once it was viewed as a platform, tacking it to the wall was an obvious step. The algorithmic stage in such problems, therefore, is inconsequential.

Although we have only seen evidence of reward hindering the discovery of insightful solutions, it is nonetheless possible for reward to facilitate performance on such problems in the case where the algorithm is made obvious. Glucksberg (1962, 1964) demonstrated this using both the candle and the circuit-completion problems. To make the solution to the candle problem obvious, he emptied the tacks from the box and so left the box as an isolated stimulus item on the table. To make the circuit-completion solution obvious, he painted the blade of the screwdriver the same color as the two wires that were to be joined. In both these cases, reward subjects were faster than nonreward subjects to produce the solution.

By increasing the salience of relevant items in the functional-fixedness problems, Glucksberg in effect eliminated the heuristic stage. One could do the same thing using the other tasks we have considered. In concept attainment, for example, posing a problem in which the stimuli varied on but a single dimension would have the effect of eliminating the heuristic stage. The same effect could be achieved also by enhancing the salience of the correct dimension. Witryol, Lowden, and Fagan (1967), for example, did this by the use of a differential reward procedure in pretraining in which child subjects were rewarded for responding to, say, a color but not to a form dimension. This predifferentiation subsequently enhanced the performance of reward subjects on a two-choice, three-dimensional discrimination problem in which color was the correct dimension. In perceptual recognition, the heuristic stage could be eliminated by similar salience training—one form of which is to tell the subject precisely what to see as in the case of studies requiring subjects to find x. Giving a paired-associate task that would eliminate the need for creative mnemonics—as, for example, a task with pairs like table–chair, cat–dog, etc.—would be an operation in verbal learning that would be analogous to Glucksberg's method of eliminating the heuristic stage in a functional-fixedness problem.

The Special Case of Incidental Learning and the Question "Why"

Conspicuously absent from the discussion in this section have been the results of the incidental-learning studies reported in Section A. The reason for this is not that incidental learning cannot be fit to the aversive–attractive and algorithmic–heuristic dimensions. It fits easily. Incidental learning is heuristic, because it is by definition learning that takes place in the absence of a set to learn. It is attractive, because the learning takes place in the absence of any extrinsic incentive and therefore, by definition, is intrinsically motivated. The reason for excluding it from the discussion, though, is that we cannot proceed directly from defining incidental learning's place in the attractiveness X type solution matrix to predicting reward's effect. This is because subjects are differentially rewarded not for incidental learning but for intentional learning. With respect to the incidental material, all subjects are nonreward subjects. The detrimental effect of reward on incidental learning is, then, a secondary or mediated effect that acts independently of reward's effect on the intentional task. Incidental learning, therefore, constitutes a special case and one that is of seeming theoretical importance, because the reason reward has a detrimental effect on incidental learning may well be the reason reward has a detrimental effect on attractive tasks with heuristic solutions such as we have been considering.

What we are proposing is that reward subjects might do less well on concept formation, problem solving, and those other tasks on which we have seen reward subjects to be inferior *precisely because of* their inferiority at incidental learning. That differences in incidental learning may be at the root of it all follows from the observation that the heuristic processes we have seen as important to solving problems in verbal learning, perceptual recognition, concept formation, etc., often require attention to what is either cognitively or perceptually peripheral in order to reach a solution. To the extent that this is true, the heuristic process needed for some intentional-task solutions can be said to feed on incidental thoughts and perceptions. Consequently, by explaining the results of studies in which reward for intentional learning was found to have a detrimental effect on incidental learning, one would seem to be offering an explanation for instances of reward's detrimental effects on attractive tasks with heuristic solutions as well.

SUMMARY AND CONCLUSION

In Section A we reviewed studies that show reward to have a detrimental effect and found that the evidence for a detrimental effect comes from a wide variety of tasks in which a large number of subject and methodological parameters have been varied. In Section B we considered the question of when reward would prove to be detrimental and when facilitating. A comparison of tasks on which there is facilitation with tasks on which there is a detrimental effect seemed to suggest that there are two important dimensions along which a task must be scaled before a prediction for the effect of reward on performance can be made. These were the attractive–aversive and algorithmic–heuristic dimensions.

If a task is aversive to the subject, then reward cannot be expected to disrupt performance. To the contrary, it will improve it. But it is not sufficient for a task to be attractive to the subject. It must also be designed such that the subject who is superior at heuristic behavior· will have a performance advantage. In verbal learning, therefore, the task had to be designed so that subjects could considerably shorten the associative learning process by developing mediating and coding strategies of their own to relate otherwise dissimilar items. In concept formation, the task had to be one employing enough dimensions that breaking down the stimuli into mere concatenations of stimulus values would not be an obvious way to proceed. In the more complex, problem-solving tasks, there was the similar requirement that direct discovery of the first step for the solution be somehow blocked. In perceptual recognition, the requirement was that subjects neither have nor be given a set for what they are to perceive.

In concluding Section B, it was noted that incidental learning formed a special case in that the effect of reward on incidental learning was mediated by the offer of reward for intentional learning. Because it may be "incidental learning" that accounts for the superior performance of nonreward subjects on tasks requiring heuristic solutions, it was suggested that determining the reason for reward's effect in the incidental-learning paradigm may provide an explanation for reward's detrimental effect elsewhere.

Having come all this way in laying out what appear to be the crucial features for determining when a task will be susceptible to a detrimental effect of reward, it is haunting to think that much of this has been said before. Yet it is the case that Spence's (1956) use of the position of the correct response in the habit family hierarchy as a determinant of the effect of incentive on performance covers much of what we mean by making the nature of the solution (algorithmic or heuristic) a determinant of reward's effect. Algorithmic solutions would translate as responses that are readily available at the top of the hierarchy, and heuristic solutions would be those that are initially low in the hierarchy. Spence's prediction, then, that incentive (K) would retard discovery of the correct solution when it was low in the hierarchy but facilitate it when high in the hierarchy is our prediction that heuristic solutions will be slowed but algorithmic solutions facilitated by the offer of reward. In a like manner credit for first focusing on the attractive-aversive distinction also lies elsewhere, because Lepper and Greene (1975) used it in explaining when reward would show a detrimental effect on level of motivation. Their distinction was the same, except that they used the terms *work* and *play* to describe it.

But even though the algorithmic-heuristic and aversive-attractive dimensions have been implicated before and so are not completely original, we can lay claim to having developed them more extensively than before. Also unique is the two-factor prediction model which has been developed to account—*post hoc*, at least—for reward-nonreward performance differences that have appeared in a large number of studies employing a wide variety of tasks. These contributions, along with the literature review, will hopefully give some currency to the phenomenon of detrimental effects of reward on performance.

A final word is reserved for the importance of research on reward's detrimental effects. Although provisions for the detrimental effects of reward have been with us for some time in our theoretical orientations—in addition to Hull–Spence theory there is the Yerkes–Dodson Law—detrimental effects appear to have been overlooked in our research emphases. Almost exclusively, research into reward's effects has focused on studies within the aversive–algorithmic task sector. From our view and that of the other contributors to this book, this is a mistake, because the attractive–heuristic sector is certainly as widely represented by tasks outside the laboratory. An implication that can be drawn from this is that reward's detrimental effects are potentially as widespread as its benefits. If that is so, psychology is certainly late in announcing this fact to the parents, teachers, and businessmen who would surely like to know it.

ACKNOWLEDGMENTS

Preparation of this manuscript as well as the research by McGraw and McCullers it reports was supported by NIMH, PHS/DHEW Grants MH 22041-01A1 and MH 26359-01, -02 to the University of Oklahoma, and MH 30570-01 to Oklahoma State University, John C. McCullers, Principal Investigator.

REFERENCES

Bahrick, H. P. Incidental learning under two incentive conditions. *Journal of Experimental Psychology*, 1954, *47*, 170–172.

Bahrick, H. P., Fitts, P. M., & Rankin, R. E. Effects of incentive upon reactions to peripheral stimuli. *Journal of Experimental Psychology*, 1952, *44*, 400–406.

Condry, J. The role of initial interest and task performance on intrinsic motivation. In J. C. McCullers (Chair), *Hidden costs of reward*. A symposium presented at the American Psychological Association Convention, Chicago, 1975.

Cuvo, A. J., & Witryol, S. L. The influence of incentives on memory stages in children. *The Journal of Genetic Psychology*, 1971, *119*, 289–300.

Davis, R. T., & Lovelace, W. E. Variable rewards and peripheral cues in discriminations by irradiated and nonirradiated monkeys. *The Journal of Genetic Psychology*, 1963, *103*, 201–205.

Dornbush, R. L. Motivation and positional cues in incidental learning. *Perceptual and Motor Skills*, 1965, *20*, 709–714.

Duncker, K. On problem solving. *Psychological Monographs*, 1945, *58* (5, Whole No. 270).

Glucksberg, S. The influence of strength of drive on functional fixedness and perceptual recognition. *Journal of Experimental Psychology*, 1962, *63*, 36–41.

Glucksberg, S. Problem solving: Response competition and the influence of drive. *Psychological Reports*, 1964, *15*, 939–942.

Goyen, J. D., & Lyle, J. G. Effect of incentive upon retarded and normal readers on a visual-associate learning task. *Journal of Experimental Child Psychology*, 1971, *11*, 274–280.

Haddad, N. F., McCullers, J. C., & Moran, J. D. Satiation and the detrimental effects of material rewards. *Child Development*, 1976, *47*, 547–550.

Harley, W. F., Jr. The effect of monetary incentive in paired-associate learning using a different method. *Psychonomic Science*, 1965, *2*, 377–378. (a)

Harley, W. F., Jr. The effect of monetary incentive in paired-associate learning using an absolute method. *Psychonomic Science*, 1965, *3*, 141–142. (b)

Jeffrey, W. E., & Skager, R. W. Effect of incentive conditions on stimulus generalization in children. *Child Development*, 1962, *33*, 865–870.

Johnson, R., & Thomson, C. Incidental and intentional learning under three conditions of motivation. *American Journal of Psychology*, 1962, *75*, 284–288.

Kausler, D. H., Laughlin, P. R., & Trapp, P. E. Effects of incentive-set on relevant and irrelevant (incidental) learning. *Child Development*, 1963, *34*, 195–199.

Kausler, D. H., & Trapp, P. E. Effects of incentive-set and task variables on relevant and irrelevant learning in serial verbal learning. *Psychological Reports*, 1962, *10*, 451–457.

Kruglanski, A. W., Friedman, I., & Zeevi, G. The effects of extrinsic incentive on some qualitative aspects of task performance. *Journal of Personality*, 1971, *39*, 606–617.

Lepper, M. R., & Greene, D. Turning play into work: Effects of adult surveillance and extrinsic rewards on children's intrinsic motivation. *Journal of Personality and Social Psychology*, 1975, *31*, 479–486.

Luchins, A. S. Mechanization in problem solving: The effect of Einstellung. *Psychological Monographs*, 1942, *54* (6, Whole No. 248).

McCullers, J. C., & Martin, J. A. G. A reexamination of the role of incentive in children's discrimination learning. *Child Development*, 1971, *42*, 827–837.

McGraw, K. O., & McCullers, J. C. The distracting effect of material reward: An alternative explanation for the superior performance of reward groups in probability learning. *Journal of Experimental Child Psychology*, 1974, *18*, 149–158.

McGraw, K. O., & McCullers, J. C. Use of a non-counterbalanced discrimination problem to determine whether reward subjects are less solution-oriented than KOR subjects in probability learning. Unpublished manuscript. 1975. (a)

McGraw, K. O., & McCullers, J. C. Monetary reward and concept attainment: Further research on the detrimental effect of reward. Unpublished manuscript. 1975. (b)

McGraw, K. O., & McCullers, J. C. Monetary reward and water-jar task performance: Evidence of a detrimental effect of reward on problem solving. Paper presented at the meeting of the Southeastern Psychological Association, New Orleans, 1976. (a)

McGraw, K. O., & McCullers, J. C. Monetary reward and mental multiplication: Further research on the detrimental effect of reward. Unpublished manuscript, 1976. (b)

McNamara, H. J., & Fisch, R. I. Effect of high and low motivation on two aspects of attention. *Perceptual and Motor Skills*, 1964, *19*, 571–578.

Mechanic, A. Effects of orienting task, practice, and incentive on simultaneous incidental and intentional learning. *Journal of Experimental Psychology*, 1962, *64*, 393–399.

Miller, L. B., & Estes, B. W. Monetary reward and motivation in discrimination learning. *Journal of Experimental Psychology*, 1961, *61*, 501–504.

Pikulski, J. Effects of reinforcement on word recognition. *The Reading Teacher*, 1970, *23*, 518–522.

Renne, C. M. The influence of monetary reward on intentional and incidental learning, irrelevant motor responding, and attending responses in children: A test of the generalized drive interpretation of incentive motivation. Doctoral dissertation, St. Louis University, 1965. *Dissertation Abstracts International,* 1965, *26,* 482–483. (University Microfilms No. 65-7055.)

Rosenkrantz, A. L., & Van de Riet, V. The influence of prior contact between child subjects and adult experimenters on subsequent child performance. *Journal of Genetic Psychology,* 1974, *124,* 79–90.

Rubin, B. M., Shantz, D. W., & Smock, C. D. Perceptual constriction as a function of incentive motivation. *Perceptual and Motor Skills,* 1962, *15,* 90.

Schere, R. A. Differential reinforcement with exceptional children. (Doctoral dissertation, New York University, 1969.) *Dissertation Abstracts International,* 1970, *31,* 1088–A. (University Microfilms No. 70-15, 981.)

Shantz, D. W., Rubin, B. M., & Smock, C. D. Utilization of visual information as a function of incentive motivation. *Perceptual and Motor Skills,* 1962, *15,* 357–358.

Smock, C. D., & Rubin, B. M. Utilization of visual information in children as a function of incentive motivation. *Child Development,* 1964, *35,* 109–117.

Spence, J. T. The distracting effect of material reinforcers in the discrimination learning of lower- and middle-class children. *Child Development,* 1970, *41,* 103–111.

Spence, J. T. Do material rewards enhance the performance of lower-class children? *Child Development,* 1971, *42,* 1461–1470.

Spence, J. T., & Dunton, M. C. The influence of verbal and nonverbal reinforcement combinations in the discrimination learning of middle- and lower-class preschool children. *Child Development,* 1967, *38,* 1177–1186.

Spence, J. T., & Segner, L. L. Verbal versus nonverbal reinforcement combinations learning of middle- and lower-class children. *Child Development,* 1967, *38,* 29–38.

Spence, K. W. *Behavior theory and conditioning.* New Haven: Yale University Press, 1956.

Staat, J., & McCullers, J. C. The distracting effect of material reward on the recall of incidentally acquired R–S associations. Paper presented at the meeting of the American Psychological Association, New Orleans, August 1974.

Terrell, G., Jr. The role of incentives in discrimination learning in children. *Child Development,* 1958, *25,* 231–236.

Terrell, G., Jr., Durkin, K., & Wiesley, M. Social class and the nature of the incentives in discrimination learning. *Journal of Abnormal and Social Psychology,* 1959, *59,* 270–272.

Terrell, G., Jr., & Kennedy, W. A. Discrimination learning and transposition in children as a function of the nature of the reward. *Journal of Experimental Psychology,* 1957, *53,* 257–260.

Underwood, B. J. The representativeness of rote verbal learning. In A. W. Melton (Ed), *Categories of human learning.* New York: Academic Press, 1964.

Viesti, C. R., Jr. Effect of monetary rewards on an insight learning task. *Psychonomic Science,* 1971, *23,* 181–182.

Ward, W. C., Kogan, N., & Pankove, E. Incentive effects in children's creativity. *Child Development,* 1972, *43,* 669–676.

Weick, K. E. Reduction in cognitive dissonance through task enhancement and effort expenditure. *Journal of Abnormal and Social Psychology,* 1964, *68,* 533–539.

Weinstein, L. Effects of reduction in reward magnitude on active avoidance behavior in humans. *Psychonomic Science,* 1971, *25,* 205–206. (a)

Weinstein, L. Effects of an increment in monetary incentive magnitude on instrumental responding and repeated increases in reward magnitude in humans. *Psychonomic Science,* 1971, *25,* 235–236. (b)

Weinstein, L. Negative contrast with humans as a function of emotionality. *The Journal of Psychology,* 1972, *80,* 161–165.

Witryol, S. L., Lowden, L. M., & Fagan, J. F. Incentive effects upon attention in children's discrimination learning. *Journal of Experimental Child Psychology,* 1967, *5,* 94–108.

Wray, N. The effects of attention, incentive, and sequential repetition upon intentional and incidental learning in seventh grade girls. Doctoral dissertation, The University of Wisconsin, 1966. *Dissertation Abstracts International,* 1967, *28,* 1244B–1245B. (University Microfilms No. 66–4592.)

4 Intrinsic Motivation and the Process of Learning

John Condry
James Chambers
Cornell University

INTRODUCTION

The purpose of this chapter is to place in perspective the research we have been doing at Cornell on the topic of intrinsic motivation and to suggest a theoretical rubric for analysis. Actually, our research to date has been relatively atheoretical. We have felt that a good, theoretical explanation should account for most of the known facts but that the range and limits of the phenomena under study have yet to be established. With this in mind, we have attempted to understand the meaning of the "undermining" effect before speculating extensively on its causes. In that light, we first describe how we came to choose the problems we have studied and outline some of the limits we have worked within.

The purpose of our research program at Cornell is to apply, insofar as is possible, what is known in human development to social needs and indeed to generate knowledge in response to real human problems. As it is not possible to attend to all aspects of a problem, we have chosen to focus on those elements of the current research on "intrinsic" motivation that are most directly implicated in what we see as an issue: the use of incentives to motivate learning. Early research looked at the undermining effect of different kinds of reward (W. E. Smith, 1975) and of monetary incentives on different types of initial interest (Upton, 1973). Most recently, we have focused with some intensity on the process of task activity (Condry, 1975; Garbarino, 1975; Condry & Chambers, 1976; Chambers, 1976). Our reasoning has been that if rewards "undermine" only interest, this effect is substantially less important, at least to us, than if they "undermine" the *process* of learning.

61

We do not think of rewards as "undermining" interest or intrinsic motivation, although we recognize the popular usage of this term. Talking in this way, however, directs our thinking and theorizing; it suggests that there is an ongoing stream of intrinsically motivated behavior that is somehow "undermined" by the offer of a task-extrinsic incentive. In our research, we have conceptualized these facts differently. We have assumed that rather than undermine anything, the offer of a reward acted as a "signal" to the individual to call forth a given sequence of activity. Thus, task-extrinsic rewards are part of an informational array specifying the appropriate actions to take and perhaps the appropriate way to conceptualize the "causes" of one's behavior. The absence of a reward as well as other aspects of the situation are part of an informational array we call a "context," which elicits a different pattern of motivated behavior. We clarify our reasons and the evidence for this conceptual scheme as we proceed in this chapter. Thinking about it in this way has some advantages:

1. It takes our attention away from the reward per se and focuses it on the entire complex of information facing the individual. It allows us to keep in mind, for example, one of the original findings (Lepper, Greene, & Nisbett, 1973) that *unanticipated* rewards had no "undermining" effect (we would say they had a different informational value or meaning).

2. It avoids the conception of motivation as being *either* "intrinsic" or "extrinsic." Rather we think the information specifying these different contexts and what they "afford," what they offer, exists and is discriminated by individuals. This discrimination is reflected in both behavior and conceptualization, as we shall see. Thus, we avoid a false dichotomy (not a false distinction) and leave open the question of whether there are other informational arrays, other "contexts" that give rise to other patterns of motivated behavior.

In the chapter that follows, then, we speak of intrinsic and extrinsic contexts and the kind of things they "afford" in terms of the different patterns of behavior they elicit and the different outcomes of each pattern. We begin with a series of distinctions that limit the phenomena we hope to explain. We distinguish between acquisition and performance in the first place, and then, under the title of acquisition, we distinguish between the process and products of learning. Finally, we add a brief caveat concerning the types of knowledge that may be most affected by the offer of a task-extrinsic incentive. With these limitations out of the way, we contrast the pattern of motivated activity under different motivational contexts. That is, we see if we can establish a process of intrinsically motivated activity that is different from a process of extrinsically motivated activity. Next, we consider the products of these two separate processes, and finally we suggest directions for more research and applications of the findings already in hand.

Acquisition vs. Performance

Although it is still an open question, we assume that the effects of task-extrinsic rewards are different for the acquisition of skills and knowledge than for well-learned habits. That is, we wish to concentrate on "learning" rather than on performance. Common sense suggests the distinction is important, and it is supported by some suggestive findings from earlier research.

Bandura and Walters (1963) raise the distinction between acquisition and performance and offer repeated examples of its utility in the study of social learning and imitation. In addition, Zajonc (1965) uses the same dichotomy as the basic theoretical underpinning of his theory of social facilitation. According to Zajonc, an audience is arousing, and arousal has different effects depending on the stage of learning one has attained. Well-learned skills are facilitated by the presence of an audience; poorly learned skills are inhibited by an audience. We think a similar effect is to be found here. Professionals of all sorts (e.g., in sports) show little undermining of interest and/or performance when money is offered in exchange for whatever they do. The question of whether the individual would continue playing even when the pay was not available is an open one; but there would seem to be little common-sense support for a global statement that rewards undermine performance in all circumstances, and this seems a good place to draw the line. Well-learned skills are stable or relatively so, and the attention-diverting effects of rewards should be less "disruptive" than for less stable sequences of action. Simply put, rewards are unlikely to cause wide variation in stable performance sequences or to cause a drop in interest, although the latter is more problematic than the former.

In saying this, we are not suggesting that rewards have *no* effect on the performance of well-learned acts. The considerable literature on token economies attests to the fact that the systematic use of extrinsic rewards can and does result in temporary alterations in patterns of behavior. But whether these temporary alterations *persist* once the extrinsic rewards are no longer available (or systematically applied) is still at issue, and it is the central issue of a good part of the literature summarized in this book.

We think of skills as collections of modular acts (cf. Koslowski & Bruner, 1972) arranged, probably, in some hierarchical form (at least it seems useful to think of them this way). Poorly learned skills are variable, sloppy, show a wide latitude between effort and outcome, and are easily undermined by *any* distracting circumstance. Remember what it was like when you first learned to drive a car! With repeated practice, they became more stable, more easily controlled, less easily distracted. Arousal facilitates performance at this stage. The demand to "perform" the skill—for applause or applesauce—is often pleasurable rather than distracting when the skill is well developed and stable. For these reasons, we suggest that rewards or incentives have *different* effects depending on the degree of stability of the skill under study, and we keep our attention focused on acquisition (learning and development) rather than performance of already well-established schema.

Process vs. Product

Given that we are attending to *acquisition*, there is an even finer distinction to make. Most research to date in the learning tradition (cf. McGraw & McCullers, 1975) deals with the products of learning: with errors and problems solved, with times to solution and the ability to break set. It is equally legitimate, although we believe more difficult, to study closely the step–by–step process of problem solving and to look for differences in the sequence of interaction of the person with the task. In the same way, one might study the step–by–step interaction of one person with another, we have attempted to document the progressive actions of a person faced with intrinsic and extrinsic motivational contexts. In doing so, we believe we are studying the *process* of learning.

A common response to the material described in the book is that no one in their right minds would ''reward'' interested and curious children who learn for their ''own sake.'' The use of rewards has traditionally been associated with poorly motivated individuals. The suggestion has been that extrinsic rewards may enhance the interest and thus the learning of a person with low initial interest in the problem or task at hand, even though their use with highly motivated individuals is unwarranted. This may be so; but if, as we suspect, these rewards create a context that elicits a different pattern of interaction with the task, they may be a poor way to ''motivate'' even uninterested children. If the offer of rewards produces ''token learning'' (Levine & Fasnacht, 1974)—that is, a more superficial interaction of subject with task—then we may be loath to use them even to encourage uninterested children to ''learn.'' Underlying these notions is a conceptualization of ''development'' as essentially an *active process*. We assume that individuals seek to structure and conceptualize the world and that human behavior may be understood, at least in part, if we know something about what these cognitive structures are, how they are formed, and how they are affected by different environmental circumstances or contexts. Thus, the study of development demands the study of process, as well as the progressive cognitive, behavioral, and affective ''structures'' that result from it (Piaget, 1970).

Types of Tasks

Finally, and briefly, all of the research reviewed in this book focuses on individuals as they interact with concrete tasks—that is, as they draw, solve simple problems or anagrams, or as they beat a drum or listen to a song. What we may reasonably expect to learn from this research is how people deal with the world of *things* under different motivating circumstances. But we must recognize that the range of tasks and skills researched in these studies is necessarily limited and may be substantially unrepresentative of the range of possibilities existing in real-life contexts. In fact, there has never been a taxonomy of tasks used in this research, except for a small effort in Condry (1977). Nevertheless, it is a common observation that some tasks feed back information about one's progress and competence and that others are less informative—to mention only one dimension. Because "task-extrinsic" incentives can and often do signal information about the task and about progress and competence, there are many instances in which learning could not proceed without them, at least without *some* feedback from the outside world. It seems wise to limit our speculations to the kinds of tasks that have been studied—i.e., those that allow feedback as to competence—and to remind ourselves occasionally that there may be tasks where "extrinsic" feedback not only does not undermine performance but is, in fact, necessary for successful completion. A careful analysis of how motivational context interacts with the nature of the task is a job that is yet to be done.

In summary, we cull this material, particularly our own research, for what it tells us about the pattern of subject–task interaction under different motivational contexts. We attend, primarily, to the acquisition of cognitive and behavioral skills or schemata rather than to the performance of already established schemata. The extent to which patterns that can be differentiated emerge should extend our understanding of the subtleties of the "undermining" effect on one hand and provide a descriptive taxonomy of the process of unconstrained exploration on the other.

THE PROCESS OF LEARNING

Task activity and learning may be seen to occur in a sequence of steps. The task is *engaged* or *initiated* in some way; it is actively explored or manipulated via one or another *process;* it is eventually *disengaged* and may later be *reengaged*—beginning the cycle anew. Each of these steps occurs within a context of interrelated elements—including ego involvement, motivation, attention, expectation, etc. In this section, we examine each of these steps in the learning process under the motivational contexts we have been calling *intrinsic* and *extrinsic*. In general, we want to try to develop a picture of what this activity/ learning sequence looks like for the two different motivational contexts under examination.

Initial Engagement

Let us first consider *engagement*. The two conditions studied in research are those in which one engages in a task or activity in the absence of salient external incentives (intrinsic) and those in which incentives are anticipated from the outset (extrinsic). The extrinsic-reward context is usually characterized by a lack of choice about whether to engage in a task at all and, if so, at what level of difficulty. The typical paradigm of this research has been to study the effects of different contexts of engagement on later steps in the sequence (usually reengagement). The typical finding, well known by now, is that later engagement is less likely when the task is initiated in an extrinsic context.

Little research has been directed at questions of whether the subject would choose different problems if they were free to do so, although there is some evidence in the literature on this point. Maehr and Stallings (1972), for example, found that subjects who expected to be judged by an external source (a condition comparable to what we are calling "extrinsic") choose easier problems than subjects in an "intrinsic" evaluation condition. This was particularly true of subjects high in need for achievement. In our research, we have found a similar phenomenon (Condry & Chambers, 1976). We examined what difficulty level of tasks subjects *chose* to do under different motivational contexts. Adolescent males were left free to explore and familiarize themselves with a series of concept-attainment problems varying in difficulty. The results revealed that those who were paid for the problems did significantly easier ones than those who solved the problems without the anticipation of a reward. This suggests that the desire to obtain the incentive was the dominant motive in the extrinsic context, because easier problems were more likely to yield a quick success (cf. pp. 168–171). This is not, we think, the most conducive atmosphere for learning.

In saying this, we are returning to our earlier distinction between acquisition and performance, between well learned and poorly learned skills. We are suggesting that when a person's attention is directed to a narrow aspect of the situation, e.g., producing a specific outcome in order to get a reward, it is not (perhaps it cannot be) directed to subtle aspects of the task. Moreover, we think the effects of narrowing attention are more problematic when the skill is undeveloped. Thus, a person learning to hit a tennis ball must attend to hitting alone. If he attends to where the ball might go, he loses control of the more basic skill—of simply making contact with the ball. Eventually, of course, when he becomes more proficient at hitting the ball, he can then attend to other possibilities.

We think this happens because attention is inherently limited and because skills are hierarchically organized. The basic components of the skill must become internalized before it is possible (or useful) to attend to other aspects of the informational array. Bruner (1974), in the study of early skilled action, notes that with repeated practice, early acts become "modularized"—i.e., less variable in latency and execution and more economical. Once this occurs, "modularization frees available information processing capacity for further use in task analysis, just by virtue of constituent sub-routines requiring less attention" (Bruner, 1974, p. 172). We are suggesting that rewards often distract attention from the process of task activity to the product of getting a reward, thus undermining the development of basic skills.

In order to develop new skills, one must take some risks and try new things. Continued application of proven skills may yield superior performance, but it will not lead to development and learning. It is suggested that external incentives create a "performance" context and a concomitant narrowing of attention to specific "outcomes." This results in performance at achieved levels rather than progression to "aspired" levels. The presence of rewards implies exchange. The unit of exchange at the disposal of the payee is the product of the work. Thus, with attention focused on yielding a product, a person would engage the task in such a way as to maximize his or her ability to produce. Attention is focused on the easiest route to this "goal." This is fine when performance, or its product, is what is desired; but the truth is that rewards are all too often used as the preferred way to motivate learning, and this is questionable. Diverting or limiting attention to only certain aspects of the informational array may retard the learning process; certainly it leads to a choice of the easiest route to the goal—the receipt of the reward.

In addition to limiting future engagement and the difficulty level of what is chosen, choice of when and where to engage a task may also be affected by extrinsic rewards. Given a large block of time within which to complete a short task, would it be engaged all at once or in bits and pieces? Right away, or just before it was due? And, most importantly, would the *choice* of when and where to start make a difference in the product? If our notions about self-involvement are correct, we would expect an extrinsically rewarded task to be less "meaningful" and its engagement put off until the last minute; but evidence is lacking on this point.

Taken together, the general theme we are suggesting is that the extrinsic motivational context is associated, in the initial engagement phase, with a preference for relatively simpler activities and an orientation toward performance rather than progress. Degree of choice is severely curtailed in the "extrinsic" context. This means that the *degree of active self-involvement* is substantially less under the "extrinsic" context, under the promise of a reward or surveillance. In contrast, intrinsic contexts result in attempts at more difficult problems, more self-involvement, and an initial focus on learning and development of basic prerequisite skills.

Process

Because we are interested in development, the second stage—*process*—is most interesting for us. Most studies have looked only at the products of performance under the two contexts. This research tends to conceptualize learning as the performance of poorly learned skills without looking at the actual process of achieving the product. Recent research on the development of mathematical skills in children illustrates the problem. Herbert Ginsburg (1977) has been interviewing children in order to study the processes they go through when learning math. He has found that even when children do not *perform* well, they are often applying rules and strategies rather than haphazardly blundering through the problems. These attempts to organize and structure the world are typical of children learning about the world and need to be examined more carefully if we are to understand development. What do we say about a child who applies an erroneous rule but achieves the correct answer with it? What has been learned? At some point, the weakness of the rule will become evident, and performance will no longer be successful. Successful performance alone is of limited utility in the study of human learning. Of greater utility is the study of where attention is directed, what information is used and what is ignored, and what rules are generated by the individual.

We have taken the beginning steps in this direction in terms of both cognitive problem solving and interpersonal interactions. Studies by Condry and Chambers (1976) have been aimed at explicating the problem-solving process. Employing a modification of a concept-attainment task (Bruner, Goodnow, & Austin, 1956), subjects were first introduced to the task and then worked through one on their own. This was followed by a time period during which they chose and worked on problems from a set that varied in difficulty. The problems were designed so that subjects could gather information, guess at the answer, and obtain feedback completely at their own pace. During this free exploration time, one group was paid for each problem solved, and the other was not. Unknown to the subjects, each information choice or concept guess was recorded and later analyzed to examine progress in the development and change of their problem-solving and learning strategies.

A number of differences appeared between the two groups. Those who were paid to do the problems tackled them in a way that was more "answer oriented." More specifically, they began guessing at the answer earlier—i.e., after obtaining less information than the no-reward group—and they made proportionately more concept guesses en route to solving the problems. A concern for product over process was also reflected in the comparatively inefficient use of information in the rewarded group. They made more redundant choices and in the end required just as much or more information before achieving the correct solution. Incomplete use of information was also suggested by when guesses were made. Some choices yielded negative feedback, others positive. The proportion of positive to negative for any problem was heavily in favor of negative; yet the rewarded group most often guessed at the answer after a positive instance. This suggests poor usage and understanding of the information value of negative instances and a reliance on finding positive instances in order to find "the answer."

Differences also appeared in the use of available resources. Worksheets were provided so that notes could be made, records of choices kept, and concepts eliminated as one progressed. We found that those in the rewarded group tended to use the sheets less extensively and left them completely unused significantly more often.

Thus, it can be seen from the few examples given that there is more to solving a problem or engaging an activity than merely producing a product. The research above suggests that extrinsic contexts may sacrifice process for product. "Getting the answer" is satisfying when "success" is the central goal, but "solving the mystery" may be more important to development. Learning requires that one develop some skills and habits such as attention to specific aspects of the informational array, formation of meaningful questions, perception of relationships, and integration of information. Our research suggests that these skills, what we prefer to call *strategies of learning,* are different under the two motivational contexts we have described. Intrinsically motivated subjects attend to and utilize a wider array of information; they are focused on the *way* to solve the problem rather than the solution. They are, in general, more careful, logical, and coherent in their problem-solving strategies than comparable subjects offered a reward to solve the same problems.

These same process differences are found in social interactions under these same "motivational contexts." Garbarino (1975) looked at the effects of incentives on cross-age tutoring. His concern was not only with how well the child would learn the task but more importantly with how the older child would treat the younger one while teaching the task, i.e., on the step–by–step processes of social interaction. He found that the children who were paid to teach were characterized by an "instrumental" orientation toward these "pupils." The focus was more on the goal of receiving the reward and less on the teaching itself. The tutees were valued as a function of their utility in achieving the goal and so were devalued when they frustrated goal achievement. The "emotional tone" of the interaction was more negative in the reward group. This negative evaluation of task performance was translated into a negative evaluation of the person on the interpersonal level. In contrast, the nonrewarded tutors were less intrusive in style and fostered a "more positive emotional tone" of interaction. Their tutees responded by demonstrating significantly greater task ability and fewer errors in learning the task.

These findings are important, because many social and emotional factors (e.g., self-image) are bound up with activity and learning. How one feels about oneself in relation to learning and performance situations is crucial to continued development, we believe. Fear of negative evaluations and of making mistakes can inhibit the willingness to try new things that is essential for progress in learning. Even Harlow's monkeys (Harlow, 1950) needed to feel secure in order to freely explore and manipulate their world. More consideration should be given to the effects of different motivational contexts on the emotional components of learning, rather than focusing on learning and performance simply as cognitive processes and thus looking for cognitive explanations alone, when variations appear.

And variations *do* appear. Our study of the step–by–step sequence of actions in problem solving suggests that the offer of a reward does not simply "undermine" intrinsically motivated behavior; it results in an entirely different sequence of activity. Attention is directed to different aspects of the informational array, and the information is used differently by individuals in the different conditions. We discuss the meaning of these differences in the next section, "The Products of Subject–Task Interaction," after looking at disengagement and reengagement—the final steps in the process of task activity.

Disengagement

The third step in the sequence is that of *disengagement*. At some point, activity is terminated, and one moves on to something else. Again, we want to know how the willingness to *leave* a task, to disengage it, is different under different motivational contexts. Research on this problem is sorely lacking, but we may speculate and raise some issues.

When reward is involved, termination typically occurs when the desired product is achieved—usually the receipt of the offered reward. Ordinarily, when engagement is for intrinsic reasons, the point of disengagement is determined by the individual. This may be because the "questions" leading to initial activity have been answered, a sense of mastery (for the time being) has been achieved, the novelty has worn off, or other interests and demands have become more urgent. Typically, research structures the situation so that neither group really has a choice in termination. So it is difficult to tell from the research so far what facts and considerations lead to disengagement in the intrinsic context. A suggestion would be that at least in real-life circumstances a skill is developed to the level of "normative" demand. That is, one learns to drive, or speak "proper" grammar, or whatever to the level "required" by the other people in one's immediate surroundings. How these social forces operate or what additional factors must be considered are not well understood.

These considerations suggest that the phase of disengagement is a most interesting and complex one, and it deserves more attention than it has gotten so far. For the moment, the central consideration is whether the different motivational contexts produce a different pattern of activity at each phase in the learning process. It is clear that this is the case with disengagement, also. We do not know the variety of reasons a person may have for disengaging an "intrinsically motivated" sequence of action, but they are certainly *not* because of the receipt of an extrinsic reward. Perhaps the simplest description would be that intrinsically motivated activities are disengaged when *self*-satisfaction (in some form) is achieved, whereas extrinsically motivated activities are terminated with "other" satisfaction (Condry, 1977).

What occurs during the process of activity may also affect disengagement. The level of understanding that one attains during the process of task involvement may bear on the ability to accurately gauge when termination is appropriate (i.e., when the question has been answered, when novelty is exhausted, when mastery is attained, etc.). Relevant data may be found in Chambers's (1976) study previously discussed. In the process of working on the problems, the "answer orientation" of the rewarded subjects resulted in significantly fewer cases of a problem being worked all the way through. In other words, the "extrinsic" group did not experience the gathering and integrating of the relevant information before finishing the problems. Instead they short-cut the process by guessing at the answer, and they did so repeatedly. This strategy is important in that it reduces what one learns about one's own problem-solving abilities. In this case, there is less experience with knowing when enough information is in hand to be sure of the answer. Chambers (1976) also has evidence bearing on this: When asked to work out a problem and not offer answers until they were sure, significantly more of those in the extrinsic-context group guessed before they logically had sufficient information.

Finally, the conditions of disengagement may also affect aspects of subsequent reengagement. In original work on the Zeigarnik effect, Ovsiankina (1928) found that if behavior was interrupted before reaching its natural end, there was a desire to return to it. In the present research, the experimenter ends the behavior either with or without a reward. Neither group is allowed to choose the endpoint. If left to exhaust their own interest, subjects in both conditions may demonstrate patterns of subsequent interest different than those currently being found.

Reengagement

We now consider reengagement more carefully, in relation to the entire sequence of activity. The willingness to persist—or to return to a task later—is the focus of the bulk of the research to date on this topic (Lepper, Greene, & Nisbett, 1973; Deci, 1975; Calder & Staw, 1975). As mentioned earlier, the standard paradigm has looked at willingness to return to a task after engaging in it under either extrinsic or intrinsic motives. Most of the research to date has been done in standard laboratory situations. This basic format has been extended to a naturalistic field setting by Upton (1973) and to the application of social incentives by W. E. Smith (1975). Upton studied the effect of the offer of an incentive (or not) on the willingness of people at different levels of initial interest (high vs. low) to donate blood to a bloodmobile. The total number of subjects, all adult, in Upton's study was 1200 (approximately 300 in each of the four treatment conditions), and the incentive offered and given was $10. This represents an enormous sample size for research of this sort and a more powerful incentive than is usually the case. The results indicated that blood donors who were offered money to give blood were less likely to actually do so than those who simply volunteered. Reward interacted with interest, but most of the effect was due to the fact that the high-initial-interest subjects volunteered substantially less when money was offered (65%) than when it was not (93%), whereas the reverse (87% to 83%, respectively) was true of low-initial-interest subjects. W. E. Smith's (1975) study was designed to test two findings reported by Deci (1975):

1. Social reward or feedback increases "intrinsic" motivation.
2. Females are more influenced by social feedback than males.

In both studies (by Deci), only unanticipated reward was studied. Smith conducted a lab study in which *both* anticipated and unanticipated feedback were compared and for two types of reward: social and monetary. He found lower subsequent interest in returning to the task associated with *anticipated* reward of both types and no sex differences comparable to those reported by Deci.

These two studies were attempts to extend and elaborate the existing corpus of research. The ability to demonstrate laboratory phenomena in the real world is always an issue, and additional evidence concerning social incentives is useful and important. Behavior often occurs within the context of social contracts (approval, acceptance, influence), rather than in that of concrete, tangible rewards. Obviously, a full appreciation of the effects of different contexts must consider these types of incentive as well.

There are, however, many issues of interest left unexamined. In the first place, between the phases of engagement and reengagement are those of *process* and *disengagement*. Because examination of the effects of the circumstances of initial engagement (intrinsic vs. extrinsic) on these two stages has been limited, we don't have a very good idea of the process at work that leads to less reengagement in reward groups. Overjustification, the original hypothesis, focuses on attribution during engagement that is applied upon opportunity for reengagement. A different conceptualization results if we examine the *process* stage more carefully. If the processes of task involvement lead to different experiences and feelings of mastery, understanding, self-involvement, and satisfaction, then it would not be surprising to find differing enthusiasm for returning to the task. If one does something for external incentives, the experience may become constrained. One must attempt to discern what behavior is appropriate and will fit the others' expectations. To the extent that those expectations conflict with the needs of the self, the task may become a burden and unpleasant. This results in a decrease in meaningfulness, enjoyment, and the desire to return to it. The task itself may become negatively evaluated and a poor vehicle for self-expression.

The association of reward with a task does not appear to make the task itself attractive—i.e., in behaviorist terms, to give it "secondary reinforcing" qualities. Cognitive explanations for these facts fail to test whether children employ the reasoning demanded by their explanation, and there is some suggestion in the literature that young children (before about 7 years of age) *cannot* employ this level of reasoning (M. C. Smith, 1975). It seems more likely that Karniol and Ross (1976) are closer to the truth when they assert that some children do reason in this way (i.e., apply the discounting principle) and some children do not. Still, those who apply no systematic causal schema and those who apply an "additive" (the more "reward," the better) schema do pose something of a problem for "attributional" theoretical analyses.

The alternative conception suggested here—that self-initiated tasks have a greater meaning to the individual and result in a different pattern of motivated activity at each stage in the learning process—does not conflict with an attributional explanation; it adds considerable detail to it. It suggests that in addition to the cognitive effects found in earlier research, behavioral manifestations revealed when the process of learning is carefully studied point to a more elaborate and detailed set of effects than is explained by appeal to cognitive restructuring alone.

We think that the use of a system of rewards and the concomitant "other direction" that this implies:

1. affects the choice of the type of problem undertaken;
2. leads to a selection of attention to those aspects of task performance that will satisfy the rewarder;
3. leads to inadequate development of basic skills due to the fact that the process of skill development (e.g., the initiation, direction, and termination of action) is under the control of forces outside of the actor;
4. leads to less of a sense of personal adequacy and control, with respect to the task;
5. as a consequence of some or all or the above, leads to a lower interest in returning to the task.

Finally, we may profit by considering which conditions people *prefer* to act under. Thus far, experimenters have provided or offered either a reward or no-reward context within which to engage an activity. A choice between the two contexts is never offered the subject. A case approximating this condition was observed by Chambers in pilot research during informal interviews with grade school children. A number of group projects were developed as part of the regular school program, and the children had a choice of which group they wanted to join. All the children were asked by the experimenter to choose between their third choice—where they would receive gold stars and a certificate for being in the group—and their first choice—which involved nothing extra. These children all preferred to be in the group with no extra prizes.

Questions such as these expand the focus past what one *does* in different motivational contexts to what one *feels* about the tasks and about one's self. It may be that a shift occurs in context preference as activity and ability progress from acquisition to performance, as we suggested earlier. Thus, we may enjoy displaying our skills, and "rewards" of various kinds are seen as simply icing on the cake when the skills are well developed. Further research is needed to probe these questions. For the moment, it is enough to note that the process of learning is substantially different in these different motivational contexts, and it is different at each phase we have studied.

THE PRODUCTS OF SUBJECT–TASK INTERACTION

If the sequence of interactions described above are the processes of learning in these different contexts (and they are substantially different, as we have seen), how might the "products" of these different patterns of action be compared? If two distinct patterns of motivated activity are suggested, what are the general outcomes of each? If intrinsically motivated learning is useful, when is it useful and why? The evidence we have collected suggests that the *self* lies at the center of the findings we have seen.

Exploration, in the absence of powerful extrinsic incentives, is characterized by greater "self" involvement—(and thus more feedback with respect to the self)—than in the extrinsic motivational context. This behavior is self-initiated, self-directed, and self-terminated.

Self-initiated activities have a "flow" (Csikszentmihalyi, 1975) to them that we believe is absent in extrinsically initiated activities.

In a sense, a person undertaking intrinsically motivated activities is more "active" if this refers to acts of the *will*. Because the extrinsic forces are minimal (by definition), the task is acted upon because of something *within* the actor. Attention is directed while performing the task by the needs of the actor as he or she relates to the task. Whatever goals are set, are set as a consequence of an internal dialogue of the person with him- or herself—about the past and the future. Attention is focused on the attainment of these self-initiated goals, and the activity is terminated when self-satisfaction has been obtained. In the same sense, the individual in the extrinsic context is passive. His actions are other initiated, other directed, and other terminated. This language is not intended to denigrate one and elevate the other but rather to specify the degree of self-involvement at each stage in the process in the different contexts described.

This leads us to suggest that one of the "products" of pressure-free, exploratory contexts is a greater "self-control of skills." Self-involvement leads to "activity" and also to a greater degree of internalization and thus *consistency* between the attitudes one has about a task and the behavior one displays toward it. In a fascinating study of the relationship between attitudes and behavior, Regan and Fazio (1977) found greater attitude–behavior consistency for individuals who were "directly" involved in an event than for individuals who were indirectly involved. These facts were demonstrated in both the field and the laboratory. Thus, we might expect people who initiate and direct learning activity on their own (as opposed to having it done by others) to be characterized by greater internalization of the component skills and greater consistency between their attitudes and their behavior than more "passively" involved individuals.

Just as one learns to control the world, so, too, one learns to be *helpless*. Neither is the "natural" state; both are responsive to the self–environment interaction.

There is evidence (Seligman, 1975) to suggest that the "passivity" engendered by learned helplessness may generalize from the circumstances in which it was originally learned to other unrelated circumstances. The same (in reverse) may be true of activity. Thus, the knowledge that one can *act* upon the world and change it is enormously exhilarating, just as its antithesis is depressing. This *feeling* of activity, efficacy, and competence is another "product" of exploratory learning, of the intrinsic pattern (White, 1959).

These are the two most potent outcomes of self-directed (vs. other-directed) activity—self-control in terms of skills and the feeling of control or power engendered by acting upon the world and observing the consequences of self-initiated actions. Actually, the former is not precise. It is better expressed as a knowledge of the interrelation between an individual's will and the environment; in the case of the research reviewed here, the interaction of a subject's self-directed actions and a *particular task*. From self-directed experience, notions of control and power arise. The type of control specified here is the awareness of a relation between willful effort and effective outcome. Seligman (1975) calls this "voluntary" control.

THEORETICAL CONSIDERATIONS

At each stage in the learning process, self-initiation, self-direction, self-disengagement, and later self-interest in returning to the activity are diminished in the extrinsic context when compared to the intrinsic context. The outcomes of the two processes parallel these findings. The theoretical account we give to these facts begins with the idea that the information specifying these different motivational contexts contains distinctive features that make the contexts discriminably different from one another. Moreover, we suggest that these contexts *are* discriminated by individuals and that they call forth different patterns of response. These differences in response are found both in terms of attitudes and in terms of behavior, and they are found at every stage of the learning process studied. The findings of the research presented in this book may be conceptualized from this perspective. In addition, taking this stance allows us to associate these findings with other research with a similar conceptual base and to point the direction for future research.

If we are correct about the role of the "self" and active control (or at least the perception of control) in this process, then several things immediately follow. First and foremost, the basic dependent variable of this research must expand to include such difficult indices as self-control, self-knowledge, and conceptions of control over the environment and the particular task at hand. If these are the most important outcomes of this process, as we have suggested, then they must be studied and compared before a complete picture of the "hidden costs of reward" emerges and before a complete theory to account for them can be devised.

Second, if this theoretical suggestion is to have meaning, a number of questions must be given more complete answers than we now have:

1. Is there information in the world to distinguish these different "contexts" from one another? What is it?
2. Do people make the distinction? Is it important to human beings to learn the distinctive features of "intrinsic" and "extrinsic" motivational contexts?
3. What difference does it make? That is, if there is a distinction and if people "use" it, how do they do so—what does it "get" them?

We believe the evidence arrayed in this chapter and in other chapters in this book provides partial answers to each of these questions. We have seen how a variety of extrinsic demands (mostly "positive" rewards) signal a specific context that is discriminated (even by very young children) and responded to differently than a condition involving the same task but a different (intrinsic) motivational context. We have devoted most of this chapter to a specification of the differences in the type of response to these two conditions when they are "signaled" by the presence or absence of reward. But let us look into each of these questions in more detail and see what other related research may be brought to bear if the phenomena are conceptualized in the way we have suggested, i.e., if the degree of "active" (self-) control is seen to be the central issue.

Information specifying self–environmental control is contained in the world, as we have seen. This information is particularly evident in what we have called the "intrinsic" context, but it is conflicted in the extrinsic context. When a task, for example, is undertaken because a powerful reward is offered, the person's initial *action* in choosing the task is constrained. Whatever outcomes are obtained from these other-initiated circumstances, they do not bear on self-initiated actions. They do not speak to the individual of one's *own* good (or bad) judgment, only of another's. If the extrinsic context leads to further differences in the *activity* with respect to the task, then, again, the individual may learn something about ability to exert effort and obtain outcomes under these constrained conditions, under "demand"; but he or she learns little about *self-directed* effort and outcomes. Of course, the individual is in part directing the activity even in the extrinsic motivational conditions, but only in part. We have described evidence from our research (Condry & Chambers, 1976) that both what information is selected and how it is used is systematically different in these different motivational contexts. The direction of the difference is to be more *self-relevant* in the intrinsic context and thus relevant to a knowledge of the active self's control of the world. Finally, information about the individual's ability to disengage a task or, for that matter, to engage it later is also very much constrained in the extrinsic context. In all of these circumstances, information concerning the interrelationship of an "active" self with the environment is greatly limited in the extrinsic context, where the offer of a reward appears to call forth a different sequence of behavior, (cf. pp. 127–137).

Additional evidence for the ability and propensity to discriminate control-relevant from control-irrelevant—active from passive—circumstances comes from the research of Rotter (1966), de Charms (1968), Zimbardo (1969), Nuttin (1973), Lefcourt (1973), Langer (1975), and Seligman (1975). The propensity to differentiate these contexts behaviorally is very widespread across species. Thus, Lefcourt (1973), in a review of some of this research, reports that animals from rats (Mowrer & Viek, 1948; Richter, 1959) to dogs (Seligman, Maier, & Solomon, 1969) to humans (Glass & Singer, 1972) are capable of differently responding to control-relevant as opposed to control-irrelevant environmental contexts. The characteristics of this differential response are discussed later, but at the very least, this evidence indicates that these informational contexts are readily discriminated by men and beasts alike.

Apparently, the effect is very powerful. Langer (1975; Langer & Roth, 1975) and her colleagues have shown in a number of studies that if the informational elements of "controllable" situations (choice, stimulus or response familiarity, passive or active involvement, and competition, according to Langer) are introduced into a patently chance situation (e.g., a lottery, or tossing a coin), people approach the situation *as if* it were controlled.

In the particular case of this series of experiments, Langer shows that confidence in the outcome is greatly increased when people can be convinced that "control" is possible. She rightly calls this effect the "illusion of control." But once again we note that if such an "illusion" is possible, it arises from a differential discrimination of and differential response to informational (situational) contexts. The illusion is created by providing conditions and information ordinarily associated with "control."

Another set of studies bearing upon the issues under consideration is found in the work of Julian Rotter and his colleagues in constructing and testing an individual difference measure of personal causation called "locus of control." This factor was first outlined by Rotter, Seeman, and Liverant (1962) as distributing individuals according to the degree to which they accept personal responsibility for their outcomes. People who perceive or expect most of their outcomes to be caused by external sources are called "externals" (EC for "external control"), and those who typically expect or perceive their outcomes as being caused by themselves are called "internals" (IC for "internal control"). Lefcourt (1966), in his review of the pertinent literature, explains it thus:

> As a general principle, internal control refers to the perception of positive and/or negative events as being a consequence in one's own actions and thereby under personal control; external control refers to the perception of positive and/or nega-

tive events as being unrelated to one's own behaviors in certain situations and therefore beyond personal control [p. 207].

Several studies have been conducted with ethnic groups to determine their location on the EC–IC scale. Battle and Rotter (1963) found that lower-class blacks are more external than middle-class blacks and whites. Lefcourt and Ladwig (1965) found that black prison inmates were more external (EC) than white prison inmates (with most of the inmates coming from the lower socioeconomic classes). And Graves (1961), in a study of a tri-ethnic community, found the Indians (American) to be most external, the Spanish–Americans next, and the whites to be most internal. From this group of studies, it is possible to conclude that groups of minimal power through their social position, either by class or race, are most external.

Another set of studies to be considered are those that show relations between the EC–IC scale and different behavioral predispositions. In studies of black students, Gore and Rotter (1963) and Strickland (1965) found that internals were more likely to express interest and involvement in social action than were their external counterparts. A number of studies by Seeman and his colleagues report differential learning and knowledge between ECs and ICs. Specifically, external patients in a tuberculosis hospital know less about their conditions than internal patients, with the groups matched on socioeconomic and hospital-experience variables (Seeman & Evans, 1962); external inmates know less in relation to "control-important" goals (factors related to achieving successful parole), whereas there was no difference between externals and internals regarding knowledge pertaining to noncontrol-related goals (Seeman, 1963); and Swedish workers who were external knew less of politics and international affairs but scored about the same on art as did internal Swedish workers. Finally, Neal and Seeman (1964) have shown that workers belonging to a union are significantly more internal than nonunion workers.

A last set of studies bears on the relation between the EC–IC scale and conformity. Odell (1959) and Crowne and Liverant (1963) found that EC was significantly related to conformity, that externals were more conformist than the ICs. Liverant and Scodel (1960) demonstrated that internals take more moderate risks and show a greater tendency toward self-regulation with regard to objective probabilities than do externals. A similar finding is reported by Lichtman and Julian (1964) in a study of strategy preferences in a dart-throwing task.

It may be concluded from these studies that internals tend to learn and utilize control-relevant information to a greater extent than externals; they tend to attempt to exert more control and are more objective and confident in their assessment of the probabilities of success than externals.

The central theme running through the three areas of research outlined earlier is that the perception of personal causation is an important variable to consider in attempting to understand behavior, particularly that aspect of behavior having to do with the setting of goals and aspirations and the expenditure of effort in service of those goals.

Finally, Nuttin (1973) reports that preference for controllable situations is evident in young children even when paired, for purposes of contrast, with a highly stimulating but uncontrollable perceptual event. Clearly, there is not only evidence that different contexts specifying different degrees of personal control *are* discriminable, but people do make these discriminations and respond differently a consequence.

Let us now consider this last point in more detail. How do people respond to these different situations, these different circumstances? Again, we have seen some of the evidence described in this chapter, at least with respect to a comparison of reward and no-reward contexts. But if these conditions actually vary in the degree to which "control" is relevant, as we think, then the other research just described tells us a good deal more about the response to these different situations.

We have already indicated that human beings seem to "prefer" the "control-relevant" context as, indeed, do animals (Berlyne, 1969; Kisk, 1955; Kisk & Antonitis, 1956; Russell, 1972) and that in this context they are more persistent, creative, logical, and coherent in their task activity. Moreover, what is learned from situations where the activity of the self is salient appears to be better internalized and integrated into the individual's behavioral and conceptual schemata. In addition to the evidence described in this book, however, there is other research available where choice, the perception of control, and action involvement are the main independent variables. Thus, Zimbardo (1969) has shown how these same indices of choice, freedom, and the "perception" of control give rise to "cognitive" control of a variety of environmental stimuli that are ordinarily aversive. In general, when people can choose, and when they believe control is vested in themselves (as opposed to some outside agent), they can better control aversive stimuli of many kinds—from loud and painful noise (Glass & Singer, 1972) to electric shock (Corah & Boffa, 1970; Zimbardo, 1969). Attitudes are also affected. When people choose to do something they might ordinarily have foregone (e.g., eat grasshoppers, cf. Zimbardo, 1969), their subsequent attitudes are more internalized and consistent with their actions than if they are "forced" to commit themselves to the same behavior. These findings, in turn, are consistent with the research of Regan and Fazio (1977) mentioned earlier.

Lefcourt (1973) concludes his review of some of this same research as follows:

> . . . With respect to the response to aversive stimulation, perceived control makes a great difference. Pain or anxiety arousing stimuli are not simply to be found in the stimuli impinging on our senses. Our responses are evidently shaped and molded by our perception of those stimuli and by our perception of ourselves

vis-à-vis those stimuli. . . . The perception of control would seem to be a common predictor of the response to aversive events regardless of species [p. 424].

In short, when choice, active involvement, and the "perception of control" are studied, it appears that these conditions lead to greater attitude–behavior consistency and a greater "cognitive control" of aversive stimulation than when human beings and animals are given less choice, are passively involved, or when they perceive little control over the relationship between their efforts and their outcomes. We believe this evidence indicates that there are distinctive features of control-relevant vs. control-irrelevant conditions (the availability of a reward is one) *and* that people are capable of differentially perceiving and responding to these conditions. The most general outcome of this process is greater self-knowledge and self-control over the environment. This is reflected in greater attitude–behavior consistency and greater "activity" in the face of aversive events.

CONCLUSIONS

Let us look at some of the variety of unresolved issues that have arisen from our analysis of the effects of rewards on patterns of activity.

1. More research is needed on the various phases of the learning process, particularly the process of task engagement (e. g., what makes things interesting; is it novelty, anticipated reward, or what?) and the phase of disengagement. It is especially important to study the phase of *disengagement* when it is chosen by the subject (under intrinsically motivating circumstances). Research designs to date have not allowed an adequate test of this part of the process.

2. More research is needed on each of the three questions we raised earlier about an information-based theory:

a. What information specifies control?
b. How is it discriminated?
c. What are the consequences (behavioral and cognitive) of making this discrimination?

We have noted that some information already exists on each of these topics. Some of the kinds of information signaling the "potential for control" include: low environmental "demand," low arousal, high choice, freedom, a contingent relationship between effort and outcome, and apparent predictability of the events in the environment. When these conditions obtain, people are active in their problem solving, choose more difficult problems, have greater confidence in the outcomes, direct attention to those aspects of the task relevant to the development of basic skills, are more persistent in doing the task and more willing to return to it than when these conditions do not obtain. But these conditions are the only ones studied in research so far. Are there others? If so, what are they, and how do people come to learn that they signal the potential for control?

This second question, how are these informational elements discriminated and when (in the developmental sequence) seems most important. Some kinds of control may be present in infants, but a great deal of it must be learned within an environment. How does this learning take place? Finally, once we know something about what kinds of information signal control, and we know that people do differentiate these "contexts" from one another, we must discover how people come to respond differentially to these perceptual differences. Once again, some of this differential responsiveness may be apparent in early infancy, but it is likely that a great deal of it must be learned. If the distinction is as important as we think and if most of it must be learned, then it follows that the learning of differential responsiveness should, in some degree, "map" the learning of the perceptual distinctions. We have made a beginning to this analysis by showing how the response to the different "reward" contexts studied in this research may be viewed as differential responses to the conditions or the contexts involved. But the full range of responses to these different contexts is unknown at this time, although the literature just reviewed and contained in other chapters of this book provides a good place to start.

As can be seen, there is a good deal of research to be done before it is possible to develop a complete and accurate theory of the process of learning under different motivational contexts. In particular, the role of the "self" in the whole process needs much additional research, as well as the importance of the perception of control over events. We believe the distinctions we have raised have heuristic possibilities. They focus upon the informational context rather than reward per se—in particular, the way it is perceived and utilized by the individual and the pattern of response set off by different informational arrays. We have organized the evidence in this chapter that we believe supports such an analysis, and we hope we have opened a variety of questions for future research to undertake. Rewards are powerful ways to control behavior, we do not deny that; but the consequences of this control are just beginning to be studied. We have seen evidence to suggest that there are circumstances in which control by extrinsic forces (e.g., the systematic use of rewards) undermines the development of competence, of effective voluntary control of skilled action. The use of rewards in the "motivation" of learning is placed in doubt by the evidence reported here. The time is ripe for a different look at motivation, and particularly an individual's "control" of the process.

REFERENCES

Bandura, A., & Walters, R. H. *Social learning and personality development.* New York: Holt, Rinehart & Winston, 1963.

Battle, E., & Rotter, J. B. Children's feelings of personal control as related to social class and ethnic group. *Journal of Personality,* 1963, *31,* 482–490.

Berlyne, D. E. The reward-value of indifferent stimulation. In J. T. Tapp (Ed.), *Reinforcement and behavior.* New York: Academic Press, 1969.

Bruner, J. The organization of early skilled action. In M. P. M. Richards (Ed.), *The integration of the child into a social world.* London: Cambridge Press, 1974.

Bruner, J., Goodnow, J. J., & Austin, G. A. *A study of thinking.* New York: J. Wiley & Sons, Inc., 1956.

Calder, B. J., & Staw, B. M. Self-perception of intrinsic and extrinsic motivation. *Journal of Personality and Social Psychology,* 1975, *31,* 599–605.

Chambers, J. C. *The effects of intrinsic and extrinsic motivational contexts on problem solving and the process of learning.* Doctoral dissertation, in preparation, 1976.

Condry, J. C. The role of initial interest and task performance on intrinsic motivation. Paper presented at the meeting of the American Psychological Association, Chicago, September 1975.

Condry, J. C. Enemies of Exploration: Self-initiated versus other-initiated learning. *Journal of Personality and Social Psychology,* 1977, *35,* 459–477.

Condry, J. C., & Chambers, J. C. How rewards change the problem solving process. In preparation. 1976.

Corah, J. L., & Boffa, J. Perceived control, self-observation and response to aversive stimulation. *Journal of Personality and Social Psychology,* 1970, *16,* 1–14.

Crowne, D. P., & Liverant, S. Conformity under varying conditions of personal commitment. *Journal of Abnormal and Social Psychology,* 1963, *66,* 547–555.

Csikszentmihalyi, M. *Beyond boredom and anxiety.* San Francisco: Jossey–Bass, 1975.

de Charms, R. *Personal causation.* New York: Academic Press, 1968.

Deci, E. L. *Intrinsic motivation.* New York: Plenum, 1975.

Garbarino, J. The impact of anticipated rewards on cross-age tutoring. *Journal of Personality and Social Psychology,* 1975, *32,* 421–428.

Ginsburg, H. *Children's arithmetic: The learning process.* New York: Van Nostrand Co., 1977.

Glass, D. C., & Singer, J. E. *Stress and adaptation: Experimental studies of behavioral effects of exposure to aversive events.* New York: Academic Press, 1972.

Gore, P. M., & Rotter, J. B. A personality correlate of social action. *Journal of Personality,* 1963, *31,* 58–64.

Graves, T. D. *Time Perspective and the Deferred Gratification Pattern in a Triethnic Community.* Research Report No. 5, *Tri-Ethnic Research Project.* Institute of Behavioral Science, University of Colorado, 1961.

Harlow, H. F. Learning and satiation of response in intrinsically motivated complex puzzle performance by monkeys. *Journal of Comparative Physiological Psychology,* 1950, *43,* 289–294.

Karniol, R. and Ross, M. The development of causal attributions in social perception. *Journal of Personality and Social Psychology,* 1976, *34,* 455–464.

Kisk, G. B. Learning when the onset of illumination is used as a reinforcing stimulus. *Journal of Comparative and Physiological Psychology,* 1955, *48,* 261–264.

Kisk, G. B., & Antonitis, J. J. Unconditioned operant behavior in two homozygous strains of mice. *The Journal of Genetic Psychology,* 1956, *88,* 121–129.

Koslowski, B., & Bruner, J. S. Learning to use a lever. *Child Development,* 1972, *43,* 790–799.

Langer, E. J. The illusion of control. *Journal of Personality and Social Psychology,* 1975, *32,* 311–328.

Langer, E. J., & Roth, J. Heads I win, tails it's chance: The illusion of control as a function of the sequence of outcomes in a purely chance task. *Journal of Personality and Social Psychology,* 1975, *32,* 951–955.

Lefcourt, H. M. Internal versus external control of reinforcement: A review. *Psychological Bulletin,* 1966, *65,* 206–220.

Lefcourt, H. J. The function of the illusions of control and freedom. *American Psychologist,* 1973, *28,* 417–425.

Lefcourt, H. J., & Ladwig, G. W. The American Negro: A problem in expectancies. *Journal of Personality and Social Psychology,* 1965, *1,* 377–380.

Lepper, M. R., Greene, D., & Nisbett, R. E. Undermining children's intrinsic interest with extrinsic rewards: A test of the overjustification hypothesis. *Journal of Personality and Social Psychology,* 1973, *28,* 129–137.

Levine, F. M., & Fasnacht, G. Token rewards may lead to token learning. *American Psychologist,* 1974, *29,* 816–820.

Lichtman, C. M., & Julian, J. W. Internal versus external control of reinforcement as a determinant of preferred strategy on a behavioral task. Paper presented at the meeting of the Midwestern Psychological Association, St. Louis, 1964.

Liverant, S., & Scodel, A. Internal and external control as determinants of decision making under conditions of risk. *Psychological Reports,* 1960, *7,* 59–67.

Maehr, M. L., & Stallings, W. M. Freedom from external evaluation. *Child Development,* 1972, *43,* 177–185.

McGraw, K. O., & McCullers, J. C. Some detrimental effects of reward on laboratory task performance. Paper presented at the meeting of the American Psychological Association, Chicago, 1975.

Mowrer, O. H., & Viek, P. An experimental analogue of fear from a sense of helplessness. *Journal of Abnormal and Social Psychology,* 1948, *43,* 193–200.

Neal, A. G., & Seeman, M. Organizations and powerlessness: A test of the mediation hypothesis. *American Sociological Review,* 1964, *29,* 2, 216–226.

Nuttin, J. R. Pleasure and reward in human motivation and learning. In D. E. Berlyne & K. B. Madsen (Eds.), *Pleasure, reward, preference.* New York: Academic Press, 1973.

Odell, M. *Personality correlates of independence and conformity.* Unpublished master's thesis, Ohio State University, 1959.

Ovsiankina, M. Die Wiederaufname unterbrochener Handlungen. *Psychologische Forschung,* 1928, *11,* 302–379.

Piaget, J. *Genetic epistemology.* New York: Columbia University Press, 1970.

Regan, D. and Fazio, R. On the consistency between attitudes and behavior: Look to the method of attitude formation. *Journal of Experimental Social Psychology,* 1977, *13,* 28–45.

Richter, C. F. Sudden death phenomenon in animals and humans. In H. Feifel (Ed.), *The meaning of death.* New York: McGraw–Hill, 1959.

Rotter, J. B. Generalized expectancies for internal versus external control of reinforcement. *Psychological Monographs,* 1966. 80(Whole no. 609).

Rotter, J. B., Seeman, M., & Liverant, S. Internal versus external control of reinforcements: A major variable in behavior theory. In N. F. Washburne (Ed.), *Decisions, values, and groups* (Vol. 2). London: Pergamon Press, 1962.

Russell, A. The effects of magnitude and duration of change on the light contingent bar-pressing of hooded rats. *Australian Journal of Psychology,* 1972, *24,* 63–73.

Seeman, M. Alienation and social learning in a reformatory. *American Journal of Sociology,* 1963, *3,* 270–285.

Seeman, M., & Evans, J. W. Alienation and learning in a hospital setting. *American Sociological Review,* 1962, *27,* 772–782.

Seligman, M. E. P. *Helplessness*. San Francisco: Freeman, 1975.

Seligman, M. E. P., Maier, S. F., & Solomon, R. R. Unpredictable and uncontrollable aversive events. In F. R. Brush (Ed.), *Aversive conditioning and learning*. New York: Academic Press, 1969.

Smith, M. C. Children's use of the multiple sufficient cause schema in social perception. *Journal of Personality and Social Psychology*, 1975, *32*, 737-747.

Smith, W. E. The effects of anticipated vs. unanticipated social reward on subsequent intrinsic motivation. Unpublished doctoral dissertation, Cornell University, 1975.

Strickland, B. The prediction of social action from a dimension of internal–external control. *Journal of Social Psychology*, 1965, *66*, 353-358.

Upton, W. *Altruism, attribution, and intrinsic motivation in the recruitment of blood donors*. (Doctoral dissertation, Cornell University, 1973.) *Dissertation Abstracts International*, 1974, *34*, 6260-B.

White, R. W. Motivation reconsidered: The concept of competence. *Psychological Review*, 1959, *66*, 297-333.

Zajonc, R. Social facilitation. *Science*, 1965, *149*, 269-274.

Zimbardo, P. *The cognitive control of motivation*. Glenview, Ill.: Scott, Foresman, 1969.

5 Endogenous Attribution and Intrinsic Motivation

Arie W. Kruglanski
Tel-Aviv University

The purpose of this chapter is to explore the implications of recent developments in attribution theory (e.g., Kelley, 1967, 1971; Kruglanski, 1975) for the understanding of task motivation. The subsequent discussion dwells on the antecedents and the consequences of *intrinsic* vs. *extrinsic* motivation to an activity, i.e., of the case in which the activity is thought of as being performed for its inherent qualities vs. its being performed for contingent rewards. This particular emphasis contrasts with the traditional motivational theory that has stressed alternative aspects of task motivation, notably: (1) the general *intensity* of motivation (concern reflected, e.g., in the *drive* × habit or the expectancy × *value* formulation); and (2) the specific *direction* of motivation (apparent, e.g., in concern about the different motives and their development: the achievement motive, the curiosity motive, etc.).

ATTRIBUTION THEORY AND EPISTEMOLOGICAL REPRESENTATION

Attribution theory is addressed to the issue of lay epistemology. It is concerned with the process whereby people acquire knowledge about their physical, psychological, and social environment (cf. Kelley, 1967). The relevance of attribution theory to problems of motivation and emotion rests on what might be called the *assumption of epistemological representation*. Specifically, motives or emotions are assumed to be represented in phenomenology; i.e., they are assumed to constitute kinds of knowledge that people may have about themselves. Accordingly, a common statement about an emotional event is assumed transformable into a statement about an epistemological event. For example, when we say that "John has a toothache," we actually mean that "John is aware, or knows of (his) toothache" or even that "John interprets his particular experiences in terms of the 'toothache' concept."

Furthermore, the epistemological content of one's motives and emotions is assumed to exert significant influence on one's behaviors. Thus, if John had known his experiences for a "toothache," he might have set up a dental appointment; whereas if he had known them for the "pangs of sinus," he may have arranged to see a laryngologist instead.

In sum, the application of attribution theory to motivational and emotional phenomena assumes that the psychological significance of such phenomena derives from their epistemological character. Epistemological accounts of emotion are exemplified in the pioneer works of Stanley Schachter (cf. Schachter & Singer, 1962; Nisbett & Schachter, 1966). The present chapter applies the epistemological approach to the domain of task motivation.

The Content and Logic of Attributional Analysis

The fundamental assumption of attribution theory is that the lay process of knowledge acquisition is similar in crucial respects to the scientific process. In science, it is useful to distinguish between the content of knowledge and the logical method whereby the knowledge in question is validated. Similarly, in lay knowledge, it is possible to separate the content of hypotheses generated by the layman in order to explain some events from the logic whereby he or she might assess the validity of those explanations. Furthermore, in the same way that the content of scientific knowledge (the theories and hypotheses investigated) varies greatly from one domain of study to the next, the lay concepts used to explain events also vary greatly across situations. For instance, Weiner, Frieze, Kukla, Reed, Rest, and Rosenbaum (1971) have demonstrated how concepts like "ability," "luck," "effort," and "task difficulty" apply to specific situations involving success and failure (but, presumably, not to alternative situations). Similarly, it will be shown subsequently how the concepts "ends" and "means" apply to situations in which some voluntary action is being explained and how these concepts affect one's motivation toward a task.

Unlike the protean domain of content, the logic of validating specific hypotheses of interest is assumed invariant across situations. Broadly speaking, this is the logic of *consistency*. In other words, a given concept will be accepted as a valid explanation of some event (e.g., an action) to the extent that it is consistent with the event in question (where "consistent" means that the event is logically deducible from the explanation).[1] Furthermore, when the evidence is con-

---

[1]For a detailed discussion of the logical relation between an explanation and the empirical evidence, see, in particular, Popper, 1959, pp. 59–62.

sistent with more than one mutually incongruent (i.e., logically contradictory) explanation, the attributor will tend to *discount* each explanation as compared with the case where it alone was consistent with the evidence (cf. Kelley, 1971).

Once a given explanation (attribution) of some effect has been adjudged as valid, so are adjudged all the implications deducible from this explanation. In what follows, several motivational implications are deduced from the layman's specific explanations of his or her own (or another's) actions, or *voluntary* behaviors. The present analysis is not considered applicable to the explanation of *occurrences,* i.e., events (like success or failure on some task) that potentially contain a considerable nonvoluntary (or externally based) conponent. For further discussion of the differences between actions and occurrences, see Kruglanski (1975).

THE ENDOGENOUS-ATTRIBUTION THEORY OF INTRINSIC MOTIVATION

Postulate 1: *For the naive attributor (an actor or an observer of someone else's action), actions are explicable in terms of "reasons" or "purposes."*

Corollary to Postulate 1: *Insofar as all actions are assumed purposive, any action may be conceived of as either its own end or as means to a further end.*

Definition 1: *Let the term* endogenous attribution *of an action denote the case where an action is attributed to itself as reason. In other words, endogenously attributed action is an "end in itself."*

Definition 2: *Let the term* exogenous attribution *of an action denote the case where action is perceived as means that mediates a further goal.*

Postulate 2: *Subjective freedom consists in the attainment of goals.* One does not freely choose to have needs. Those are determined for the individual (by biological constitution, societal norms, ethical injunctions, etc.). But granting the existence of needs, one would then freely decide to fulfill them, e.g., to eat when feeling hungry, etc.

Postulate 3: *The decision to act is based on the judgment that there exists sufficient reason for the action.* Substituting the term *goal* for *sufficient reason,* it may be stated that the decision to engage in (persist at, or resume) an activity is occasioned by the judgment that this action is either a goal in itself or is means to another goal. In turn, the judgment that some entity constitutes a goal is partially determined by prior attributions of behavior to the entity in question.

Several psychological analyses of information processing (e.g., Kanouse, 1971; Kelley & Thibaut, 1969; Miller, Galanter, & Pribram, 1960) suggest the following final postulate of the present theory.

Postulate 4: *Attributional (informational) analysis is more likely to be initiated when the individual is dissatisfied (vs. being satisfied) with current outcomes.*

Implications of Endogenous and Exogenous Attributions

The central thesis presently advocated is that several motivational implications follow when evidence available to the attributor favors an endogenous (vs. an exogenous) attribution of an action. Let me first spell out the implications of endogenous and exogenous attributions and then discuss the nature of the requisite evidence for such attributions.

Derivation 1 from Definition 1: *To the extent that an action is attributed endogenously, it implies the actor's positive affect (enjoyment, contentment, satisfaction, etc.).* This follows from the common definition of the "end" concept as a state of affairs that the actor desires. Thus, its attainment (an endogenously attributed action) represents the fulfillment of one's desire, a situation creditable with positive feelings of enjoyment and satisfaction.

Derivation 2 from Definition 2: *To the extent that an action is exogenously attributed, it implies the actor's negative affect, as "means" is not something that the actor desires.* In the case of an exogenously motivated action, the actor is doing something that he or she does not want to do. The action signifies the overcoming of an obstacle that forestalls the direct gratification of the actor's need (the attainment of the goal). In this sense, then, the action is inseparable from a frustrating event accompanied by negative affect. Note that the endogenous–exogenous variable is not assumed to constitute the exclusive determinant of positive or negative affect. An action is endogenous or exogenous with respect to a single goal, whereas the degree of satisfaction–dissatisfaction is assumed contingent on the totality of the person's goals (or needs)—notably, on the degree to which they are fulfilled or frustrated. Thus, the above two derivations (1 and 2) need to be supplemented by a *ceteris paribus* proviso whereby the inferences of enjoyment vs. disenjoyment are a monotone function of the endogenous–exogenous variable only when the state of the person's remaining goals (needs) is held constant.

Derivation 3 (from Postulate 2 and Definition 1): *To the extent that an action is attributed endogenously, it affords the inference of subjective freedom attendant on the performance of the action.* That is because such action constitutes the attainment of a goal (fulfillment of a need), an event assumed to signify freedom.

Derivation 4 (from Postulate 2 and Definition 2): *To the extent that an action is attributed exogenously, it affords the inference of compulsion attendant on the action's performance.* In the case of means (vs. ends), the actor is not pursuing an action that is inherently desirable. One does not want to, but is compelled to, enact it by the situational constraints that pose barriers in the way of immediate need satisfaction.

Thus far we have dealt with the cognitive elements: the actor's inferences of enjoyment and of freedom while pursuing an activity. But are the implications of attributional analysis restricted to the cognitive level? Is our attributor, like the proverbial rat in Tolman's learning theory, forever buried in thought? This does not seem to be the case. Actual (overt) behavior is linked to attribution and the mediating link is the actor's *decision*. Thus we have:

Derivation 5 (from Postulate 3 and Definition 1): *When an action cannot be assumed to constitute a means to some end, the likelihood of decision to engage in it, persist at it, or resume it will be a positive function of it being the target of endogenous attributions made in the past.*

It has been proposed that the actor would be more satisfied with an endogenously (vs. exogenously) attributed activity. This notion coupled with the assumption that the motivation to engage in an informational analysis is inversely related to satisfaction suggests:

Derivation 6 (from Postulate 4 and Derivations 1 and 2): *Given a situation in which action attribution has been made, continued attributional analysis will be more likely to take place in the case of an exogenous (vs. endogenous) attribution. The intent of such analysis will be to identify those aspects of the activity that are absolutely indispensible to goal attainment.*

In other words, for an exogenously (vs. endogenously) attributed bahavior, there will take place a "shrinkage" in the actor's conception of the relevant activity, or the "means." Combined with the earlier "action" postulate (3), this implies directly:

Derivation 7 (from Postulate 3 and Derivation 6): *Granting the same initially defined activity, more restricted portions thereof will come to be enacted in the exogenously vs. the endogenously attributable case. Furthermore, the specific portions enacted will be the instrumental ones, i.e., those perceived as indispensable to the attainment of the exogenous goal.*

So far, the *content* of endogenous (vs. exogenous) attributions has been shown to yield implications on levels of *cognition* (inferences of enjoyment and of freedom), *decision* (to engage in, persist at, or resume an activity), and *performance* (of specific, instrumental subparts versus wholes of initially conceived activities). But the various implications may obtain in specific situations only after the attributor has applied the *consistency logic* to conclude that an endogenous or an exogenous attribution was warranted by the evidence. Let us consider now what the requisite evidence might be for endogenous (or exogenous) attributions.

Evidence Categories for Endogenous (Exogenous) Attributions

By our definitions (1 and 2), an endogenous attribution will be made when the action is considered its own reason, and an exogenous attribution when the reason is extrinsic to the action. These definitions contain three distinct components: the action, its reason, and the relation of endogeneity (or exogeneity) assumed to span these two. Correspondingly, the evidence for endogenous (exogenous) attribution is naturally classifiable into that affecting the *action* (its perceived identity) the action's perceived reason, and the reason's perceived endogeneity to the action. These three categories of evidence are next examined at some length.

The action's reason.   By Postulate 1 of the present theory, a layman would consider an action as explained once its reason or goal[2] has been confidently identified. Thus, given an action to be explained, some goal is postulated *consistent* with information that this goal was salient (for the actor) at the time the action was taking place and that the action was aimed at an attainment of the goal. Accordingly, evidence regarding an action's reason would be of two broad types: (1) historical and (2) instantial. Historical evidence is required to establish that a given entity may occasionally constitute a goal for the actor. For example, given information about the actor's past, it might be reasonable (or unreasonable) to surmise that ''attendance at a classical concert'' might be goal for this person. Or, given the actor's (history of) membership in the Western culture, one may venture to assume that money is this person's important goal. Instantial evidence is required to establish that the goal in question was operative at the instance to be explained and that the action could be assumed to further the goal's attainment. For example, a monetary reward would not qualify as a cogent explanation of an action if in order to perform it at the instance in question the actor had foregone much higher pay. Also, a reward would not provide a compelling explanation of an action if this reward was forthcoming regardless of the action's occurrence.

In sum, an explanation of an action would be adjudged valid to the extent that there existed historical and instantial evidence regarding the reason for the action. Thus, an endogenous attribution might be made if, based on prior knowledge, some currently performed action (say the consumption of an exotic meal) could be assumed to constitute plausible reason for the actor, and to the extent that this reason could be assumed salient at the instance in question. For example, the consumption of an exotic meal would be less likely to appear as an end in itself given that the actor (eater) had already completed a particularly opulent dinner. Furthermore, confidence in a given explanation of an action might be lowered to the extent that historical and instantial information implicated an alternative reason for the action. For example, an endogenous attribution would be less likely to the extent that there existed also plausible, exogenous reason for the action.

The action.   The problem of explanation has received considerable attention within attribution theory (see, e.g., Kelley, 1967, 1971, 1972, 1973). By contrast, little discussion has been accorded to the problem of *identification,* i.e., to the way an ''effect'' to be explained (in our case, an action) is conceptualized. It

---

[2]Throughout the present discussion, the terms *reason, goal, desire,* or *need* are treated as synonymous.

is presently suggested that the lay person's knowledge of an action's identity is conjectural or conceptual in the same sense as one's knowledge of an action's reason. Thus, a person confronted with an event or sequence of events is assumed to generate hypotheses about the conceptual identities of these phenomena. Stated differently, the same physical events are assumed amenable to several disparate identifications. The same sequence of behaviors may be conceptualized as different actions (see also, Lepper & Greene, pp. 125–131, 238–239). For example, the same sequence of behaviors might be variously interpreted to mean that the actor is: (1) sweeping the floor; (2) practicing shuffleboard; (3) helping mother; (4) earning money; etc. It follows that *given a constant reason for these behaviors, the attribution of endogeneity would vary according to whether they were conceptualized in terms of this reason or in terms foreign to the reason.* For instance, given that a person's reason for an action is to "help mother," an endogenous attribution would be indicated if the action had been similarly identified, and an exogenous attribution if it had been identified, e.g., as "sweeping the floor."

But what may be the conditions for assigning a given identity to an action? The assumption that identity attributions are conjectural or hypothetical suggests the applicability of the consistency logic of attributional analysis. Thus, a given identity hypothesis would be adopted to the extent that it cohered with current fact and background assumptions, and it would be discounted to the extent that alternative hypotheses manifested such consistency. For example, the actor's conclusion that he or she is "playing a game of tennis" vs. "giving a tennis lesson" would be affected by his or her background knowledge (e.g., regarding the degree of experience as a tennis pro) and by evidence regarding the partner's relative ability, willingness to accept our actor's recommendations, etc.

The endogeneity question. Thus far, our discussion of evidence for endogenous (vs. exogenous) attributions has been addressed to the actor's conceptions of the action or of the reason as they may affect the perceived similarity between the two. But an alternative category of evidence seems implicit in the relation of endogeneity itself. Specifically, the endogeneity concept connotes an action's inherence to or inseparability from its goal. As with the inference of the action's identity, or its reason, endogeneity is assumed inferable according to the consistency logic, i.e., to the extent that the endogeneity concept provides the best fit to the available evidence. For example, the endogeneity assumption would be consistent with evidence of recurrent temporal association of action and goal or of the goal's dissociation from alternative actions and the action's dissociation from alternative goals.

By now we have discussed both the implications of endogenous (exogenous) attributions and the several evidence categories relevant to such attributions. Thus, the groundwork has been laid for the examination of specific experimental findings within the present scheme. The various research studies to be reviewed are discussed in rough accordance with the specific evidence category manipulated experimentally. Let us discuss first those studies in which the implicated reason of an action was varied along the endogenous–exogenous dimension.

Endogenous Causality and Intrinsic Motivation

Throughout subsequent discussion, the term *intrinsic motivation* is taken to mean the actor's degree of motivation to perform the task *as such*. It is assumed that intrinsic motivation would be reflected in the actor's verbal statements about an interest in, enjoyment of, and freedom at the activity as well as in (the actor's) overt behavior—notably, persistence at or resumption of the activity in circumstances where this does not appear to mediate exogenous rewards. In the subsequent review, studies with verbal measures are considered first, followed by studies with behavioral measures.

Intrinsic motivation studies with verbal measures.   A typical experimental paradigm employed to study intrinsic motivation involves an actor in an activity in return for (vs. without) contingent exogenous rewards, and the effects of these manipulations on intrinsic motivation toward that activity are observed. From the present perspective, the presence of exogenous reward introduces a plausible alternative to an endogenous explanation of an action; hence, it renders it less likely. Consequently, a greater degree of intrinsic motivation is expected in the no-reward (exogenous) than in the reward condition. Consistent with the above prediction are the findings of Kruglanski, Friedman, and Zeevi (1971). These investigators induced high school children to perform a series of tasks involving verbal skills. Half of the subjects were promised an exogenous reward (a visit to the university) for the execution of the tasks, whereas the remaining half were not promised such a reward. As expected, subjects in the no-reward condition reported subsequently a greater interest in the tasks than did subjects in the reward condition.

Further evidence for the adverse effect of exogenous reward on stated interest in a task comes from two studies reported by Kruglanski, Riter, Amitai, Margolin, Shabtai, and Zaksh (1975). In one of the studies, teen-age boys at youth centers constructed models according to pictures. In the second study, high school students acted as managers of (fictitious) athletic teams and attempted to maximize their teams' winnings by a judicious allocation of athletes to events. In each study, half of the subjects received monetary rewards for successful performance, and the remaining half of the subjects received points. In both experiments, the unpaid subjects rated the tasks as more interesting and expressed greater preference for them over alternative activities than did the paid subjects.

In a yet different study, Kruglanski, Alon, and Lewis (1972) involved elementary school children in team competitions with verbal tasks. *Following* the completion of the contest, half of the winning subjects (the reward condition) were falsely led to believe that they had been previously promised attractive prizes for winning. No false beliefs about a previous promise of prizes were induced in the remaining half of the winning subjects (the no-reward condition). It turned out that the no-reward subjects reported subsequently greater interest in the competitive games than did the reward subjects. It is noteworthy that the Kruglanski et al. (1972) findings furnish a particularly strong support for the present attributional implication whereby task enjoyment is *inferred* from evidence extant at the time rather than being *given directly* via experience with the task.

Studies discussed so far pertain to Derivation 1, which links endogenous (vs. exogenous) attributions with positive affect (e.g., enjoyment, interest) toward a task. Let me turn now to experimental evidence for Derivations 3 and 4, whereby endogenous (vs. exogenous) attributions of action imply the actor's greater freedom. In one relevant study (Kruglanski & Cohen, 1973), subjects received information about a choice made by another individual. In the "in-character" condition, the choice was consistent with this person's past preference, suggesting that in the current instance, too, it was endogenously attributable. In the "out-of-character" condition, the choice was inconsistent with the actor's past preferences, implying that it had originated in exogenous circumstance. As expected, subjects with the "in-character" information attributed greater freedom to the actor than did subjects with the "out-of-character" information.

In another similar research (reported in Kruglanski, 1975), hypothetical actors' preexisting preferences were consistent with a specific, exogenous circumstance of their current acts versus being consistent with the acts' endogenous aspects. For instance, in one of the situations formulated, the actor, a high school student, decides to attend a concert. In the *endogenous* condition, the actor is known for his (past) delight in classical music; and in the *exogenous* condition he is known for his interest in Ann, an attractive girl also known to attend the concert. When questioned about the actor's subjective freedom and enjoyment at performing the action (e.g., listening to the concert), subjects imputed to him greater freedom (as well as enjoyment) when the evidence favored an endogenous (vs. an exogenous) attribution.

Intrinsic-motivation studies with behavioral measures. According to Derivation 5 of the present framework, when an action cannot be assumed to constitute a means to some end, the tendency to engage in it, persist at it, or resume it will be positively related to it being the target of endogenous attributions made by the person in the past. Evidence pertinent to this derivation comes from research by the Deci (e.g., 1971) and the Lepper and Greene teams (e.g., Greene, 1974; Greene & Lepper, 1974; Lepper, Greene, & Nisbett, 1973). In the experimental paradigm commonly employed by these investigators, a baseline is measured of the subjects' tendency to pursue some activity; then a reward is dispensed (vs. not dispensed) for performance of the activity. Finally, the tendency to pursue the activity in a subsequent situation devoid of the reward is measured. The recurrent finding in such experiments is that the introduction of exogenous rewards lowers the subjects' tendency to engage in the activity for its own sake. This is readily interpretable in terms of Derivation 5, given the familiar assumption that exogenous rewards lower the likelihood of the activity being attributed endogenously.

Greater persistence at an activity under conditions in which an endogenous (vs. an exogenous) attribution would seem more likely has been observed in the series of experiments by Kruglanski, Riter, Arazi, Agassi, Monteqio, Peri, and Peretz, (1975b). In this research, subjects performed either an interesting or a dull task for (the same) monetary reward. In one of the experimental studies, subjects were required to work at the task for a specified time that qualified them for the reward. As expected, subjects with the interesting task (i.e., in circumstances where an endogenous attribution would be more likely) persisted at the activity longer than did subjects with the dull task.

Endogenous Attribution and Extrinsic Motivation

Findings already reviewed support the prediction that evidence for exogenous (vs. endogenous) attribution of task performance would lower *intrinsic* motivation toward the task. But the present theoretical framework also implies the complementary prediction that evidence for endogenous (vs. exogenous) attribution of task performance would lower inferred *extrinsic* motivation toward the task. Support for the latter proposition derives from the experimental series by Kruglanski et al. (1975b) referred to in the preceding section. Recall that in both conditions of this design, subjects performed dull or interesting tasks for identical monetary rewards. As expected, subjects with the interesting task (high intrinsic reward) attached less importance to the monetary payment (e.g., recommended a lower amount of pay increase and donated a greater proportion of their pay to charity) than did subjects with the dull tasks (low intrinsic reward). These findings were interpreted to reflect the greater tendency of the low- (vs. the high) intrinsic-reward subjects to attribute their performance of the task to the exogenous reward and, hence, to attach greater value to the reward in question.

Endogenous Attribution and Performance

The present Derivation 7 implies that the performance of exogenously (vs. endogenously) attributed activities will be confined to aspects judged indispensable to reward attainment. In other words, an actor who attributes her activity exogenously may be expected to do the bare minimum sufficient for the acquisition of reward. Direct evidence for this prediction comes from a recent study by Kruglanski, Stein, and Riter (1977). Unlike the previously reviewed research, this study did not contrast the endogenous vs. exogenous cases. Instead, both the exogenous reward and the activity were kept constant across the experimental conditions, and the variable manipulated was the specific aspect of the activity on which the reward had been made contingent. The subjects in this experiment were college students solicited to perform a job for a monetary remuneration. There were three experimental conditions in which the task was described identically as the transmission of research data onto computer coding forms. In addition, subjects in all conditions were informed that they had 45 minutes at their disposal and that within this interval the standard performance was 20 rows of data. In the time-contingent condition, subjects were informed that the payment was contingent on their spending the 45 minutes on the task; in the standard-contingent condition, subjects were told that the payment was contingent on their completion of the standard 20 rows; and in the output-contingent condition, that the payment was contingent on the quantity of output. It turned out that subjects in the time-contingent condition deviated least from the 45-minute limit, as compared with subjects in the remaining conditions. Subjects in the standard-contingent condition deviated least from the specified output standard of 20 data columns, and subjects in the output-contingent condition produced the highest amounts of output. These data were interpreted as consistent with the hypothesis that extrinsically motivated workers act in accordance with a minimax strategy: They minimize their performance of a task by restricting it to aspects deemed indispensable to attainment of the contingent reward; and when possible, they perform in ways designed to maximize the reward in question. The minimization tendency has been manifest in the time-contingent and the standard-contingent conditions of this research, where subjects closely adhered to the minimal performance requirements specified as sufficient for reward attainment. Recall that the requirements in question marked the lower bounds of satisfactory performance, which could have been exceeded with impunity in the upward direction. Thus, the subjects' close approximations of the sufficiency requirements seem not only to reflect their concern about attaining the reward but also their intent to do the *bare minimum* sufficient for that purpose. The maximization tendency was manifest in the output-contingent condition where the subjects' performance was apparently aimed at securing the greatest possible amount of reward.

The restriction of activities to aspects perceived directly instrumental to attainment of the exogenous goal could result in performance decrements on tasks that require unobvious, indirect approaches for a successful execution. Support for the above hypothesis was obtained in the experiment by Kruglanski, Friedman, and Zeevi (1971) mentioned earlier. In this research, high school students who expected to be exogenously rewarded for the performance of verbal tasks manifested lesser creativity and worse recall (of the tasks' details) than did subjects who did not expect reward. Similarly, Garbarino (1975) found that tutors who anticipated exogenous reward for successful teaching adopted a direct, intrusive teaching style and were generally less effective in communicating the pertinent concepts to their students than were tutors to whom no rewards had been promised. Finally, McGraw and McCullers (1975) found that incidental learning was less likely to occur where exogenous (monetary) rewards were made contingent on the performance of a verbal-learning task.

This research suggests that reward will adversely affect the performance of tasks that require an unobvious or creative (vs. explicit or direct) approach to their solution. In a sense, this seems congruent with the learning-theory prediction that intense motivation or drive (presumed positively related to reward magnitude) will impair performance on difficult tasks in which the incorrect responses are high in the habit hierarchy (cf. Spence, 1956). But a noteworthy conceptual difference between the present formulation and learning theory is that the latter speaks of reward magnitude in general, whereas the former makes the fundamental distinction between rewards that are endogenous vs. exogenous to the task. According to the rationale of learning theory, large rewards of all types would be detrimental to the performance of difficult tasks. By contrast, according to the endogenous attribution theory, only large exogenous—but not large endogenous—rewards would be so detrimental. Thus, for a person intensely interested in some difficult problem, finding the solution may constitute a large endogenous reward; yet it seems unlikely that this fact would impair the person's problem-solving performance.

Identity, Endogeneity, and Intrinsic Motivation

Except for the research by Kruglanski, Stein, and Riter (1977), all of the studies reviewed thus far manipulated the actor's implied reason for behavior along the endogenous–exogenous dimension. Let me now describe in some detail the research by Kruglanski, Riter, Amitai, Margolin, Shabtai, and Zaksh (1975) in which endogenous (vs. exogenous) attributions were created by changing the action's implied identity so as to make it more vs. less endogenous to its reason. In both studies contained in this research, one experimental variation had to do with the presence (vs. the absence) of monetary rewards contingent on the successful performance of the task. The above variation was orthogonally crossed with the nature of the task. In experiment 1, subjects in one condition (money–endogenous condition) played a coin-toss game, i.e., performed an activity to which possible monetary gain is (commonly assumed to be) an inherent feature. In the second (money–exogenous) condition, subjects played a model-construction game, i.e., performed an activity to which monetary gain is not inherent. In terms of the present framework, an attempt was made to vary the identity of the activity in such a way as to render monetary gain endogenous vs. exogenous to the activity.

Beside the differential endogeneity of money, the coin-toss and model-construction games vary on a host of other characteristics (e.g., the degree of interest that they may evoke or the type of skill that they may require). In order to reduce this irrelevant variability, subjects in Experiment 2, in both task conditions engaged in *exactly the same behaviors,* which were interpreted differently, notably as stock-market operation in the money–endogenous conditions and as athletic-management in the money–exogenous conditions. Again, then, the action's implied *identity* has been varied so that in one case it has been rendered close to the idea of monetary reward and in a second case rendered remote (exogenous) from that idea. The central interest in both experiments revolved about the effect of monetary rewards (their presence vs. absence) on intrinsic motivation in each of the task conditions, i.e., where money would be apprehended as a task-endogenous vs. a task-exogenous feature. The present theory suggests that when money is exogenous to a task, its presence would lower endogenous attribution and thus lower intrinsic motivation. However, when a salient goal such as money is endogenous to the task, its presence should enhance endogenous attribution and thus enhance intrinsic motivation. The degree of intrinsic motivation was inferred from the subjects' verbal reports of interest in the game and from their stated preference for it over possible alternatives. The data of both experiments strongly supported the present predictions: When money was endogenous to the task, its presence (vs. absence) enhanced intrinsic motivation; and when it was exogenous to the task, its presence depressed intrinsic motivation. A similar conclusion seems suggested by the findings of Staw, Calder, and Hess (1974). These investigators manipulated norms for payment as well as the actual payment of money for performing an interesting task. They found an interaction of norms and payment such that the introduction of an extrinsic reward decreased intrinsic interest in a task only where there existed a situational norm for no payment, i.e., a norm that highlighted the separateness (exogeneity) of the payment from the task.

The evidence so far pertained to changes in the action's perceived *identity* or *reason* as they affect intrinsic motivation in accordance with the endogenous attribution hypothesis. No direct data known to this writer bear on the possible effects on intrinsic motivation of shifts in perceived endogeneity *as such.* An experiment designed to test for such effects would need to hold constant the action's identity and reason and to vary factors influencing the judgment that the two are endogenous (or exogenous) to each other. It is possible to speculate here about two separate cases, one in which the action concept is well established (as with familiar activities like eating, swimming, or reading) and the second in which the action concept is newly being formed. In case of a familiar action, the attributor already knows which features inherently belong to the action and which features do not so belong. But the perception of endogeneity or exogeneity could be sharpened by enhancing the saliency of the endogeneity relation (e.g., by explicitly inviting the subject to attend to the endogeneity question). Such a manipulation of saliency should enhance intrinsic motivation for endogenously related actions and reasons and decrease intrinsic motivation for exogenously related actions and reasons.

For an action concept that is newly being formed, the impression that a given feature (e.g., the action's reason) is endogenous to the action might be created, e.g., by the provision of evidence regarding temporal association between instances in which a given action label is suggested to apply and the feature in question is present. It should be noted, however, that temporal association (between a feature and an action label) is merely a necessary condition for the endogeneity hypothesis, not a sufficient condition. A feature that is endogenous to an action must be inevitably present whenever the action occurs, but the mere association of an activity and a feature does not logically compel the endogeneity hypothesis.

Reversals in the Effects of Rewards on Attitudes

According to the present analysis, rewards may have either positive or negative influence on motivation toward an activity, depending on whether they are apprehended as endogenous or exogenous to this activity. This implication is congruent with the experimental evidence for reversal in the effect of rewards on attitudes (see, e.g., Chapter 2, this volume). Though not previously deduced from a unified conceptual framework, the conditions for the reversal have been characterized in terms of some empirical variables. It is, therefore, of interest to speculate about the possibility that these variables are coordinable to the endogenous–exogenous dimension. In particular, I should like to consider two major variables that have been proposed as moderators of the relation between rewards and motivation: (1) the actor's perceived degree of choice, and (2) the extent of temporal association between the reward and the behavior. As for the former variable, Linder, Cooper, and Jones (1967) have shown that when the actor is given free choice about performing (vs. declining to perform) an unpleasant activity, there obtains a negative relation between the magnitude of an exogenous reward and liking (or, intrinsic motivation) for the activity; however, when the actor is given no choice—the relation is positive. These results may be understood if it is assumed that rewards have two contradictory effects on enjoyment:

1. Their mere presence (or the promise of their delivery) enhances current enjoyment.
2. Their identification as exogenous reasons of the activity depresses enjoyment (see Derivation 2 discussed earlier).

The "free-choice" condition represents a situation in which two plausible reasons for the activity seem implied—the activity's endogenous properties and the exogenous reward. In these circumstances, the magnitude of the exogenous reward should directly influence the subject's tendency to attribute his or her activity exogenously rather than endogenously. The decrement of enjoyment due to exogenous attribution may override the increment of enjoyment due to the promise of reward, so that the net effect would be a negative relation between the magnitude of reward and enjoyment.

By contrast, in the "no-choice" condition, the subject's wish to obey the experimenter's instruction seems so compelling a reason for performing the activity as to render possible alternative reasons implausible by comparison. If this is so, the subject's tendency to attribute the activity exogenously should no longer vary as a function of the reward's magnitude, for in all cases now the underlying reason for the activity would appear to be obedience rather than reward. Under these circumstances, the only effect of reward on enjoyment would be the positive one, and it would grow monotonically with increases in the magnitude of reward.

Or, consider the temporal association between task and reward. Recently, Reiss and Sushinsky (1975) have argued that novel reward introduces a disruptive influence that results in negative affect, but a reward's protracted association with an activity promotes the development of positive affect toward the activity. In present terms, novel reward that has not been associated with the activity in the past is, therefore, apprehended as exogenous; so its effect on liking for the activity should be negative. By contrast, a reward continually associated with the activity might become assimilated thereto or apprehended as part of the activity, in which case its effect on liking for the activity would be positive. It is reiterated that temporal association between a feature (e.g., a reward) and an activity is not a sufficient condition for the perception of endogeneity. Temporal association is merely consistent with such a perception; hence, it may render it more likely in situations where the individual's existing concepts did not strongly indicate exogeneity.

Circumstantially Contingent and Circumstantially Independent Consumption of Rewards

Let me now consider an intriguing implication of the endogenous-attribution theory for the effects of *qualitatively different* rewards on task motivation. Generally, it is possible to distinguish three broad ways whereby the relation between rewards and motivation has been conceptualized so far. One conceptualization may be dubbed the "absolutist view," as it implies that the relation between reward and motivation to an activity is uniform regardless of the nature of the reward or of the activity. For example, the absolutist view is reflected in claims (reviewed in Kruglanski, Chapter 2 of the present volume) that the relation between reward and motivation is uniformly positive. The second view may be called "genericist," as it divides the various rewards into those that are generically extrinsic to activities (e.g., money, food, status,) and those that are generically intrinsic to activities (e.g., achievement, mastery, curiosity, self-enhancement) (see, e.g., Super, 1962). Correspondingly, it has been sometimes implied that provision of intrinsic reward would introduce intrinsic motivation, whereas provision of extrinsic reward would promote extrinsic motivation. Finally, the third view is implied in the present framework and it may be called "relativist," as it relativizes the effects of rewards on motivation to perceived endogeneity between activity and reward. The relativist view suggests that rewards do not have uniform effect on activities, nor may certain categories of rewards, because of their generic qualities, have such unitary effects; but rather the effects of reward would depend on whether it is endogenous or exogenous to the activity.

Actually, the "relativist" view of the relation between rewards and motivation is not as incompatible with the "genericist" view as at first it may appear. In particular, some rewards may be "generically" more endogenous to all activities than other rewards. To be sure, there can be no purely exogenous rewards. At the very least, any reward is endogenous to the consummatory behavior of which it is the target. Yet some rewards simply cannot be made *exogenous* to activities with which they may be linked. Consider, for instance, rewards inherent in assuming oneself to be "a good person" or in "helping one's friend." Depending on the specific circumstances, any activity at all (carrying a suitcase, driving a car, raking the leaves) could be sometimes interpreted to signify the attainment of such goals. In other words, activities that a priori have nothing to do with the particular goal could become circumstantially endogenous thereto. For example, a goal of "being a good person" is attained *in the very act* of giving one's blood for the benefit of others. This is quite unlike the case in which "giving blood" is subservient to the receipt of monetary payment, a goal attained *only following* the completion of the instrumental act.

The above notions suggest the classification of rewards or goals into those whose mode of consumption is *circumstance contingent* and those whose mode of consumption is *circumstance independent*. The examples just considered (of "helping" or "being good") identify circumstantially contingent goals, i.e., ones whose mode of consumption (or attainment) would depend on the specific circumstances. By contrast, the consumption of circumstantially independent goals would be relatively invariant across different circumstances. Thus, "eating" would be recognizable as such (i.e., be fairly invariant) regardless of the attendant situational specifics; ditto the receipt of money, a good grade, or prestige. To reiterate, a goal whose consumption is circumstantially contingent would warrant the endogenous attribution of any activity performed in its service, despite the absence of an inherent relation between the action and the goal. By contrast, an independently consumable goal would lead to an exogenous attribution of unrelated activities performed in its service.

The above ideas were tested in unpublished research by Vardah Wiesieltier of Tel-Aviv University. Wiesieltier intuited that *altruistic goals* belong in the circumstantial-consumption category whereas *egoistic goals* belong in the independent-consumption category. For example, compare the altruistic act of driving another person to the airport to help him with the same act performed now (e.g., by a cabby) for the egoistic goal of monetary remuneration. In advance of the specific circumstances, "driving" is as unrelated to "helping" as it is to "earning money." However, the cabby's goal of earning money is accomplished only upon being paid by the customer; whereas the goal of helping is realized (consumed) in the very activity of driving itself. Accordingly, Wiesieltier hypothesized that the same activities will be apprehended as more intrinsically motivated when performed in the service of altruistic vs. egoistic (utilitarian) goals.

In her experiment, Wiesieltier presented subjects with two sets of 12 sentences. In each of the sentences a protagonist performs an action in the service of some goal. The same 12 actions were used in the two sets, such that each action was once conjoined with an altruistic goal and the second time with an egoistic one. Each set of 12 sentences included an equal number of egoistic and altruistic goals, and an action that appeared in one set with goal in the egoistic category appeared in the remaining set with goal in the altruistic category. Thus, one item in the egoistic set read "a girl studies medicine in order to gain high income," and the comparable item in the altruistic set was "a girl studies medicine in order to help cure cancer patients."

After having read each of the items, the subject rated the perceived degree to which the actor enjoyed the behavior and was performing it freely. The results provided an impressive support for the research hypothesis: On the average, actions coupled with altruistic goals were rated as (1) more enjoyable and as (2) accompanied by a greater freedom ($p < .001$, for both enjoyment and freedom ratings) than the same actions coupled with egoistic goals. This finding has been since replicated with several demographically diverse samples of the Israeli population.

Wiesieltier's results and the relation between the endogeneity variable and the circumstantial contingency of goals' attainment might merit a close attention. For one thing, it jibes nicely with the finding (reported, e.g., by Deci, 1971; McGraw & McCullers, 1975) that verbal rewards enhance intrinsic motivation where material rewards seem to suppress it. In the present terms, "verbal rewards" are those whose consumption is circumstantial: Under specific circumstances, any activity could be defined as approvable (i.e., to warrant "verbal rewards"). In other words, the role of some "verbal rewards" may be that of pinpointing, under specific circumstances, those activities that are approvable. The actor who performs such behaviors is ipso facto accomplishing a goal of being an approvable, worthwhile person; hence, his (her) behavior may be attributed endogenously. On the other hand, the consumption of material rewards is independent of the circumstances. Hence, numerous activities performed in the service of material goals might be apprehended as exogenously motivated.

In general, the relation of verbal rewards to intrinsic motivation should depend entirely on the meaning conveyed by the particular verbalizations. For example, in the preceding discussion, the *content* of verbal rewards tagged specific activities as representing the attainment of socially approvable ends (e.g., of helping other people); and this was assumed critical for mediating the effects of verbal statements on intrinsic motivation. Furthermore, the perceived *sincerity* of the rewards would seem of great importance for the type of influence that they may exert on intrinsic motivation: A verbal reward exposed as insincere would be thereby divested of its pleasure-eliciting capacity. Finally, it should make a considerable difference whether the verbal reward is apprehended as relevant or irrelevant to its target activity. In particular, verbal reward perceived as relevant to its target activity is therefore more endogenous to the activity than reward perceived as irrelevant. For instance, consider a pianist who is complimented on a performance by an expert critic or by a sexually attractive person who happens to understand little about music. The compliment may be equally enjoyable on both occasions, but in the first case it may seem highly relevant (hence endogenous) to the pianist's actual performance and in the second case as somewhat irrelevant (hence exogenous) to the performance. According to this analysis, attribution of behavior to relevant praise would promote intrinsic motivation to the behavior in question; whereas attritubtion of behavior to an irrelevant praise would lower intrinsic motivation. That verbal rewards may lower intrinsic motivation in circumstances where they may seem irrelevant (hence exogenous) to performance seems suggested by Smith's recent dissertation (1975) at Cornell University. Smith found that verbal rewards anticipated in advance and somewhat routinized may lead to decrements in intrinsic motivation. In terms of the present analysis, routinized and a priori announced verbal rewards may appear somewhat irrelevant (hence exogenous) to actual performance, which may lead to the observed decrements in intrinsic motivation.

Finally, Deci's finding (Deci, Cascio, & Krusell, 1973) that the intrinsic motivation of the males increased and of females decreased under the influence of verbal rewards is explicable if the sexes may be assumed to have different perceptions regarding the relevance of such rewards to performance. As Deci (1975, pp. 145–146) has implied, because of differential socializations the males may be more strongly motivated than are the females to attain competence at numerous activities, and the females may be more strongly motivated than are the males to gain interpersonal approval. Thus, the males may respond primarily to the *content* of verbal rewards that is relevant to competence at the experimental activity, and the females may respond primarily to the interpersonal *mode* of the reward's delivery that is largely irrelevant to the specific experimental activity. These differences in perceived relevance (or endogeneity) may account for the differential effects of verbal rewards on intrinsic motivation of males versus females.

Several practical benefits of using goals whose consumption is circumstantially contingent (vs. independent) are readily apparent, e.g., benefits accruing from the greater sense of enjoyment and of freedom while performing activities for goals in the former category. However, I should like to call attention to the additional implication that the employment of such goals might be a particularly effective means of instilling new motives, because an activity performed in the service of a goal whose consumption is circumstantially contingent is thereby defined as an *end in itself*. Such analysis seems consistent with Hoffman's (1970) conclusion that the parental disciplinary technique of induction is a more efficient means of producing the internalization of moral values than are the techniques of love withdrawal or power assertion. According to Hoffman (1970): ''... induction includes techniques in which the parent gives explanations or reasons for requiring the child to change his behavior ... [p. 286].'' Examples are appeals to the child's pride, striving for mastery, and to be ''grown up,'' and concern for others. By contrast, ''... love withdrawal techniques are those in which the parent simply gives direct but nonphysical expression to his anger or disapproval of the child for engaging in some undesirable behavior.'' Examples are ignoring the child, turning one's back on him, refusing to speak or listen to him, explicitly stating a dislike for the child, and isolating or threatening to leave him. Finally, ''... Power assertion includes physical punishment, deprivation of material objects or privileges, the direct applications of force, or the threat of any of these ... [p. 285].''

Assuming that moral values are goals whose consumption is circumstantially contingent, it becomes understandable why induction is superior to both power assertion and love withdrawal as an instrument of internalization. Induction must explicitly spells out to the child *what specific acts* signify the implementation of the larger moral goals. By contrast, with power assertion the larger moral value does not get as explicitly articulated. In latter circumstances, the objective of the morally appropriate action becomes the avoidance of physical harm or material deficit, objectives that may well be assumed to be circumstantially independent. With power-assertive techniques, then, the moral action may be perceived as means to an exogenous goal and with induction as an end in itself. Love withdrawal (or resumption) is in and of itself an affect-laden event, and in this sense it is a circumstantially independent punishment or reward. On the other hand, more so than impulsively delivered physical punishments, love manipulations may convey the parent's considered evaluation of the action in reference to the moral code. In this sense, then, love manipulations are circumstantially contingent rewards that identify some actions as (moral) ends in themselves. All of this would account for the intermediate efficiency of love withdrawal as an instrument of internalization.

RECAPITULATION AND CONCLUSION

This paper outlined a novel theoretical approach to the study of task motivation premised on the assumption that task motivation is explicable as inference that may be drawn from past (or ongoing) behavior and that may determine future behavior oriented toward the task. Specifically, intrinsic motivation has been assumed to follow from endogenous (vs. exogenous) attribution of task performance, i.e., from the attributor's judgment that performance of a task is an end in itself vs. being a means to a further end. Furthermore, past attribution of behavior (endogenously vs. exogenously) was assumed to affect the enactment of this behavior in future situations where it could not be assumed to mediate exogenous rewards.

The inference of motivation has been regarded as epistemologically nonunique, i.e., as subject to the underlying logic of all inference. This is the logic of consistency whereby an inference: (1) is adopted when the available evidence is consistent with the attribution from which it may be deduced; and (2) is weakened when the evidence is consistent with alternative (incompatible) attributions.

The theory of endogenous attribution has been shown to furnish a good fit to the manifold of empirical data pertinent to task motivation. The theory has been congruent with findings diverse with respect to: (1) the attributor's relation to the behavior being explained, notably of the actor or the observer of another's actions; (2) the content of inferences mediated by endogenous attribution, notably the inferences of enjoyment and of subjective freedom; and (3) the psychological categories affected by a person's attributional analysis, notably the categories of *inference, action,* and *performance.*

Besides its consistency with findings generated so far, the theory of endogenous attribution could provide a useful framework for future research on task motivation. For example, a possible direction for such research might be an extension of the presently initiated analysis of *circumstantially* vs. *independently* consumable rewards and their relation to task motivation. An entirely different line of research might explore the *epistemological implications* of the present analysis for the relevance of cognitive needs (e.g., the need for consistency) and abilities (e.g., the ability to detect inconsistencies) to motivational phenomena, etc.

Finally, a broad significance of the present framework derives from its explicit commitment to the view that intrinsic motivation may be profitably understood from the *subjective* vantage of the attributor (as opposed to the *objective* vantage of the scientist). According to this view, the prediction of intrinsic motivation requires that the scientist combine knowledge of the attributional logic with *conjecture* about the actor's specific ideas formulated under the circumstances of interest. Let me elaborate on this final point at some length. The earlier discussion of evidence categories for endogenous or exogenous attribution merely characterized the *necessary* conditions for such attributions, derivable from the general concepts "action," "reason," and "endogeneity." This discussion did not attempt to specify the *sufficient* conditions for endogenous (vs. exogenous) attributions; i.e., it did not fully characterize the circumstances in which the attributions in question would follow inevitably. The reason for this apparent omission is that in any particular instance, the attribution rendered would depend on: (1) the specific situational context; (2) the attributor's specific background knowledge (i.e., his (her) total repertory of concepts and beliefs in which terms the situational context would be interpreted); and (3) the mysterious and whimsical process whereby the attributor may apply to the specific context a given subset of concepts and beliefs out of the vast epistemological repertory at his (her) disposal. It seems that all three matters are so decisively particularistic that they may not be included in any universal (or nomothetic) theory of human nature.[3] No person may ever know someone to the extent of fully predicting what the latter would think or do in a specific instance, let alone predicting what *anyone* would. Harry Stack Sullivan (1972) perceived this clearly:

> There's an essential inaccessibility about any personality... Years of intimacy with another does not put the most devoted friend in a position such that he can predict every act of the other one. No amount of effort at self-revelation conveys the whole unique totality of one's personality. There's always ample residuum that escapes analysis and communication... No one can hope fully to *understand* another. One is very fortunate if he approaches an understanding of oneself... [p. 5].

All this notwithstanding, an approximate outguessing of another's thoughts or actions is quite commonplace. One example among myriad are the numerous experiments reported in this volume that time and again corroborated the experimenters' hypotheses. It should be clear, however, that in addition to reflecting on the validity of the nomothetic psychological theory being tested in such experiments (e.g., the theory of endogenous attribution), their success reflects on the experimenter's culturally specific, hence idiographic, knowledge of the subjects' conceptual frameworks involved in the specific experimental contexts. The former (theoretical) knowledge is where psychology constitutes a science, whereas the latter (contextual) knowledge is where it constitutes an art.

ACKNOWLEDGMENTS

Research reported in this chapter was supported in part by Ford Foundation Grant 7 (through Israel Foundation Trustees) to the author.   This chapter was prepared while the author was on a leave from Tel-Aviv University and at Vanderbilt University, Nashville, Tennessee.

REFERENCES

Campbell, D. T. Unjustified variation and selective retention in scientific discovery. In F. J. Ayalla & T. Dobzhansky (Eds.), *Studies in philosophy of biology*. New York: Macmillan, 1974.

---

[3]D. T. Campbell (e.g., 1974) insists that this process is properly classifiable as *random*.

Deci, E. L. Effects of externally mediated rewards on intrinsic motivation. *Journal of Personality and Social Psychology,* 1971, *18,* 105–115.

Deci, E. L. *Intrinsic motivation.* New York: Plenum, 1975.

Deci, E. L., Cascio, W., & Krusell, J. Cognitive evaluation theory and some comments on the Calder and Staw critique. *Journal of Personality and Social Psychology,* 1973, *31,* 81–85.

Garbarino, J. The impact of anticipated reward on cross-age tutoring. *Journal of Personality and Social Psychology,* 1975, *32,* 421–429.

Greene, D. Immediate and subsequent effects of differential reward systems on intrinsic motivation in public school classrooms. (Doctoral Dissertation, Stanford University 1974). *Dissertation Abstracts International,* 1974, *35,* 4626B. (University Microfilms No. 75-6854.)

Greene, D., & Lepper, M. R. Effects of extrinsic rewards on children's subsequent intrinsic interest. *Child Development,* 1974, *45,* 1141–1145.

Hoffman, M. L. Moral development. In P. H. Mussen (Ed.), *Carmichael's manual of child psychology.* New York: Wiley & Sons, 1970.

Kanouse, D. *Language, labeling and attribution.* Morristown, N.J.: General Learning Press, 1971.

Kelley, H. H. Attribution theory in social psychology. In D. Levine (Ed.), *Nebraska Symposium on Motivation* (Vol. 15). Lincoln; University of Nebraska Press, 1967.

Kelley, H. H. *Attribution in social interaction.* Morristown, N.J.: General Learning Press, 1971.

Kelley, H. H. *Causal schemata and the attribution process.* Morristown, N.J.: General Learning Press, 1972.

Kelley, H. H. The processes of causal attribution. *American Psychologist,* 1973, *28,* 107–128.

Kelley, H. H., & Thibaut, T. W. Group problem solving. In G. Lindzey & E. Aronson (Eds.), *Handbook of social psychology* (Vol. 4). Reading, Mass.: Addison–Wesley, 1969.

Kruglanski, A. W. The endogenous–exogenous partition in attribution theory. *Psychological Review,* 1975, *82,* 387–406.

Kruglanski, A. W., Stein, C., & Riter, A. Contingencies of exogenous reward and task performance: On the "minimax" principle in instrumental behavior. *Journal of Applied Social Psychology,* 1977, *7,* 2, 141–148.

Kruglanski, A. W., Alon, S., & Lewis, T. Retrospective misattribution and task enjoyment. *Journal of Experimental Social Psychology.* 1972, *8,* 493–501.

Kruglanski, A. W., & Cohen, M. Attributed freedom and personal causation. *Journal of Personality and Social Psychology,* 1973, *26,* 245–250.

Kruglanski, A. W., Friedman, I., & Zeevi, G. The effects of extrinsic incentives on some qualitative aspects of task performance. *Journal of Personality,* 1971, *39,* 608–617.

Kruglanski, A. W., Riter, A., Amitai, A., Margolin, B., Shabtai, L., & Zaksh, D. Can money enhance intrinsic motivation: A test of the content-consequences hypothesis. *Journal of Personality and Social Psychology,* 1975, *31,* 744–750. (a)

Kruglanski, A. W., Riter, A., Arazi, D., Agassi, R. M., Monteqio, T., Peri, I., & Peretz M. The effects of task-intrinsic rewards upon extrinsic and intrinsic motivation. *Journal of Personality and Social Psychology,* 1975, *31,* 699–705. (b)

Lepper, M. R., Greene, D., & Nisbett, R. E. Undermining children's intrinsic interest with extrinsic rewards: A test of the overjustification hypothesis. *Journal of Personality and Social Psychology,* 1973, *28,* 129–137.

Linder, D. E., Cooper, J., & Jones, E. E. Decision freedom as a determinant of the role of incentive in attitude change. *Journal of Personality and Social Psychology,* 1967, *6,* 245–254.

McGraw, K. O., & McCullers, J. C. Some detrimental effects of reward on performance in traditional laboratory tasks. Paper presented at the meeting of the American Psychological Association, Chicago, 1975.

Miller, G. A., Galanter, E., & Pribram, K. H. *Plans and the structure of behavior.* New York: Holt, Rinehart & Winston, 1960.

Nisbett, R. E., & Schachter, S. Cognitive manipulation of pain. *Journal of Experimental Social Psychology,* 1966, *2,* 227–236.

Popper, K. R. *The logic of scientific discovery*. New York: Basic Books, 1959.

Reiss, S., & Sushinsky, L. W. Overjustification, competing responses, and the acquisition of intrinsic interest. *Journal of Personality and Social Psychology*, 1975, *31*, 1116–1125.

Schachter, S., & Singer, J. E. Cognitive, social and physiological determinants of emotional state. *Psychological Review*, 1962, *69*, 379–399.

Smith, W. F. The effects of social and monetary rewards on intrinsic motivation. Unpublished doctoral dissertation, Cornell University, 1975.

Spence, K. W. *Behavior theory and conditioning*. New Haven: Yale University Press, 1956.

Staw, B. M., Calder, B. J., & Hess, R. Situational norms and the effect of extrinsic rewards on intrinsic motivation. Unpublished manuscript, University of Illinois, Urbana-Champaign, 1974.

Sullivan, H. S. *Personal psychopathology: Early formulations*. New York: Norton, 1972.

Super, D. E. The structure of job values in relation to status, achievement, interests and adjustment. *Journal of Applied Psychology*, 1962, *46*, 231–239.

Weiner, B., Frieze, I., Kukla, A., Reed, L., Rest, S., & Rosenbaum, R. *Perceiving the causes of success and failure*. Morristown, N.J.: General Learning Press, 1971.

6

Overjustification Research and Beyond: Toward a Means–Ends Analysis of Intrinsic and Extrinsic Motivation

Mark R. Lepper
Stanford University

David Greene
SRI International

In the many years since Thorndike's formulation of his "Law of Effect" (1911) an enormous amount of research has been devoted to the study of the manner in which rewards increase, and punishments decrease, the subsequent probability of responses that precede them. Recently, however, psychologists have begun to ask a quite different question, one concerning the effects of "extrinsic" rewards on "intrinsic" motivation as indicated by a person's subsequent attitude toward the activity, willingness to engage in that activity in the later absence of extrinsic contingencies, and/or the quality of performance while engaged in the activity. The resulting experimental literature suggests that when a person engages in an intrinsically interesting activity, under certain conditions, the imposition of superfluous extrinsic rewards may have detrimental effects on his or her intrinsic motivation (Condry, 1977; Deci, 1975; Kruglanski, 1975; Lepper & Greene, 1976; Lepper, Greene, & Nisbett, 1973; Ross, 1976).

The central theme of this chapter is an examination of the processes by which these detrimental effects may be produced and the conditions under which such "hidden costs" of reward can be observed. More specifically, we begin the present chapter by summarizing the results of our own research program. In so doing, we both discuss the conditions under which detrimental effects of extrinsic rewards on subsequent intrinsic motivation appear to occur and make explicit several critical features of the basic experimental paradigm from which these conclusions are drawn. In the remainder of the chapter, we seek to place these findings in two broader contexts: (a) by presenting a more complete, process-oriented account of the mechanisms by which extrinsic constraints may produce detrimental effects on intrinsic motivation; and (b) by presenting a more comprehensive, general model of how these processes may interact with others to determine the net effects of any particular reward system on subsequent behavior.

THE OVERJUSTIFICATION PARADIGM

Theoretical Background

We begin, then, with a brief review of our own research program and related work growing out of the social-psychological research traditions outlined earlier in this volume by Kruglanski (Chapter 2). Historically, as Kruglanski notes, experimental interest in the inverse relation between an individual's "attitude" toward an activity and the salience of extrinsic justification for engaging in it began with cognitive-dissonance research on the effects of psychologically insufficient justification (cf. Aronson, 1966). In this research, typically, individuals are induced to engage in attitudinally inconsistent behavior under conditions of either clearly sufficient or psychologically inadequate justification. Subsequently, subjects given little extrinsic justification act as if their actions had been intrinsically motivated rather than externally constrained.

In one classic series of studies, for example, it has been repeatedly demonstrated that the *less* powerful or salient the extrinsic constraints employed to induce children to comply with an adult's prohibition of a particular activity, the *more* likely they are to show subsequent "internalization" of that prohibition in their attitudes toward the activity (Aronson & Carlsmith, 1963; Carlsmith, Ebbesen, Lepper, Zanna, Joncas, & Abelson, 1969; Zanna, Lepper, & Abelson, 1973) and their later willingness to engage in the activity in situations where the activity has not been prohibited (Freedman, 1965; Pepitone, McCauley, & Hammond, 1967). Indeed, prior compliance with a prohibition under conditions of minimal justification in one setting has been shown to produce significant decreases in children's willingness to cheat at a different activity, in a quite different setting, several weeks later (Lepper, 1973).

Though initially derived within a dissonance framework, these findings were subsequently reinterpreted by Bem (1967, 1972) and by Kelley (1967, 1973) in terms of self-perception or self-attribution processes, whereby a person's attitude toward an activity is hypothesized to be determined in part by one's perception of his or her reasons for engaging in the activity. To the extent that external reinforcement contingencies controlling one's behavior are salient, unambiguous, and sufficient to explain it, the person will be likely to attribute his or her behavior to these constraints. But if external contingencies are seen as weak, unclear, or psychologically insufficient to account for one's actions, the person will attribute those actions to his or her own dispositions, interests, or desires. The findings from insufficient justification studies are therefore explained as the result of a self-directed "inference" process rather than the reduction of an aversive emotional state. In low-justification conditions, inferences from behavior in the apparent absence of external pressure suggest that the behavior must have reflected the subject's own wishes; in high-justification conditions, the subject infers that his or her behavior was determined by the external pressures in the situation.

Whether the self-perception model provides the best account of this prior literature on insufficient justification remains a topic of some debate (e.g., Fazio, Zanna & Cooper, 1977; Greenwald, 1975; Zanna & Cooper, 1976). Casting this literature in attributional terms, however, had the heuristic benefit of leading us to consider the possibility that conceptually analogous effects might be obtained in situations where unnecessarily powerful and salient extrinsic pressures are applied to induce an individual to engage in an activity of initial intrinsic interest. To the extent that the extrinsic incentives are sufficiently salient and seemingly "oversufficient," an attributional analysis suggested, the individual might attribute his or her behavior to these compelling extrinsic contingencies rather than to an intrinsic interest in the task and would therefore be less likely to regard the activity as interesting in itself. We termed this proposition the *overjustification* hypothesis to emphasize its conceptual relationship to the insufficient-justification literature.

In focusing on an individual's perception of the reasons for his or her actions, moreover, this analysis suggested that it was not simply the association of extrinsic rewards with an activity but rather the perception of extrinsic instrumentality that would be necessary to produce a decrease in intrinsic motivation. Contracting explicitly to engage in an interesting activity to obtain a reward, therefore, should be relatively likely to undermine interest in the activity. By contrast, receipt of an unforeseen reward after engaging in an activity should be relatively less likely to produce a detrimental effect, because such a procedure should not typically lead subjects to see their previous behavior as having been directed toward attainment of the reward. Were subjects provided with a subsequent opportunity to engage in the activity in the absence of salient extrinsic constraints, subjects in the former but not the latter case would be expected to show less intrinsic interest in the activity than nonrewarded control subjects.

Initial Demonstrations

A paradigmatic initial investigation of this hypothesis was performed by Lepper, Greene, and Nisbett (1973). To obtain a measure of "intrinsic" motivation, we arranged to introduce an attractive drawing activity into regular preschool classrooms on several days, during explicit "free-play" periods, when children were free to choose continuously among a vast array of attractive alternatives. This target activity was set out by the children's regular teachers as part of the normal school program, without intrusion by research personnel, in classrooms where we could record covertly the amount of time each child in the class spent with the activity from behind a one-way mirror. On the basis of these baseline measures, children showing initial intrinsic interest in the activity were selected for the experiment.

In individual experimental sessions in a different setting, these children were asked to engage in the activity under one of three conditions. In the Expected Award condition, subjects were first shown an extrinsic reward, a "Good Player" certificate, and were asked if they wished to engage in the drawing activity in order to win this award. This procedure was designed to induce subjects to see their engagement in the activity as instrumental to an extrinsic goal. In the Unexpected Award condition, subjects were asked to engage in the activity without mention of any reward but unexpectedly received the same award and the same feedback after they had finished with the activity. This procedure provided a control for task engagement and receipt of the reward without providing the conditions likely to promote a perception of task engagement as instrumental to an ulterior goal. Finally, in the No Award control condition, subjects neither expected nor received a reward but otherwise duplicated the experience of subjects in the other conditions. Two weeks later, to provide a measure of children's subsequent intrinsic interest in the activity, the target activity was again placed out in the children's classrooms for several days, and postexperimental interest in the activity was unobtrusively observed, in the absence of any expectation of further extrinsic rewards, as during the baseline period.

From a self-perception perspective, we predicted that subjects in the Expected Award condition would show less subsequent interest in the activity than subjects in either the Unexpected Award or No Award conditions. The results strongly supported this prediction. Subjects who had agreed to engage in the activity in order to obtain the award subsequently spent significantly less time playing with the materials than did subjects in the other two conditions. Relative to uniform, high levels of baseline interest, Expected Award subjects showed a significant decrease in interest in the activity from baseline to postexperimental observations, whereas subjects in the No Award and Unexpected Award conditions showed no significant change in overall interest.

This pattern of results, suggesting the importance of subjects' perceptions of their activity as a means to an extrinsic goal—as opposed to the simple association of the activity with the reward per se—has proven an experimentally robust finding. In subsequent experiments employing the same general paradigm (Greene & Lepper, 1974; Lepper & Greene, 1975; Lepper, Sagotsky, & Greene, 1977a), for example, these findings have been replicated across substantial variations in the nature of the contingency imposed, the target activity, and the reward employed. Similarly, Smith (1976), using a paradigm patterned closely after Deci's (1971) procedure, has demonstrated decrements in subsequent intrinsic interest from expected but not unexpected rewards with a college sample. In this study, moreover, generally comparable results were obtained with both monetary and social rewards, providing additional evidence that the critical variable is the salience of the means–end relationship between the activity and the reward rather than the association of a particular type of reward with engagement in the activity.[1]

Further data consistent with this analysis have been provided by studies examining the effects of explicit variations in the salience of an expected extrinsic reward on subsequent intrinsic motivation (Ross, 1975). In a first study, the perceptual salience of the extrinsic reward was varied. In this study, preschool children in two experimental groups were offered an unspecified "prize" for engaging in an activity of initial interest. In one group, no further mention was made of this reward; in the other, an opaque box ostensibly containing the promised prize was placed on the table in front of the subject. Relative to nonrewarded control subjects, subjects who were merely promised an unspecified prize showed no decrement in subsequent intrinsic interest. When the reward remained unspecified but was made perceptually salient, however, subjects showed significantly less subsequent interest in the activity.

These findings were extended in a second study, which involved a more "cognitive" manipulation of means–end salience. In this experiment, preschool children in three experimental conditions were promised an attractive food reward for engaging in an interesting activity but were given different instructional sets designed to vary the salience of this extrinsic contingency (cf. Mischel, Ebbesen, & Zeiss, 1972). In a condition designed to make the contingency particularly salient, subjects were told explicitly to "think about" the reward as they engaged in the activity; in a condition designed to decrease the salience of the contingency, subjects were told to think about a contingency-irrelevant topic; and in a third condition, subjects were given no explicit ideational instructions. Again, relative to nonrewarded control subjects, children in both the reward-salient condition and the no-instruction condition showed significant decrements in later spontaneous play with the activity, whereas subjects in the distraction condition showed no such decrease in subsequent interest.

Taken together, these studies provide empirical support for the overjustification hypothesis that engagement in an activity of initial interest under conditions that make salient to the person the instrumentality of engaging in that activity as a means to some ulterior end may lead to decrements in subsequent, intrinsic interest in the activity. There are, however, other theoretically possible explanations of these data, and several additional studies have been directed toward testing various alternative accounts of these initial overjustification studies.

---

[1]Additional demonstrations of a detrimental effect of expected and salient tangible rewards on subsequent intrinsic interest, relative to no-reward control procedures, have been reported in a number of other investigations (e.g., Anderson, Manoogian, & Reznick, 1976; Calder & Staw, 1975; Deci, 1975; Kruglanski, Riter, Amitai, Margolin, Shabtai, & Zaksh, 1975; Pittman, Cooper, & Smith, 1977; Swann & Pittman, 1977).

Further Research Issues

Immediate vs. subsequent effects.   One class of issues raised by these initial studies concerns the role of possible differences in task performance, during the treatment period when rewards were available, in mediating adverse effects of extrinsic rewards on subsequent, intrinsic interest in the activity. That is, given the evidence that rewards may sometimes impede rather than facilitate immediate task performance (cf. McCullers, Chapter 1; McGraw, Chapter 3), one might ask whether such initial performance decrements provide a necessary and/or sufficient condition for the observation of subsequent decreases in intrinsic interest. Indeed, in our own first studies (Lepper et al., 1973; Greene & Lepper, 1974), we obtained some evidence of immediate performance decrements. Children expecting a reward during the experimental sessions tended to draw more pictures that, given a constant time period, were individually of lower quality on the average than drawings made by subjects not expecting a reward. Moreover, these performance measures during experimental sessions showed small but significant correlations with subsequent interest in the activity in subjects' classrooms and hence provided a potential focal point for explaining the subsequent behavioral data. Of course, such immediate performance decrements are not inconsistent with the hypothesis that the expected reward procedure may decrease intrinsic motivation. They do suggest, however, that the subsequent effects may be dependent upon these prior, qualitative differences in task performance.

With this issue in mind, further research has attempted to examine subsequent intrinsic interest following expected reward procedures that do not produce immediate performance effects. At this point, it seems reasonably clear that performance decrements do not necessarily precede subsequent decrements in interest. On the one hand, adverse effects on behavioral measures of subsequent, intrinsic interest have been obtained in a number of experiments in which there was evidence of neither qualitative nor quantitative performance differences (Amabile, DeJong, & Lepper, 1976; Deci, Cascio, & Krusell, 1975; Lepper, Sagotsky, & Greene, 1977b, 1977c; Ross, 1975; Ross, Karniol, & Rothstein, 1976) and in experiments in which evidence of significant increases in task engagement were obtained without accompanying decrements in task quality (Colvin, 1971; Lepper et al., 1977a). In our own studies, for example, when the subject's task during the experimental sessions has been more clearly defined than in our initial experiments—e.g., as the completion of a specified number of drawings (or puzzles) or as engagement in the task until some specified temporal criterion has been reached—performance decrements have not been found; yet comparable results on measures of subsequent engagement in the activity have been obtained. On the other hand, factors that produce decrements in immediate task performance do not necessarily produce decreases in subsequent intrinsic interest; nor do measures of immediate performance necessarily correlate with measures of subsequent behavior (Ross, 1976; Ross et al., 1976). Thus, immediate performance decrements appear to be neither a necessary nor a sufficient condition for the production of effects on subsequent behavioral measures of intrinsic interest.

Salience of instrumentality vs. salience of reward. A second class of theoretical issues raised by our initial findings has concerned the possibility that the presence of salient, expected rewards per se may produce responses that impede a subject's enjoyment of an activity during experimental sessions. Thus, the presence or expectation of attractive rewards, not immediately available to the subject while engaged in the activity, has been hypothesized to produce "distraction," "frustration," "anxiety," or other affective states that might lead to decrements in subsequent enjoyment of the activity quite apart from the subject's perception of engagement in the activity as instrumental to the reward. Several studies have provided evidence relevant to these alternative accounts.

For example, to test the "distraction" hypothesis, Reiss and Sushinsky (1975, Experiment 1) varied orthogonally: (a) the promise of a reward, contingent upon task engagement; and (b) the salient, physical presence or absence of this reward, along with other potential distractors (a timer and buzzer). In the former case, presumably, a variety of possible competing responses may be confounded with expectations of a reward for task engagement; in the latter case, however, possible competing responses generated by the salient rewards and other distractors are not confounded with perceived instrumentality, providing a means for examining the effects of competing responses per se. The results of this study, as expected from an attributional perspective, indicated that promise of a contingent reward produced significant decrements in subsequent interest, whereas the presence of the same, salient but noncontingent reward produced no effect. Thus, as in Ross's (1975) data, explicit but contingency-irrelevant distractors appeared not to affect subsequent interest in the activity.

Both this distraction hypothesis and the related hypothesis that "frustration" produced by waiting to receive an attractive, expected reward may account for decrements in subsequent, intrinsic interest were examined in a further experiment by Ross, Karniol, and Rothstein (1976). In this study, rewards were promised as contingent upon either: (a) engagement in an activity of initial interest; or (b) simply waiting for a fixed time period while incidentally engaged in the same activity. When the reward was contingent upon task engagement, a decrement in subsequent interest would be predicted by an attributional analysis and possibly by a competing response model as well; when the reward was contingent simply upon the passage of time, however, the presence of an attractive and potentially frustrating, conflict-producing, and/or distracting reward during task engagement is not confounded with subject's perceptions of extrinsic motivation, allowing a direct test of the competing-response model. Again, as suggested by an attributional model, the data indicated that when rewards were presented as contingent upon task engagement, children showed less subsequent engagement in the task;

however, when the reward was present and salient but presented as contingent simply upon waiting, as in many studies of the frustrative effects of delayed rewards, subsequent interest in the task was nonsignificantly increased. These findings, which provide evidence of the importance of the stated contingency between task engagement and the receipt of expected rewards, have been replicated, moreover, with both adult (Deci, 1971, 1972) and child (Swann & Pittman, 1977) populations.

Similar conclusions also appear in an experiment by Lepper et al. (1977b) that attempted to examine the theoretically minimal conditions sufficient to produce an overjustification effect by investigating the effects of the imposition of a merely "nominal" contingency between two activities of equal, high, initial interest designated as "means" and "ends." In this study, two groups of subjects were asked to engage in two activities of initially equivalent interest value, with both activities present and visible throughout the experimental session. In one condition, one of the activities was presented as a means of obtaining the opportunity to play with the other activity; in a second condition, no such contingency was stated. In the first case, potential responses of distraction or attentional conflict are confounded with perceived instrumentality; in the second case, such potential competing responses are not confounded with perceived instrumentality. The results indicated that presentation of one activity as a means of winning a chance to play with the other decreased subsequent interest in the activity presented as a "means," whereas engagement in the two activities under otherwise identical conditions did not affect subsequent interest.

Conceptually, the results of these studies seem to permit a simple summary, indicating—as an attributional model would suggest—that the critical variable is the presentation of an activity in a manner that makes salient to the individual the instrumentality of his or her engagement in the activity as a means to some extrinsic goal (Kruglanski, 1975). Thus, when engagement in the task is presented as a means to some ulterior end, significant decrements in subsequent interest in the task have been shown. When salient and potentially distracting, frustrative, embarrassing, exciting, or attentionally-conflicting rewards are presented in a noninstrumental fashion, decrements in subsequent interest do not appear. At the same time, as competing responses of different sorts may be hypothesized to account for any set of results following procedures that employ expected extrinsic rewards, these data may not constitute the strongest form of the argument.

In this context, perhaps the most compelling existing evidence on this issue comes from an ingenious study by Kruglanski, Alon, and Lewis (1972), which demonstrates a detrimental effect of *unexpected* rewards on subsequent, reported intrinsic interest in the task. In this study, two groups of subjects engaged in a series of games without expectation of any extrinsic reward. Under such conditions, presumably, competing responses as a function of the expectation or sight or thought of reward are in principle absent. Subsequently, however, subjects in one group were led erroneously to attribute their engagement in the games to a reward they received after finishing the activity, through a procedure in which subjects were falsely informed that the reward had initially been promised to them.

Theoretically, of course, this procedure differs fundamentally from the unexpected reward procedure employed by Lepper et al. (1973), because it involves an explicit attempt to convince subjects that they had been informed of the reward prior to their agreement to engage in the task. It is not surprising, therefore, that the two procedures have quite different effects. With their explicitly deceptive procedure, Kruglanski et al. (1972) found that subjects who received unanticipated prizes allegedly promised beforehand reported less intrinsic interest than subjects who did not receive prizes. Because the adverse effect of the extrinsic reward was almost entirely accounted for by subjects who described themselves (mistakenly) as having been motivated to engage in the games in order to obtain the reward, the data provide further evidence consistent with an attributional analysis. Thus, although unexpected rewards should not typically lead an individual to view his or her behavior as having been directed toward attainment of that reward, these results indicate that unexpected reward manipulations that produce appropriate retrospective misattributions (cf. Loftis & Ross, 1974) of task engagement as a means to an ulterior goal can undermine intrinsic interest in the task in the absence of any effects of reward expectancy per se.[2]

Multiple-trial reinforcement procedures. Taken together, the preceding studies define a paradigm in which the imposition of rewards, in a manner that makes salient to a person the instrumentality of engagement in an activity, can be shown with some consistency to have adverse effects on subsequent willingness to engage in the activity in the absence of further rewards. At the same time, however, it is obvious from the large literature on token economy programs (Kazdin, 1975) that such detrimental effects are not a necessary or routine consequence of the use of rewards in applied or clinical settings. Hence, the potentially significant differences between these two literatures have become a focus of concern (Greene, Sternberg, & Lepper, 1976; Lepper & Greene, Chapter 11).

---

[2]In a similar vein, Pittman, Cooper, and Smith (1977) have attempted to demonstrate directly the relevance of self-perception processes in an overjustification paradigm by showing that the detrimental effects of superfluous extrinsic rewards may be moderated by manipulations designed to induce subjects to attribute their engagement in an activity to either intrinsic or extrinsic factors. In this study, college subjects engaged in an activity of initial interest either with or without expectation of a monetary reward contingent upon task performance. Within the three expected-reward conditions, subjects in two groups were provided with false physiological feedback ostensibly indicative of either the subject's interest in the task itself (intrinsic attribution) or the subject's interest in winning money by engaging in the task (extrinsic attribution); subjects in a third reward group (no feedback) received rewards without any such feedback. As anticipated, subsequent behavioral measures of interest in the task indicated that the detrimental effect of expected reward demonstrated in the no-feedback condition was significantly decreased when subjects had been provided with feedback suggesting an "intrinsic" attribution and nonsignificantly increased when an "extrinsic" attribution had been made salient.

One such difference, which has received considerable empirical investigation, is directly relevant to our present discussion of alternative accounts of the overjustification studies.

Several authors (e.g., Feingold & Mahoney, 1975; Reiss & Sushinsky, 1975) have noted that studies demonstrating negative effects of extrinsic rewards on intrinsic interest typically differ from studies of applied-reward programs in the nature of the reward procedure employed. Thus, in contrast to applied-reinforcement programs, where multiple-trial reinforcement procedures (demonstrably effective in altering children's behavior during the treatment phase) have been employed, studies demonstrating an overjustification effect have typically employed reward procedures that have not been specifically shown to produce increases in the rewarded response. Since such effects literally define a stimulus as an empirical "reinforcer," it has been argued that detrimental effects of reward procedures will not occur when demonstrably effective multiple-trial reinforcement procedures are employed.

Two studies (Feingold & Mahoney, 1975; Reiss & Sushinsky, 1975, Experiment 2) have provided single-group demonstrations of multiple-trial reinforcement procedures that resulted in continued *increased* subsequent task engagement following the withdrawal of tangible rewards in the same or a closely related situation. In the Reiss and Sushinsky study, for example, nine kindergarten children were differentially rewarded during a brief experimental session with poker chips, exchangeable for an attractive reward, for listening to one of three songs playing simultaneously. Two days later, in a different room, subjects were confronted with the same three songs, arranged in a manner identical to the treatment phase. Subjects were instructed to do whatever they wanted, and their behavior was recorded by two adult observers stationed in the same room. In this situation, six subjects continued to listen to the song for which they had previously received rewards. From these data, it was concluded that multiple-trial procedures will not decrease subsequent interest.

This study differs from previous demonstrations of overjustification effects in the use of a multiple-trial reinforcement procedure. There is, however, a second and potentially critical difference between this and previous studies in the dependent measures employed, which may account for the data obtained. From an attributional perspective, inferences concerning an individual's subsequent intrinsic motivation can be made only when that person's behavior is observed in a situation in which further tangible or social rewards are not expected; thus, great care was taken in the initial investigations of the overjustification hypothesis to create a situation in which *intrinsic* interest might be observed. Children were therefore observed unobtrusively over three 1-hour sessions during normal free-play periods in their regular classrooms several weeks following the experimental sessions by observers stationed behind a one-way mirror. This dissociated post-test measure, assessing the child's choice to engage in the target activity relative to a wide variety of other attractive alternatives and in the absence of any expectation of reward or knowledge of being observed, was designed to allow an examination of subjects' interest in the activity per se, in the absence of salient extrinsic constraints.

By contrast, in the Reiss and Sushinsky experiment, children were confronted in the posttest with a novel situation similar to the previous experimental session, and behavior was observed for a 10-minute period by observers visible to the subjects. In fact, it appears that subjects were not even explicitly informed that tangible rewards would no longer be available in this second session. Under such conditions, continued engagement in the task may have been perceived as having continued instrumentality in eliciting social approval or even further tangible rewards; therefore, one simply cannot draw conclusions from these data concerning subjects' intrinsic interest in the absence of such possible expectations. Indeed, from an attributional model, one might predict quite different results if more appropriate, unobtrusive measures of intrinsic interest had been employed.

A recent study by Lepper, Sagotsky, and Greene (1977a) addressed these issues experimentally. Children, selected for initial intrinsic interest in a target activity, were exposed to a multiple-trial, contingent-reward or noncontingent-reward procedure. In one set of conditions (multiple-activity conditions), contingent-reward subjects were differentially rewarded with tokens over trials for engagement in the target activity in preference to three other available alternatives; noncontingent-reward subjects received rewards for engagement in any of the activities. These conditions provided an analogue to the multiple-trial procedure of Reiss and Sushinsky and allowed for the demonstration of a "reinforcement" effect as a function of differential reinforcement. In a second set of conditions (single-activity conditions), contingent-reward subjects were rewarded over trials for engagement in the target activity in the absence of other alternatives; noncontingent-reward subjects received the same reward unexpectedly. These conditions provided a conceptual analogue to previous overjustification studies but with a multiple-trial reinforcement procedure, and provided a control for the effects of increased task engagement per se. A fifth control condition in which subjects were not exposed to the target activity during the experimental sessions provided a baseline for comparison.

Several weeks later, two different measures of subsequent task engagement were obtained. Subsequent intrinsic interest in the target activity was assessed through extended, dissociated, and unobtrusive measures of free-choice behavior in subjects' regular classrooms—the same measure obtained by Lepper et al. (1973). Subsequent task engagement was also observed for a brief period in a situation similar to that in which rewards had previously been available and in which children were aware that their behavior was being observed, providing a measure conceptually analogous to that obtained by Reiss and Sushinsky. Comparisons of subjects' choices in these two situations, then, provided a test of the extent to which previously conflicting results may have been a function of the difference between: (a) extended and unobtrusive measures of intrinsic interest obtained in a situation where perceived external constraints were minimized; and (b) brief and obtrusive measures of interest in a situation containing a variety of potential demand characteristics that might influence subjects, independent of their intrinsic interest in the activity, to continue to select the activity for which they had been previously rewarded.

The results demonstrated two basic effects. First, significant detrimental effects of demonstrably effective, multiple-trial, contingent-reinforcement procedures, compared to noncontingent-reinforcement and control procedures, were evident when children's subsequent engagement in the activity was observed unobtrusively in their regular classrooms. In the multiple-activity conditions, contingent-reward subjects who had previously shown increased engagement in the target activity during the experimental sessions without decrements in performance quality also showed significantly less interest in the activity during subsequent classroom observations. Analogous negative effects of a multiple-trial reward procedure on subsequent intrinsic interest, obtained in the single-activity conditions where engagement with the activity was equated by design, indicated further that this detrimental effect was not dependent upon differences in prior task engagement. By contrast, when children were returned to the experimental room for a brief session in which their choices among a limited set of activities were observed in the presence of an adult observer, these same contingent-reward procedures produced significant increases in engagement in the activity. In this situation, where social demands could reasonably be inferred, even though children had been explicitly informed that tangible rewards were no longer available, contingent-reward subjects continued to engage in the activity that had previously produced tangible reward and adult approval.

In short, it is not the simple distinction between single-trial and multiple-trial procedures (or between rewards and reinforcers) that appears to determine whether detrimental effects of reward procedures will be observed. Several studies have shown that demonstrably effective reinforcement procedures may sometimes result in decrements in subsequent intrinsic interest (e.g., Colvin, 1971; Greene et al., 1976).[3] Certainly, however, the results of the Lepper et al. (1977a) study make clear that the data one obtains will depend significantly on the context in which subsequent task engagement is assessed. To allow inferences concerning the child's intrinsic interest in the activity, the situation in which subsequent task engagement is assessed must be one in which potential demands and expectations of continued instrumentality have been minimized.

---

[3]In fact, as noted in the final section of this chapter, there are a number of reasons to suggest that long-term, applied reinforcement may be less likely to produce detrimental effects than short-term laboratory studies (cf. Lepper & Greene, Chapter 11). Our point here is merely that the simple distinction between single-trial and multiple-trial reward procedures is not sufficient to account for the differences in results across and within existing studies. Very recent evidence providing further support for this contention is reported by Smith and Pittman (1978).

Rewards vs. constraints.   A vast majority of the research on overjustification has concentrated on the effects of rewards on subsequent intrinsic interest in an activity. It should be clear, however, that the theoretical model underlying these studies is not specifically concerned with the effects of rewards but rather deals more generally with any sort of salient extrinsic control that may lead an individual to see his or her behavior as extrinsically motivated. Consequently, one final line of research in this area has sought to demonstrate that the hypothesis may have considerably greater breadth than is implied by the above literature focusing on the effects of rewards on intrinsic motivation.

In particular, the evidence suggests that other forms of external constraint may produce the same kind of effects as rewards. Lepper and Greene (1975), for example, have demonstrated that imposition of salient adult surveillance over a child's engagement in an activity of initial interest can produce a decrease in subsequent interest in the activity in the absence of surveillance. In a related vein, Amabile, DeJong, and Lepper (1976) have shown that the imposition of a temporal deadline on the performance of adult subjects on an inherently interesting task can decrease subsequent motivation to engage in this task in the absence of extrinsic constraints. Similarly, Rosenhan (1969) has reported that "enforced rehearsal" of charitable behavior, previously displayed by a model, under direct adult surveillance was effective in radically increasing "donations" during the surveillance period, but significantly decreased the probability that children would donate anonymously to charity when solicited to do so by their classroom teachers several weeks after these experimental sessions. In an important sense, then, this evidence suggests that it is the subsequent effects of salient extrinsic contraints—rather than the effects of rewards, or surveillance, or deadlines—that are illuminated by this literature.

Summary

On an empirical level, the literature just reviewed provides considerable evidence that the imposition of salient extrinsic constraints on an individual's engagement in an activity of initial intrinsic interest can, under certain conditions, undermine that individual's subsequent intrinsic motivation to engage in the behavior in the absence of salient constraints. Theoretically, these data provide consistent support for the overjustification prediction that—other things being equal—a decrease in subsequent intrinsic motivation will be likely to occur when an individual is presented with an activity of initial intrinsic interest under conditions that make salient the instrumentality of his or her engagement in that activity as a means to some ulterior end. On a metatheoretical level, however, it is also important to note that these studies, in their shared theoretical presuppositions, serve to define a research paradigm that is quite different from that typically employed in experimental investigations of reinforcement processes (Lepper & Greene, 1976; Chapter 11). It is critical, therefore, to make these underlying assumptions explicit and to define the issues to which these demonstrations are relevant.

Intrinsic vs. extrinsic motivation.   In the first place, because these studies have shared a common framework that distinguishes between intrinsic and extrinsic motivation, considerable efforts were made in these experiments to design a dependent measure that would compel, in so far as possible, an inference of intrinsic motivation—i.e., a measure of task engagement in a situation in which salient extrinsic contingencies had been deliberately minimized (Lepper & Greene, 1976). Thus, as noted earlier, our own studies with children attempted to capitalize on the structure of the children's daily environment to provide measures of interest in the target activity in the absence of any expectation of tangible rewards for engaging or not engaging in the activity by having teachers introduce the activity into the classroom during regular "free-play" periods, without intrusion by research personnel. In addition, these measures were obtained completely unobtrusively by observers behind a one-way mirror to minimize any potential expectation that adult social approval would be contingent upon engagement in the activity. Similarly, in Deci's studies with adult subjects (cf. Deci, 1975, Chapter 7), an intricate and ingenious cover story was developed to make it believable to subjects that they were being left alone, that the experimenter would neither know nor care what they did during that period, and that the experiment was finished so that there would be no possible instrumental value to subjects in working further on the puzzles. Were the dependent measures in these studies to have been obtained in situations where engagement in the activity might be perceived as having continued instrumental value in producing tangible or social rewards, as Lepper et al. (1977a) have demonstrated, a predictably different pattern of results might have been obtained.

Cognitive vs. behavioral variables.   By the same token, it is also important to emphasize that the conceptual independent variable of interest in these studies is a cognitive event—the perception of one's engagement in an activity as a means to a salient external end—rather than a reinforcement procedure. Hence, although overjustification effects have been demonstrated as a consequence of the imposition of demonstrably effective, tangible reinforcement procedures (Colvin, 1971; Greene et al., 1976; Lepper et al., 1977a; Ross, 1976), it is also clear, both theoretically and empirically, that the production of an overjustification effect need not depend upon a demonstration that the extrinsic reward actually "controlled" subjects' behavior during the experimental sessions. Indeed, the demonstration that the subsequent behavioral effects of manipulations of extrinsic incentives do not depend upon the immediate effects of these manipulations on behavior during the experimental sessions is of considerable theoretical significance, because it allows the elimination of a number of possible alternative explanations (e.g., satiation, practice, familiarity) of these subsequent effects. In fact, it is the predictable success of salient, tangible rewards in producing cognitive consequences of theoretical interest, rather than an interest in rewards per se or the effect of reinforcement procedures, that has dictated their use in much of the overjustification research. As a result, it is also of considerable theoretical interest that the imposition of other forms of salient external constraints, not involving extrinsic rewards, have also been shown to produce overjustification effects (Amabile et al., 1976; Lepper & Greene, 1975; Lepper et al., 1977b; Rosenhan, 1969).

Theoretical vs. applied research.   In addition, it should be clear that these studies, on the whole, have been intended as theoretical demonstrations carefully designed, as Lepper, Greene, and Nisbett (1973) noted, to discover evidence of overjustification effects. Subjects, for example, have been drawn from "normal" and typically middle-class populations rather than from problematic or historically recalcitrant populations often involved in applied research on extrinsic reward systems. Similarly, activities were chosen that had high initial-interest value for subjects, in contrast to the low-probability behaviors typically selected for treatment in applied settings. Moreover, activities were employed for which subjects already possessed the requisite skills to engage in the activity and experience its satisfactions without need for additional training. Thus, these studies have dealt with performance rather than acquisition processes. These choices were carefully contrived, in combination with the theoretical considerations noted above, to permit demonstrations of decreases in intrinsic motivation under appropriate conditions.

Finally, and perhaps more fundamentally, it should be stressed that the self-perception process suggested by the overjustification hypothesis is explicitly presumed to be only one of a number of processes by which rewards may affect subsequent behavior (Deci, 1975; Lepper & Greene, 1976; Ross, 1976). The theoretical questions posed in this research, therefore, can only be answered by an assessment of the effects of particular treatment conditions *relative* to appropriate control groups engaging in the same activity under different circumstances, with other potentially relevant factors held constant. Without the necessary information provided by such control conditions, a self-perception model is not intended and does not presume to make absolute predictions about the effects of any particular reinforcement program in which such "other factors" are not constant. To do so will obviously require a specification of the manner in which a number of potentially competing factors in a single situation may combine to determine an individual's subsequent behavior, as we discuss in more detail in the final section of this chapter.

BEYOND OVERJUSTIFICATION

In the first half of this chapter, then, we have reviewed a number of experiments within the general framework of an attributional analysis of "means" and "ends." Now we would like to go beyond this analysis, which—in spite of its heuristic value in generating research—is clearly incomplete in two respects. First, by itself the attributional analysis is essentially mute with respect to the variety of data in this volume and elsewhere concerning the possible detrimental effects of extrinsic rewards on immediate task performance. Though neither necessary nor sufficient to explain the previous literature on the effects of extrinsic rewards on measures of subsequent intrinsic motivation, such immediate performance decrements under conditions of extrinsic motivation are frequently correlated with subsequent measures; therefore, the relationship between these two classes of findings warrants further attention. Second, the attributional analysis is also incomplete in that it ignores a variety of other variables that will also partially determine the effect of any particular reward system on subsequent behavior. In the remainder of this chapter, then, we address these two general issues, first presenting a more complete model of the cognitive processes that may account for the effects of extrinsic constraints on both choice and performance indices of intrinsic motivation and then placing these findings in a broader, applied context of the multiple processes by which rewards may exert both positive and negative influences on subsequent behavior.

Choice and Engagement: Toward a Means–Ends Analysis

Choice Processes.

Consider first a simple model of the processes underlying choice behavior. Given a set of possible alternatives in a specific setting, we make the initial assumption that a person's choice to engage in a particular activity is determined by the relative incentive value of the perceived alternatives. Of course, this basic premise is common to a variety of conceptually analogous "expectancy × value" models of motivation (e.g., Atkinson, 1964; Bandura, 1976; Lewin, Dembo, Festinger, & Sears, 1944; Tolman, 1932; Vroom, 1964; Weiner, 1972), all of which account for a person's choices in terms of the net expected utilities of various alternatives. For our purposes, however, it is useful to distinguish between: (a) the kinds of decision-making strategies that might be postulated in any such model; and (b) the kinds of information to which such strategies are applied.

In terms of strategies per se, the evidence suggests that decision makers adopt different heuristics on different occasions, depending on the number and complexity of the available alternatives (Payne, 1976). In a two-alternative situation, for example, individuals may consider each alternative in turn and arrive at a decision reflecting a trade-off among several dimensions. When a choice among alternatives is sufficiently complex, however, persons often employ "satisficing" (Simon, 1957) rather than optimizing decision strategies. In any comprehensive account of choice processes, of course, the conditions under which various heuristics are used and the properties and limits of these heuristics require attention. In this chapter, however, we wish to focus on the "data base" to which any decision heuristic would be applied.

For this purpose, it is helpful to think of a person's store of information about various activities as a collection of conditional propositions, or "if . . . then" statements. For example, a child's "image" (cf. Miller, Galanter, & Pribram, 1960) of drawing with magic markers might include any or all of the following propositions:

1. "If an adult researcher is watching while I draw a picture, I might get a reward afterward."
2. "If I draw a representational picture of my house and show it to my teacher, she will probably be pleased and say something nice to me."
3. "If the tips are not too worn, I will probably enjoy drawing whatever comes to mind."
4. "If I draw a picture of my baby brother, it will make me feel good."

From an attributional perspective, propositions of this sort are amenable to a division into two broad categories, along the lines of the intrinsic–extrinsic or endogenous–exogenous (Kruglanski, 1975) partition. Extrinsic incentives are valued outcomes that do not inhere in task engagement itself, as exemplified by Propositions 1 and 2. In both these examples, a task-extrinsic cue is part of the antecedent condition, identifying a goal exogenous to engagement per se. By contrast, intrinsic incentives inhere in task engagement itself or are psychologically inseparable from it, as in Propositions 3 and 4. In these examples, the antecedent conditions make reference only to the quality of the task materials or the subject of the picture itself, identifying goals endogenous to task engagement. The crucial difference between the second and fourth examples is the child's degree of perceived control over the criteria that would guide his or her engagement in the drawing activity, as we discuss specifically later in this chapter.

Although some activities may be associated with only extrinsic or only intrinsic incentives, the majority are probably associated with a mixture of both. The net incentive value of any activity in a particular setting, therefore, should depend to some degree on which of several possible characterizations of the activity is evoked in that specific context. For example, the same act of cleaning up spilled water may be regarded as a courtesy to one's roommate, insurance against permanent damage to furniture, or a wide variety of other descriptions, each of which evokes a different context with its own set of associations and priorities (Kruglanski, Chapter 5; Lepper & Greene, Chapter 11). Thus, how an act is construed at least partially determines which of many potential consequences come to mind, the contingencies relevant to these consequences (and hence the probability that they will occur, or be attained), and the potential satisfaction or value connected with each of them. These kinds of information about activities, together with the opportunities perceived in a particular setting, determine the expected utility or incentive value, of the various alternatives in that setting.

Accordingly, in a situation containing discriminative cues suggesting that one or another activity may lead to extrinsic rewards, an individual's choice should depend on both the extrinsic and intrinsic incentives perceived to be associated with the various alternatives. In situations without such cues, however, the individual's choice should depend only on the intrinsic incentives seen as inherent in task engagement, other relevant factors (e.g., fatigue, satiation) held constant.

Of course, the propositions associated with an activity in one's memory will vary as a function of one's social learning history. An individual's direct experience with an activity or related activities in various situations, observations of the apparent responses and outcomes experienced by others, and a variety of more indirect forms of communication may all provide information relevant to his or her expectations concerning both the extrinsic and the intrinsic incentive value of particular activities. Moreover, these expectations should be revised or "updated" whenever a person's experience with an activity provides salient new information potentially relevant to future engagement in the activity. In particular, significant changes in the instrumental context in which an activity is undertaken should affect both the intrinsic and the extrinsic value of that activity.

Perceived instrumentality and extrinsic motivation.   Perhaps the most obvious information typically conveyed by the imposition of contingent extrinsic rewards concerns the probability that engagement in an activity may continue to be instrumental to the attainment of further extrinsic goals in subsequent similar situations. That is, the extrinsic value of an activity will be increased by reward procedures to the extent that they imply that the activity will continue to be instrumental to the attainment of extrinsic rewards (Bandura, 1976; Estes, 1972; Mischel, 1973). It should be emphasized, however, that the information relevant to the continued instrumentality of an activity is not restricted to one's expectations concerning the availability of any particular reward. Receipt of a reward from some agent, for example, typically implies that the agent values and will continue to respond positively to one's engagement in the activity. Thus, even in the absence of explicit tangible contingencies, the expected extrinsic value of the activity, as a means of obtaining social approval, may be increased in the presence of this agent. Indeed, the precise set of cues sufficient to evoke an expectation of instrumentality on a subsequent occasion—as a function of prior rewards in other settings—should be expected to vary across individuals. It may be possible to operationalize the extremes of the distribution, that is, situations in which either virtually all or virtually no subjects will perceive engagement as likely to produce further extrinsic rewards. However, many situations contain considerable uncertainty, such that subjects' reactions will depend on the manner in which they have coded the conditions under which rewards should be expected.

As a theoretical matter, moreover, it should be clear that the issue is not one of the simple physical stimulus overlap between "training" and "posttest" situations. Rather, the critical issue is whether a particular procedure leads subjects to believe that continued engagement in an activity for which rewards were previously offered will continue to elicit social or tangible rewards in particular subsequent situations. Such expectations of continued instrumentality are likely to depend not only on the gross similarity of the two situations but also on the particular instructions given to subjects, the presence or absence and salience of observers, and the nature of the reward procedure employed (Estes, 1972; Lepper et al., 1977a).

Perceived instrumentality and intrinsic motivation.   In addition to the information rewards typically convey concerning the potential extrinsic value of subsequent engagement in an activity in the presence of particular situational cues, we assume that engagement in a task as an explicit means to some extrinsic goal may simultaneously provide information that will affect the expected intrinsic incentive value of the activity. Of particular interest in the context of this chapter, of course, are the processes by which engagement in an activity undertaken as an explicit means to an extrinsic goal appears to decrease the expected intrinsic value of subsequent task engagement.

In terms of an attributional analysis, other things being equal, the imposition of extrinsic incentives is hypothesized to lead to decrements in the perceived intrinsic value of the activity when the total context in which the activity has been presented leads the individual to view his or her actions as extrinsically rather than intrinsically motivated. In other words, to the extent that individuals can be led to perceive their behavior as a function of extrinsic incentives and to consider the activity as a "means" to an extrinsic "end," they will be correspondingly less likely to perceive themselves as intrinsically motivated or to consider the activity as an "end" in itself (Bem, 1967, 1972; Kruglanski, 1975; Lepper et al., 1973). Such a change in how the activity is coded or represented in memory should influence people's responses in subsequent encounters with the activity.

Of course, the precise process by which such changes occur is a fascinating question. The attributional account suggests that a change in the label a person attaches to his or her engagement in an activity (e.g., "means" vs. "ends," "work" vs. "play," or "extrinsic" vs. "intrinsic") is sufficient to change its intrinsic incentive value. Certainly, evidence that overjustification effects can be produced through the imposition of a purely "nominal" contingency (Lepper et al., 1977b) or through retrospective, overt "mislabeling" of an individual's motives (Kruglanski et al., 1972) provides support for this contention, as does the evidence that these effects may be moderated by manipulations providing an individual with putative direct attributions concerning his or her motivational state

(Pittman, Cooper, & Smith, 1977). Whether this effect is best conceptualized in terms of a restructuring of the incentive value of the activity in line with a "discounting" schema (Kelley, 1973; Kruglanski, 1975) or perhaps a simpler assimilation of the value of the activity to some more global, but fundamental, distinction between pursuits coded as "work" or as "play" deserves further attention.

The fact that conceptually analogous "overjustification" effects have been observed in preschool as well as older school-age and college populations, of course, raises a number of interesting issues concerning the cognitive capabilities requisite for such effects to occur. Certainly, on a highly abstract level, there is evidence that very young children frequently do not employ any consistent "discounting" principle in drawing inferences concerning the attitudes of hypothetical others (Karniol & Ross, 1976; Shultz, Butkowsky, Pearce, & Shanfield, 1975; Smith, 1976). It is not at all clear, however, that the sophistication of children's ability to apply inferential principles in hypothetical social situations is necessarily a good index of their sophistication in applying those same principles to concrete situations involving themselves as actors. Instead, one might argue that children's use of abstract principles applied to social perception are developed in part through a process of generalization from their own experiences in concrete social situations (cf. Piaget, 1932; Ross, 1976; Shultz et al., 1975). In the related realm of children's understanding of concepts of intentionality, for example, it appears that young children are likely to make use of intentionality as a criterion for judging the actions of others at an earlier age when the action is presented in a relatively more vivid and concrete fashion than when it is presented in a verbal and hypothetical fashion (Chandler, Greenspan, & Barenboim, 1973); moreover, children appear to make use of this same criterion in judging their own actions at an even earlier point than they do in judging the actions of others in similar concrete contexts (Hoffman, 1976). Similar findings, with more specific reference to young children's usage of "discounting" principles in social inference, have recently been reported by Shultz and Butkowsky (1977).

That hypothetical, social reasoning abilities may develop as successively more abstract generalizations from initially concrete, social schemas seems both intuitively reasonable and theoretically consistent with recent formulations of how social knowledge is represented and accessed. Abelson and Schank (Abelson, 1976; Schank & Abelson, 1975), for example, have suggested that much of our social knowledge is organized in terms of "scripts": i.e., organized and coherent event sequences anticipated in the presence of particular situational cues, reflecting an individual's extrapolations and expectations concerning apparent regularities in his or her social environment. In this model, relatively hypothetical and categorical scripts (e.g., "When someone offers me an extrinsic reward for doing something, that something is probably boring or unpleasant") are derived by abstraction of common features from a set of relatively more concrete and lower-level "episodic" scripts (e.g., "When my mom tells me I can't have my dessert until I finish what's on my plate, what's left on my plate is usually yuckky"). Indeed, though a detailed consideration of the question is beyond the scope of this paper, a reconsideration of many issues in terms of script theory and conceptually related models (e.g., Rumelhart & Ortony, 1977) may be useful in clarifying a number of the potential difficulties inherent in the overly rational model of man (and child) presented by classical attribution theory (cf. Ross, 1977).

An analysis of the detrimental effects of extrinsic constraints on intrinsic interest in terms of the assimilation of particular activities to prototypic "scripts" that embody the distinction between "work" and "play" is, in many respects, indistinguishable from an attributional analysis of these effects. Nonetheless, such an approach may have heuristic value. A script account, for example, appropriately stresses that children's understanding of social control processes derives primarily from their own direct social experience, and is only subsequently generalized and articulated in its application to understanding the behavior of others. Similarly, although issues of volition versus constraint remain central to the phenomenological distinction between work and play (cf. Jackson, 1968, pp. 28–33), a script model implies that associated or collateral parameters may influence the child's perceptions of the activity as well. Thus, a child's perceptions of the value of an activity may be affected by both situation-specific (e.g., arithmetic vs. art classes) and more general (e.g., quiet and serious vs. more noisy and boisterous atmospheres) characteristics of the setting in which it is encountered. Close surveillance and temporal deadlines, like contractual tangible rewards, are characteristics of settings usually associated with "work" rather than "play." More generally, an analysis in terms of social scripts alerts us to the potentially central role of broader contextual factors in determining the individual's perceptions of activities and his or her reasons for engaging in them (cf. Lepper & Greene, Chapter 11).

In any case, however, an attributional account implicitly presumes the operation of two interrelated but conceptually distinct processes. First, the context in which the activity is undertaken in the presence of rewards must be one that leads individuals to consider their actions in attributional terms, i.e., to "think about" the reasons for their engagement in the task (Wixon & Laird, 1976). Second, given that individuals do engage in the appropriate "cognitive work" (cf. Abelson, 1959; Lepper, Zanna, & Abelson, 1970), the context of their engagement in the activity must be such that they will construe their own behavior in terms of incentives extrinsic or exogenous to the task rather than in terms of incentives inherent in the task itself.

Most current research and theorizing, of course, has dealt primarily with the latter issue and has presumed the former. Hence, when the question is framed as one of whether an individual will make an intrinsic or extrinsic attribution, considerable theoretical attention has been directed to a specification of the conditions likely to affect this process (e.g., Ross, 1976; Staw, 1976). These conditions, hypothesized to determine the "salience point" at which an individual will begin to see his or her engagement in an activity in the presence of extrinsic constraints as extrinsically motivated, include the physical and ideational salience of the extrinsic incentives, the ratio of extrinsic to intrinsic incentives, the individual's expectations reflecting social norms concerning rewards (cf. Folger, Rosenfield, & Hays, 1978, for recent data relevant to this issue), and, perhaps above all, the psychological "visibility" of the extrinsic incentive (cf. Kelley, 1967). As an example, an attributional analysis would predict that the salience point should be reached relatively quickly when extrinsic incentives are tangible and arbitrary (such as tokens or monetary rewards) and relatively slowly when extrinsic incentives are intangible or somewhat related to the activity itself (such as attention or diffuse social approval).[4]

On the other hand, little attention has been paid to the conditions that may be necessary to produce *any* consideration of the reasons for one's engagement in a particular task. Although such an approach has not noticeably hindered laboratory research in this area, our suspicion is that in the applications of these findings to less constrained and more familiar situations, the first stage of the process is likely to assume greater importance. Thus, as others have argued in related contexts (cf. Abelson, 1972; Bem, 1970; Greene, 1976; Thorngate, 1976), most people may prove much less likely to engage in the cognitive work entailed in maintaining attitude–behavior consistency in their daily lives than our models of behavior—based on data from laboratory settings designed explicitly to elicit such responses—might imply. Instead, it may prove the case that these hypothesized attributional processes typically occur only when "triggered" by some factor that produces explicit attention to the appropriate attributional questions. Such factors as the following may prove critical in inducing the sort of restructuring of one's perceptions of an activity that we have been discussing: (a) the extent to which the imposition of extrinsic constraints on engagement in an activity provides a disconfirmation of the individual's specific or normative expectancies (Abelson, 1968); (b) the extent to which the offer of extrinsic incentives is accompanied by some explicit choice or acknowledgment by the individual of his or her ulterior motives for engaging in the activity (Aronson, 1966); or (c) the extent to which the context in which extrinsic incentives are offered provides some explicit cues to suggest the relevance of one's behavior in

---

[4]The issue of the effects of verbal or other social rewards on subsequent intrinsic motivation raises a number of interesting questions. For example, although there is some evidence that verbal rewards can undermine subsequent interest (e.g., Deci, Cascio, & Krusell, 1975; Smith, 1976), it appears that verbal reinforcement is generally less likely to produce detrimental effects than reinforcement procedures involving tangible rewards (Anderson et al., 1976; Deci, 1971; Deci et al., 1975; Swann & Pittman, 1977). In part, of course, it is simply difficult to imagine everyday situations in which one explicitly "contracts" to engage in an activity in order to obtain social approval. More generally, howhowever, it is a fundamental presupposition of an attributional model (cf. Kelley, 1967; Bem, 1972) that social contingencies are typically less psychologically salient than tangible rewards. Hence, social pressures typically do not appear to provide a sufficient explanation for one's actions unless they are made unusually explicit and salient (cf. Kruglanski, Chapter 5, pp. 99–103).

that situation for one's subsequent attitudes and behavior (Kiesler, Nisbett, & Zanna, 1969; Ross, Lepper, Strack, & Steinmetz, 1977). Finally, as Condry and Chambers (Chapter 4) have suggested, in a different context, the degree to which any particular experience is likely to result in a reorganization of one's perceptions of the value of an activity seems likely to be a function of the extent and consistency of one's prior experience with the activity and the resultant stability of one's prior attributions concerning the activity.

Engagement Processes

In the preceding section, we have outlined a model of the processes by which the imposition of salient extrinsic contingencies may affect a person's subsequent intrinsic and extrinsic motivation, independent of the effects of perceived instrumentality on immediate task performance. As a variety of other literature discussed in this volume indicates, however, these processes do not provide the whole story of how extrinsic rewards may produce detrimental effects on intrinsic motivation. For example, they do not speak to the evidence that anticipation of salient extrinsic incentives may sometimes have adverse effects on potential "concurrent" measures of intrinsic motivation, as evidenced by decrements in the quality of immediate task performance during the period when extrinsic rewards are available. Nor do they allow for the fact that performance decrements, when obtained, may themselves produce negative effects on subsequent motivation. At this point, then, we turn our attention to the factors that guide an individual's engagement in an activity that he or she has chosen to undertake and the effects on task engagement parameters of the presence or absence of perceived extrinsic constraints.

Perceived instrumentality, goals, and subgoals. Given a model of behavior as goal directed, the most obvious consequences of a person's perception of his or her engagement in an activity as either a means to some extrinsic end or as an end in itself concern the manner in which the individual's goal in engaging in the activity will control the nature of performance at the task. Differences in perceived intrinsic or extrinsic motivation, in this sense, should be reflected in the individual's engagement in the activity in three related ways.

First, the individual's perceived goal may influence the manner in which he or she approaches the activity. Frequently, depending on the degree of structure or definition inherent in a task, a person has a number of options concerning the level at which to approach an activity. In the absence of extrinsic constraints, this level will depend on the perceived intrinsic value of those options as some function of the individual's perception of the possibilities afforded by the task and his or her own competencies and current circumstances (cf. Csikszentmihalyi, 1975). In the presence of salient extrinsic contingencies, however, the level at which the task is approached will depend on both the perceived intrinsic value of the options and the perceived extrinsic value of these options in attaining the desired extrinsic goal, introducing, as Shapira (1976) and Condry and Chambers (Chapter 4) have suggested, a general "bias" toward engagement in the task on a level perceived likely to insure attainment of the extrinsic goal. Whether a child provided with an opportunity to draw pictures with a particular set of materials will draw a line, a box, a house, or a city, for example, will depend in the former case on the child's perception of what would be most pleasing. In the latter case, however, the decision should also depend on his or her expectations concerning the sorts of products that will be successful in obtaining rewards or approval from some adult observer.

Second, this same control of a person's choices among options by his or her goals should operate hierarchically. For example, one might view the ongoing process of engagement in an activity, given some initial goal, as a series of component choices among alternative responses directed by subgoals selected for their utility in achieving either one's own, self-imposed goals or those extrinsic goals imposed on one's activity by another person. Thus, a subgoal might be the selection of the next color to add to a drawing in progress. If the goal is approval from an observer, the criterion for choosing the color might be correspondence to objective reality—if the individual believes that the observer will judge drawings at least partly on how representational they are. If the goal is self-satisfaction, of course, the same criterion might be used; and, other things being equal, an identical picture might be drawn. However, the artist is completely free to set and vary his or her own goals and criteria, whether they happen to be the same as some external agent's criteria or not.

Finally, an individual's perceived goal effectively constitutes the exit criterion or stop-rule for terminating engagement in the activity. If one is drawing in order to obtain an award, a marshmallow, or mother's approval, attainment of that goal is a sufficient condition for returning control to the executive program. By contrast, a person drawing solely for the pleasure derived from engagement in the activity per se will continue until he or she is no longer having that experience. In the latter case, our hypothetical young artist may decide that the house he or she has drawn would be nicely complemented by a family residing therein. In the former instance, he or she may be more likely to stop drawing if it appears the house itself will be sufficient to obtain a proffered reward or more likely to continue if it appears that this effort will be rewarded only when the house, family, and garage have been completed.

Considering these factors alone, then, one might predict performance differences as a function of differences in an individual's perceived intrinsic or extrinsic motivation to be determined largely by the congruence or discrepancy between the series of goals and subgoals the individual would generate independently (in the absence of extrinsic constraints) and those he or she generates given a consideration of the possible instrumental consequences of his or her actions. Frequently, these goals may be virtually identical, particularly when the activity contains some inherent structure that defines success at that task (e.g., solving a puzzle or winning a game). With activities of less inherent structure, however, the overlap between these two sets of goals will depend much more on the individual and the nature of the specific contingency imposed on the performance. This potential "match" or "mismatch" between spontaneous and imposed criteria, which seems likely to be influenced not only by the inherent structure or definition of the task but also by individual factors and the specificity of the extrinsic constraints, is, we believe, an important factor in determining performance variation under conditions of intrinsic and extrinsic motivation. There are, however, two further and equally important differences between intrinsically and extrinsically motivated behavior that deserve consideration.

Attentional consequences of perceived instrumentality.   The first of these factors concerns attention. From an information-processing point of view, the control of attention is the most important function of motivation (cf. Simon, 1967). In this context, the process of engagement in an activity consists of generating responses and repeatedly testing them, as in Miller, Galanter, and Pribram's (1960) "TOTE" units. Attention is directed toward those aspects of both the activity and the environment that provide feedback appropriate to these tests. In the present model, the difference between intrinsic and extrinsic motivation lies in the tests or criteria that guide engagement in an activity toward its goal.

Whatever the goal of an activity, some attention will obviously be directed toward monitoring feedback from the activity itself. Thus, a child drawing a picture will have to devote some of his or her attention to closing figures that should be closed, keeping the picture on the paper, and trying not to break the drawing implements. The difference between intrinsic and extrinsic motivation in this context lies in where the rest of attention is directed. If enjoyment is the goal, the rest of attention may be directed anywhere but often will be directed toward monitoring more subtle aspects of the activity itself, such as the shading of contours, balance of colors and shapes, and other flourishes that are not necessary but may enhance enjoyment. Where the goal is extrinsic to the activity, however, at least some attention must be directed toward monitoring progress toward that extrinsic goal.

Depending on the nature of the activity and the extrinsic contingency imposed, this process may lead to a focusing of attention on those specific aspects of the activity perceived as potentially instrumental, to the relative exclusion of attention to other incidental aspects of performance not expected to have instrumental value (cf. Easterbrook, 1959). In such a case, parameters of performance not seen as instrumental to the extrinsic goal may be adversely affected (Amabile, 1977; Condry & Chambers, Chapter 4; Kruglanski, Friedman, & Zeevi, 1971; Kruglanski, Chapter 5; Kruglanski, Stein, & Riter, 1977; McGraw, Chapter 3). In more extreme cases, the presence of salient extrinsic constraints may produce perseverance in previously functional but currently maladaptive strategies (McGraw & McCullers, 1975, 1976) or may prove so generally distracting as to impair task performance on "central" as well as incidental task parameters (Spence, 1970). Under many circumstances, therefore, the consequences of this difference in attention may be a relative decrement in qualitative indices of task performance under conditions of salient extrinsic motivation (McGraw, Chapter 3). Whether such performance differences should be taken as evidence of decreased intrinsic interest in the activity per se, rather than shift in the relative weights of intrinsic and extrinsic factors occasioned by the addition of further extrinsic incentives, is an interesting theoretical issue. The point to be made here is simply that when immediate performance differences are obtained under such conditions, these differences themselves may exert an influence on subsequent interest in the task.

Affective consequences of perceived instrumentality.   A second potentially critical difference between intrinsically and extrinsically motivated behavior lies in a person's degree of perceived control over the criteria that guide engagement in an activity. We suggest that the affective consequences frequently associated with intrinsic and extrinsic motivation are in large measure attributable to this aspect of engagement processes.

For a person whose goal is enjoyment, the criteria for selecting subgoals are either intrinsic to the activity itself or contingent upon subjective states. The person can take risks, rationalize, redefine, or restructure the activity at will. The exercise of these prerogatives carries no liability, save self-imposed. By contrast, for an individual engaging in an activity to attain some extrinsic goal, either of two undesirable sets of contingencies may exist. On one hand, criteria defined by an extrinsic goal may frequently be ambiguous or subject to unpredictable revision. For example, the "correct" answer to a teacher's question often seems to depend on that elusive factor—what the teacher "has in mind." On the other hand, extrinsic contingencies may conversely turn out to be too rigid or inflexible; in such cases, engagement in an activity to satisfy externally-imposed criteria may effectively preclude engagement in the activity in the manner likely to maximize enjoyment per se. If a person decides to take the scenic route rather than the fastest route, for example, he or she may risk being late for the occasion. Either way, a lack of perceived control over the criteria that guide engagement in an activity appears to be a frequent characteristic of extrinsic motivation.

Other things being equal, we assume that an individual's affective response to engagement in an activity will be relatively less positive when associated with the perception of extrinsic contingencies as unpredictable, ambiguous, or unnecessarily constricting. Certainly, in other related contexts, there is considerable evidence to support the proposition that variations in perceived control may have significant effects on indices of both affect and performance (e.g., Condry & Chambers, Chapter 4; Nuttin, 1973; Seligman, 1975; Wortman & Brehm, 1975). At the same time, however, in interpreting an individual's more general affective response to an activity that has proved successful as a means of obtaining a desirable reward, we must consider that the individual's reported satisfaction and interest may depend on both the intrinsic and extrinsic incentives involved. As Salancik's (Salancik, 1976; Salancik & Conway, 1975) ingenious demonstrations have shown, both the structure and the content of an individual's reported attitudes toward an activity may vary dramatically as a function of the salience of extrinsic rewards and the prior instrumentality of the activity in the context in which attitudes are measured. In particular, attitude measures obtained in a context in which the instrumentality of one's previous actions has been made salient are predicted better by the perceived extrinsic instrumental value than the perceived intrinsic value of the activity for the subject, and are less positive, on the whole (Salancik, 1976).

Summary

In Table 6.1, we summarize our general model of the processes by which an individual's perception of his or her behavior as extrinsically motivated may produce detrimental effects on both subsequent motivation to engage in an activity in the later absence of salient extrinsic constraints and performance while engaged in the activity.

In interpreting this framework, two prefatory comments seem in order. First, its limited purpose is to identify several processes that may explain *detrimental* effects of the imposition of extrinsic constraints on measures of immediate performance and subsequent engagement. Consequently, this model is not intended as a "complete" account of the processes by which rewards may affect subsequent motivation. Our discussion of processes by which rewards may have a *positive* influence on subsequent intrinsic motivation, through the acquisition of new task-relevant skills or effects on an individual's perception of his or her competence or ability, has been postponed until the following section of this chapter.

Second, for purposes of discussion, we have presented our framework in terms of a simple, unidimensional dichotomy between "means" and "ends." In reality, however, it is clear that a single activity may often explicitly serve a number of functions for an individual at the same time. Thus, the behavioral effects attributed to extrinsic or intrinsic motivation in this framework are relative rather than absolute differences, and no single effect is by itself unambiguously sufficient to identify either intrinsic or extrinsic motivation apart from the context in which it occurs. Rather, as noted earlier, a single act may be both an end in itself and a means to some other end at the same time. Kruglanski (1975) provides the instructive example of riding a bicycle to work, which is both a means of transportation and good exercise in its own right. Clearly, an activity with sufficient intrinsic value can be deliberately chosen by a person as the best of available alternatives to serve some other need without diminishing its intrinsic value.

Given these provisos, it is relatively easy to summarize the thrust of our position. We begin with two critical distinctions. The first distinction concerns the difference between intrinsic and extrinsic incentives. This distinction we believe to be: (a) a precondition for any analysis dealing with intrinsic motiva-

TABLE 6.1.
A Theoretical Framework for Understanding the Effects of Perceptions of Intrinsic and Extrinsic Motivation on Choice and Engagement Processes

Background factors	Initial intrinsic interest, operationally defined as spontaneous engagement in an activity in the presence of attractive alternatives and the absence of salient extrinsic constraints or incentives. Hypothesized to be a function of: A. Properties of the activity, e.g., complexity, novelty, challenge, etc. B. Person variables, e.g., task-relevant skills, perceived competence, internalized standards, prior representation of task in memory, etc.	
Experimental manipulations	Manipulation of subject's perception of the task as a "means" or "end." Hypothesized to depend on the manner and context in which the activity is presented: A. Whether procedure leads subject to consider his motives for task engagement. B. Whether subject led to see his or her actions as intrinsically or extrinsically motivated, depending on salience/sufficiency of extrinsic constraints.	
	Intrinsic motivation	*Extrinsic motivation*
Theoretical constructs	Self-perception of intrinsic motivation, "endogenous attribution," goal psychologically identified with activity itself.	Self-perception of extrinsic motivation, "exogenous attribution," goal psychologically distinct from activity itself.
Hypothesized intervening processes	A. Activity viewed as "end" in itself, engagement as inherently interesting. B. Decisions to initiate and terminate activity based on criteria generated by person or task itself. C. Subgoals or component decisions based on self- or task-generated criteria. D. Attention controlled by task- and self-generated goals, general orientation to exploration, self-expression. E. Freedom to control engagement, rationalize, redefine, etc.; potential relatively positive affect.	A. Activity viewed as "means" to extrinsic goal, engagement as less inherently interesting. B. Decisions to initiate and terminate activity based on perceived availability and probability of attainment of extrinsic goal. C. Subgoals or component decisions based on criteria derived from extrinsic contingencies. D. Attention controlled by extrinsic constraints and focused on constraints and instrumentally relevant parameters, general "instrumental" orientation. E. Control over engagement limited by extrinsic contingencies; potential relatively negative affect if criteria unpredictable or inflexible.
Observable consequences	Potential effects on immediate performance measures, hypothesized to depend upon nature of activity and nature of contingency: A. Potential increments on contingency-relevant and decrements on contingency-irrelevant performance dimensions, under extrinsic motivation, if differences between self-imposed and externally-imposed goals. B. Potential general performance decrements under extrinsic motivation, if extrinsic incentives sufficiently salient, or task sufficiently complex. Potential effects on subsequent choice measures, hypothesized to depend upon situation in which choice is assessed: A. Potential decreases in subsequent task engagement under extrinsic motivation in situations where extrinsic contingencies are perceived to be absent. B. Potential increases in subsequent task engagement under extrinsic motivation in situations where engagement is perceived to have continued instrumental value.	

tion; and (b) empirically mandated by data suggesting that the same extrinsic constraints may simultaneously increase subsequent task engagement in a situation similar to that in which rewards were previously delivered yet decrease subsequent task engagement in a situation in which salient extrinsic constraints are lacking (Lepper & Greene, 1976; Lepper et al., 1977a; Rosenhan, 1969). The second critical distinction concerns the difference between the processes that affect subsequent choice and those that guide immediate engagement in the activity. This distinction we view as: (a) theoretically necessitated by the fact that immediate performance measures—unlike subsequent indices of intrinsic motivation—are necessarily obtained in situations where both intrinsic and extrinsic factors are present and likely to exert joint effects on performance; and (b) empirically justified by data that suggest that decrements in immediate task performance, which sometimes accompany subsequent effects, appear to be neither necessary nor sufficient for the production of decrements in subsequent behavioral or attitudinal measures of intrinsic motivation (Amabile et al., 1976; Calder & Staw, 1975; Kruglanski et al., 1972; Lepper et al., 1977a; Ross, 1976).

In this model, then, perception of one's engagement in an activity as a means to some extrinsic end is hypothesized potentially to have both: (a) direct consequences for subsequent intrinsic motivation, in terms of the individual's restructuring of the perceived intrinsic and extrinsic incentives associated with task engagement as a function of the manner in which he or she has coded or labeled the activity; and (b) possible indirect consequences for subsequent intrinsic motivation, via the processes by which salient extrinsic goals may influence the individual's initial performance or enjoyment of the activity. The former process seems likely to depend on the presentation of an activity under conditions that lead the subject both to consider his or her motivation in undertaking the activity and to perceive his or her engagement in the activity as instrumental to the attainment of some extrinsic end. The latter processes—involving the nature of the goals subjects will pursue in engaging in the activity, the direction of subjects' attention, and the feelings of control subjects have over their actions—on the other hand, seem likely to depend not only on perceived instrumentality but also on more particular relationships between an individual's initial predispositions, the nature and structure of the task, and the nature of the perceived extrinsic contingencies in the situation in which the task is undertaken. Though experimentally, at least in some contexts, it is possible to analyze these processes separately, the detrimental effects of superfluous extrinsic constraints on subsequent intrinsic motivation may frequently have multiple determinants outside of controlled experimental settings.

In general, we see this framework as basically consistent with the other positions developed in this volume, though in attempting to specify some of the conditions under which we would expect different detrimental effects to become apparent, we have been led to a possibly more circumscribed view of these effects. At the same time, however, we also see our framework as complementary, in its focus on attentional processes and perceptions of control, with the work of other theorists who have been concerned more specifically with the phenomenology of intrinsically motivated behavior and the manner in which individuals may become totally "immersed" in activities pursued as ends in themselves (e.g., Koch, 1956; Csikszentmihalyi, 1975). Indeed, we see this apparent theoretical convergence among researchers pursuing related questions from quite different perspectives as a positive sign that the questions raised, if not the tentative answers provided, may have broad significance for our further understanding of human motivation.

Further Theoretical Issues

The preceding discussion of the processes by which extrinsic rewards may produce detrimental effects on intrinsic motivation has, of course, ignored the complementary issues concerning the conditions under which rewards may actually enhance intrinsic motivation. In this section, therefore, we will attempt to sketch a more comprehensive picture of the factors determining the effects of any particular reward program on subsequent intrinsic and extrinsic motivation.

Perceived competence and intrinsic motivation.   Consider, first, the role of an individual's perceptions of his or her ability and competence at an activity. As attested by the importance assigned to perceptions of competence within a wide array of different theoretical approaches (e.g., Atkinson, 1957; Csikszentmihalyi, 1975; deCharms, 1968; Deci, 1975; Harter, 1977; Lepper & Greene, 1976; Ross, 1976; Weiner, 1974; White, 1959), the significance of this variable as a potential determinant of individuals' choices of activities and their performance at activities should not be underestimated.

Within our framework, the relevant parameter is the expected probability of success or failure individuals attach to attainment of any particular goal or subgoal in choosing or engaging in activities. That is, rather than postulating any unique need or drive for competence, within an expectancy × value framework we see the expected probability of success as an integral and potentially critical component of any proposition expressing the expected incentive value of engagement in an activity or the expected value of different sorts of performances at the activity. If a person has no doubt that he or she can do whatever act is contemplated successfully, the probability of either intrinsic satisfaction or extrinsic reward will be as high as other conditions permit. On the other hand, a person who believes he or she is sure to fail will not choose to engage in an activity, no matter how certain the prospect of reward or personal satisfaction would be if he or she were to succeed.

Significantly, a person's perception of competence at an activity will depend as much on the criteria by which competence is evaluated as on the objective characteristics of his or her performance. These criteria or standards of evaluation, in turn, may depend upon the nature of the individual's goals and aspirations in undertaking a task, perceptions of the standards by which his or her performance will be judged by others, and standard of reference for evaluating success (e.g., in terms of his or her own prior performance, the performance of other individuals, or demands inherent in the nature of the task). Hence, it should make a considerable difference whether one has to succeed by his or her own standards or by someone else's (Lepper et al., 1977c; cf. also Bandura, 1971, 1976).[5]

In the absence of extrinsic constraints, of course, the subjective value of success in attaining a particular goal or subgoal may frequently be inversely related to the perceived probability of success, as suggested by the extensive literature on achievement motivation (Weiner, 1972, 1974). Hence, an individual's choice of activities will reflect both factors, leading to a choice of activities that are expected to provide some "optimal" level of challenge relative to the person's perceived competence (cf. Csikszentmihalyi, 1975; Deci, 1975; Hunt, 1965). In the presence of salient extrinsic constraints, on the other hand, an individual's choice may become much more "conservative" or heavily biased toward the selection of activities that appear to have a very high probability of success. In the presence of sufficiently attractive extrinsic rewards, for example, the person may sacrifice challenge for the more certain attainment of reward (Condry & Chambers, Chapter 4; Shapira, 1976).

At the same time, particularly with activities where the criteria for success are subjective or can be defined only through some process of social comparison, rewards may convey information concerning one's competence at an activity. Thus, a number of investigators (Deci, 1975; Karniol & Ross, 1976; Lepper & Greene, 1976; Ross, 1976; Salancik, 1975) have suggested that rewards that lead an individual to believe he or she has been successful and is personally responsible for that success should enhance that individual's intrinsic motivation to engage in that activity in the future. Both by broadening the range of options the individual will be likely to see as viable in approaching and engaging in the activity and by enhancing the individual's ability to exercise control in the engagement with the activity, increases in perceived competence may increase intrinsic motivation, as reflected in approach to the activity in the absence of extrinsic constraints or in quality of performance at the task.

When rewards are made contingent upon performance, then, so that receipt of the reward conveys relevant competence information, whether the net effect on intrinsic motivation will be positive or negative should depend on the relative salience and importance of two potentially competing processes: the perceptions of one's actions as extrinsically motivated and the perceptions of one's increased competence at the activity (cf. Deci, 1975). In contrast to the reasonably consis-

---

[5] Lepper, Sagotsky, and Greene (1977c), for example, have shown that when subjects are allowed to determine for themselves whether their performance has deserved a tangible reward, the detrimental effects of those same rewards, when delivered by an external agent, are eliminated.

tent data described earlier with respect to rewards contingent simply upon task engagement, data concerning the effects of performance-contingent rewards designed to convey competence information, when compared to no-reward control procedures, are predictably less clear (Greene & Lepper, 1974; Karniol & Ross, 1977; Ross, 1976; Salancik, 1975). In a relative sense, however, the general conclusion seems warranted that performance-contingent rewards are relatively less likely than task-contingent rewards to produce decrements in subsequent intrinsic motivation (Karniol & Ross, 1977).

Consequences of increased task engagement.   In our discussions of the effects of extrinsic rewards on people's perceptions of their motivation and competence at an activity, we have focused on theoretical questions involving relative differences among groups of subjects engaged in the same activity under different experimental conditions. In any applied context, however, where one wishes to ask questions concerning the absolute effects of a particular program of extrinsic rewards, there are a number of other factors that may assume equal importance when rewards are employed to induce individuals to engage in activities they would not have engaged in otherwise. Depending upon the nature of the activity, for example, continued engagement in an activity may produce boredom or satiation effects, decreasing, at least for a time, the expected intrinsic incentive value of the activity.

More significantly, continued engagement in an activity over some period of time may obviously result in the acquisition of new task-relevant skills or an increased proficiency in the use of previously available skills. Availability of these skills may enhance subsequent intrinsic motivation, particularly when some minimal level of competence is necessary to experience the intrinsic satisfactions of an activity, by allowing the individual to engage in the activity in a manner that increases the intrinsic value of engagement. Frequently, in the absence of constraints, an individual may actively and energetically ''practice'' in order to achieve some desired level of competence that will allow the achievement of greater subsequent satisfaction from complex activities of initial interest such as reading or playing a musical instrument. In the absence of such initial motivation, however, extrinsic rewards may provide one means of inducing sufficient practice for an individual to develop an appreciation of the intrinsic value of the activity (Bandura, 1969; Cohen, 1968; Kazdin, 1975). Certainly, an adolescent reading at a first- or second-grade level seems unlikely to find reading an intrinsically rewarding activity. If through the use of powerful reinforcement procedures, however, he or she can be led to engage in sufficient study to provide the skills that allow reading at a much higher level, it is hard to imagine that his or her intrinsic interest in reading will not have been increased by this procedure.

In the experimental literature on overjustification, of course, these factors are typically held constant by comparing experimental conditions in which all subjects engage in the activity of interest for a specified period and by employing

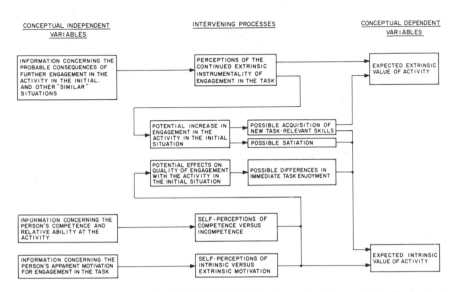

FIG. 6.1.   A conceptual analysis of the effects of reinforcement procedures on subsequent expected extrinsic and intrinsic incentive values associated with an activity.

tasks for which all subjects initially possess the skills requisite for engagement in the activity. As one moves from controlled experimental settings involving typically "normal" subject populations to applied settings in which extrinsic reward systems are employed with disturbed, destructive, or handicapped populations, to produce changes in behavior that would not occur in the absence of powerful contingencies, the role of rewards as a means of inducing engagement in particular activities may well assume paramount importance. Similarly, in the experimental literature on overjustification, little attention has been paid as yet to the possible role of "fading" procedures, commonly employed in applied settings in which rewards are gradually withdrawn, in mitigating the detrimental effects of extrinsic rewards on subsequent intrinsic motivation.[6]

---

[6]At the same time, it is important to keep clear the distinction between the practical and the theoretical issues involved here. Demonstrations that behavior change may be maintained following the gradual withdrawal of extensive reinforcement programs through the use of less extensive reinforcement programs or the contingent use of social approval or naturally available reinforcers in a particular setting (e.g., Walker & Buckley, 1972), though of considerable potential practical import, do not provide evidence concerning subsequent intrinsic motivation. Nor are demonstrations of the effectiveness of fading procedures in maintaining behavior in situations where the continued availability of extrinsic rewards may be ambiguous informative on this issue. On the other hand, there are theoretical grounds on which one would expect such techniques to be effective in minimizing the extent to which children will see their behavior as extrinsically controlled and hence reason to believe that the effects may also be apparent when appropriate measures of subsequent intrinsic motivation are obtained. Clearly, the factors governing such a process would seem to provide a fertile field for further research.

Summary. The preceding discussions have identified a number of conceptually independent factors that must be considered in any attempt to predict in an
absolute sense the effects of a particular reward program on subsequent motivation. A schematic summary of these factors appears in Figure 6.1. Obviously,
this model does not provide an easy algorithm for predicting the results of
specific reward programs. However, there are several general implications of the
point of view forwarded in this paper—concerning the conditions that are likely
to maximize the persistence and generalization of the immediately beneficial
effects of token economy programs to unprogrammed settings—that are
thoroughly consistent with suggestions already offered by thoughtful proponents
of applied reward programs (Kazdin, 1975; Kazdin & Bootzin, 1972; Kopel & Arkowitz, 1975; O'Leary & Drabman, 1971).

In this general sense, a concern with the possibility that extrinsic rewards
may have detrimental effects on intrinsic motivation suggests, for example, that
the use of powerful reward systems is most clearly indicated when dealing with
subject populations lacking in initial intrinsic motivation and for whom less
powerful and salient behavior change programs would not be effective in producing the desired behavior (O'Leary, Drabman, & Kass, 1973; O'Leary, Poulos, &
Devine, 1972). Indeed, historically, this is precisely the sort of situation in which
token economies were developed, as a treatment of "last resort" (cf. Ayllon &
Azrin, 1968). Similarly, the present approach suggests that powerful reward
systems will be most likely to show beneficial, long-term effects when focused
on behaviors likely to promote the acquisition of new skills rather than the
suppression of undesirable responses (Bandura, 1969; Kazdin, 1975; Winett &
Winkler, 1972). Finally, this approach suggests that powerful reward systems
will be most likely to produce persistent and general positive effects when the
program is specifically designed to enhance the child's feelings of competence
and self-determination (Brownell, Colletti, Ersner–Hershfield, Hershfield, &
Wilson, 1977; Drabman, Spitalnik, & O'Leary, 1973; Kopel & Arkowitz, 1975;
Lepper et al., 1977c).

Perhaps the most important practical consequence of the present framework,
however, lies less in its specific implications than in its general assertion of the
predictive utility of the distinction between intrinsic and extrinsic motivation and
the importance of obtaining unobtrusive and dissociated measures of behavior, in
the absence of perceived social or tangible rewards, in attempting to examine the
effects of any reinforcement program on *intrinsic* interest (cf. Lepper et al.,
1977a). Such measures, assessing generalization of behavior change to new
situations in which the environment has been neither socially nor materially
programmed to promote transfer, have historically been quite rare in the literature on token economies (cf. Johnson, Bolstad, & Lobitz, 1976; Kazdin, 1975;
O'Leary & Drabman, 1971). In fact, when appropriate measures of subsequent
task engagement have been obtained in situations where rewards were clearly no
longer available, decreases in task engagement analogous to the effects observed

in our laboratory research have been obtained, in some cases, following the withdrawal of reasonably long-term token-economy programs (Brownell et al., 1977; Colvin, 1971; Greene et al., 1976; Johnson et al., 1976; Meichenbaum, Bowers, & Ross, 1968; Ross & Bowers, reported in Ross, 1976; Ross, Meichenbaum, & Bowers, 1974). Such detrimental effects, we hope, will not prove a frequent concomitant of sensitively designed reinforcement programs (Greene et al., 1976). Indeed, we see the growing attention to issues of generalization to unprogrammed settings and to the process by which transfer and maintenance of behavior change can be obtained following the withdrawal of applied reinforcement programs (cf. O'Leary, in press) as extremely encouraging. At the same time, we would also hope that these findings will underscore the importance in further research of measures designed to assess intrinsic as well as extrinsic motivation, in order to determine the conditions under which long-term reward programs may undermine or enhance intrinsic motivation.

ACKNOWLEDGMENTS

Preparation of this chapter and much of the empirical research it reports was supported, in part, by Research Grants MH-24134 from the National Institute of Mental Health and HD-MH-09814 from the National Institute of Child Health and Human Development. Development of the theoretical framework presented in this paper was also facilitated by an Andrew Mellon Foundation Fellowship to the senior author. The authors wish to express their appreciation to the many colleagues who have provided thoughtful comments on an earlier version of this manuscript.

REFERENCES

Abelson, R. P. Modes of resolution of belief dilemmas. *Conflict Resolution,* 1959, *3,* 343–352.
Abelson, R. P. Psychological implication. In R. P. Abelson, E. Aronson, W. J. McGuire, T. M. Newcomb, & P. H. Tannenbaum (Eds.), *Theories of cognitive consistency: A sourcebook.* Chicago: Rand McNally, 1968.
Abelson, R. P. Are attitudes necessary? In B. King & E. McGinnis (Eds.), *Attitudes, conflict and social change.* New York: Academic Press, 1972.
Abelson, R. P. Script processing in attitude formation and decision-making. In J. S. Carroll & J. W. Payne (Eds.), *Cognition and social behavior.* Hillsdale, N.J.: Lawrence Erlbaum Associates, 1976.
Amabile, T. M. Effects of extrinsic constraint on creativity. Unpublished doctoral dissertation, Stanford University, 1977.
Amabile, T. M., DeJong, W., & Lepper, M. R. Effects of externally-imposed deadlines on subsequent intrinsic motivation. *Journal of Personality and Social Psychology,* 1976, *34,* 92–98.
Anderson, R., Manoogian, S. T., & Reznick, J. S. The undermining and enhancing of intrinsic motivation in preschool children. *Journal of Personality and Social Psychology,* 1976, *34,* 915–922.
Aronson, E. The psychology of insufficient justification: An analysis of some conflicting data. In S. Feldman (Ed.), *Cognitive consistency.* New York: Academic Press, 1966.

Aronson, E., & Carlsmith, J. M. The effect of the severity of threat on the devaluation of forbidden behavior. *Journal of Abnormal and Social Psychology,* 1963, *66,* 584–588.

Atkinson, J. W. Motivational determinants of risk-taking behavior. *Psychological Review,* 1957, *64,* 359–372.

Atkinson, J. W. *An introduction to motivation.* Princeton, N.J.: Van Nostrand Reinhold, 1964.

Ayllon, T., & Azrin, N. *The token economy.* Englewood, N. J.: Prentice–Hall, 1968.

Bandura, A. *Principles of behavior modification.* New York: Holt, Rinehart, & Winston, 1969.

Bandura, A. Vicarious and self-reinforcement processes. In R. Glasser (Ed.), *The nature of reinforcement.* New York: Academic Press, 1971.

Bandura, A. Self-reinforcement: Theoretical and methodological considerations. *Behaviorism,* 1976, *4,* 135–155.

Bem, D. J. Self-perception: An alternative interpretation of cognitive dissonance phenomena. *Psychological Review,* 1967, *74,* 183–200.

Bem, D.J. *Beliefs, attitudes, and human affairs.* Belmont, Calif: Brooks/Cole, 1970.

Bem, D. J. Self-perception theory. In L. Berkowitz (Ed.), *Advances in experimental social psychology* (Vol. 6). New York: Academic Press, 1972.

Brownell, K., Colletti, G., Ersner–Hershfield, R., Hershfield, S. M., & Wilson, G. T. Self-control in school children: Stringency and leniency in self-determined and externally-imposed performance standards. *Behavior Therapy,* 1977, *8,* 442–455.

Calder, B. J., & Staw, B. M. Self-perception of intrinsic and extrinsic motivation. *Journal of Personality and Social Psychology,* 1975, *31,* 599–605.

Carlsmith, J. M., Ebbesen, E. B., Lepper, M. R., Zanna, M. P., Joncas, A. J., & Abelson, R. P. Dissonance reduction following forced attention to the dissonance. *Proceedings of the 77th Annual Convention of the American Psychological Association,* 1969, *4,* 321–322.

Chandler, M. J., Greenspan, S., & Barenboim, C. Judgments of intentionality in response to videotaped and verbally presented moral dilemmas: The medium is the message. *Child Development,* 1973, *44,* 315–320.

Cohen, H. L. Educational therapy: The design of learning environments. In J. H. Shlien (Ed.), *Research in psychotherapy.* Washington, D. C.: American Psychological Association, 1968.

Colvin, R. H. Imposed extrinsic reward in an elementary school setting: Effects on free-operant rates and choices. (Doctoral Dissertation, Southern Illinois University, 1971). *Dissertation Abstracts International,* 1972, *32,* 5034–A.

Condry, J. C. Enemies of exploration: Self-initiated versus other-initiated learning. *Journal of Personality and Social Psychology,* 1977, *35,* 459–477.

Csikszentmihalyi, M. *Beyond boredom and anxiety.* San Francisco: Jossey–Bass, 1975.

deCharms, R. *Personal causation.* New York: Academic Press, 1968.

Deci, E. L. Effects of externally mediated rewards on intrinsic motivation. *Journal of Personality and Social Psychology,* 1971, *18,* 105–115.

Deci, E. L. The effects of contingent and noncontingent rewards and controls on intrinsic motivation. *Organizational Behavior and Human Performance,* 1972, *8,* 217–229.

Deci, E. L. *Intrinsic motivation.* New York: Plenum, 1975.

Deci, E. L., Cascio, W., & Krusell, J. Cognitive evaluation theory and some comments on the Calder and Staw critique. *Journal of Personality and Social Psychology,* 1975, *31,* 81–85.

Drabman, R. S., Spitalnik, R., & O'Leary, K. D. Teaching self-control to disruptive children. *Journal of Abnormal Psychology,* 1973, *82,* 10–16.

Easterbrook, J. A. The effect of emotion on cue utilization and organization of behavior. *Psychological Review,* 1959, *66,* 183–201.

Estes, W. K. Reinforcement in human behavior. *American Scientist,* 1972, *60,* 723–729.

Fazio, R. H., Zanna, M. P., & Cooper, J. Dissonance vs. self-perception: An integrative view of each theory's proper domain of application. *Journal of Experimental Social Psychology,* 1977, *5,* 464–479.

Feingold, B. D., & Mahoney, M. J. Reinforcement effects on intrinsic interest: Undermining the overjustification hypothesis. *Behavior Therapy*, 1975, *6*, 367–377.

Folger, R., Rosenfield, D., & Hays, R. P. Equity and intrinsic motivation: The role of choice. *Journal of Personality and Social Psychology*, 1978, in press.

Freedman, J. L. Long-term behavioral effects of cognitive dissonance. *Journal of Experimental Social Psychology*, 1965, *1*, 145–155.

Greene, D. Social perception as problem solving. In J. S. Carroll & J. W. Payne (Eds.), *Cognition and social behavior*. Hillsdale, N.J.: Lawrence Erlbaum Associates, 1976.

Greene, D., & Lepper, M. R. Effects of extrinsic rewards on children's subsequent intrinsic interest. *Child Development*, 1974, *45*, 1141–1145.

Greene, D., Sternberg, B., & Lepper, M. R. Overjustification in a token economy. *Journal of Personality and Social Psychology*, 1976, *34*, 1219–1234.

Greenwald, A. G. On the inconclusiveness of "crucial" cognitive tests of dissonance versus self-perception theories. *Journal of Experimental Social Psychology*, 1975, *11*, 490–499.

Harter, S. Effectance motivation reconsidered: Toward a developmental model. *Human Development*, 1978, *21*, 34–64.

Hoffman, M. L. Empathy, role-taking, guilt and the development of altruistic motives. In T. Lickona (Ed.), *Moral development and behavior*. New York: Holt, Rinehart & Winston, 1976.

Hunt, J. McV. Intrinsic motivation and its role in psychological development. In D. Levine (Ed.), *Nebraska Symposium on Motivation* (Vol. 13). Lincoln: University of Nebraska Press, 1965.

Jackson, P. W. *Life in classrooms*. New York: Holt, Rinehart, & Winston, 1968.

Johnson, S. M., Bolstad, O. D., & Lobitz, G. K. Generalization and contrast phenomena in behavior modification with children. In E. J. Marsh, L. C. Handy, & L. A. Hamerlynck (Eds.), *Behavior modification and families*. New York: Brunner/Mazel, 1976.

Karniol, R., & Ross, M. The development of causal attributions in social perception. *Journal of Personality and Social Psychology*, 1976, *34*, 455–464.

Karniol, R., & Ross, M. The effects of performance-relevant and performance-irrelevant rewards on children's intrinsic motivation. *Child Development*, 1977, *48*, 482–487.

Kazdin, A. E. Recent advances in token economy research. In M. Hersen, R. M. Eisler, & P. M. Miller (Eds.), *Progress in behavior modification* (Vol. 1). New York: Academic Press, 1975.

Kazdin, A. E., & Bootzin, R. R. The token economy: An evaluative review. *Journal of Applied Behavior Analysis*, 1972, *5*, 343–372.

Kelley, H. Attribution theory in social psychology. In D. Levine (Ed.), *Nebraska Symposium on Motivation* (Vol. 15). Lincoln: University of Nebraska Press, 1967.

Kelley, H. H. The processes of causal attribution. *American Psychologist*, 1973, *28*, 107–128.

Kiesler, C. A., Nisbett, R. E., & Zanna, M. P. On inferring one's beliefs from one's behavior. *Journal of Personality and Social Psychology*, 1969, *11*, 321–327.

Koch, S. Behavior as "intrinsically" regulated: Work notes towards a pretheory of phenomena called "motivational." In M. R. Jones (Ed.), *Nebraska Symposium on Motivation* (Vol. 4). Lincoln: University of Nebraska Press, 1956.

Kopel, S. A., & Arkowitz, H. The role of attribution and self-perception in behavior change: Implications for behavior therapy. *Genetic Psychology Monographs*, 1975, *92*, 175–212.

Kruglanski, A. W. The endogenous–exogenous partition in attribution theory. *Psychological Review*, 1975, *82*, 387–406.

Kruglanski, A. W., Alon, S., & Lewis, T. Retrospective misattribution and task enjoyment. *Journal of Experimental Social Psychology*, 1972, *8*, 493–501.

Kruglanski, A. W., Friedman, I., & Zeevi, G. The effects of extrinsic incentives on some qualitative aspects of task performance. *Journal of Personality*, 1971, *39*, 606–617.

Kruglanski, A. W., Riter, A., Amitai, A., Margolin, B., Shabtai, L., & Zaksh, D. Can money enhance intrinsic motivation? A test of the content–consequence hypothesis. *Journal of Personality and Social Psychology*, 1975, *31*, 744–750.

Kruglanski, A. W., Stein, C., & Riter, A. Contingencies of exogenous reward and task performance: On the "minimax" principle in instrumental behavior. *Journal of Applied Social Psychology,* 1977, *7,* 141–148.

Lepper, M. R. Dissonance, self-perception, and honesty in children. *Journal of Personality and Social Psychology,* 1973, *25,* 65–74.

Lepper, M. R., & Greene, D. Turning play into work: Effects of adult surveillance and extrinsic rewards on children's intrinsic motivation. *Journal of Personality and Social Psychology,* 1975, *31,* 479–486.

Lepper, M. R., & Greene, D. On understanding "overjustification": A reply to Reiss and Sushinsky. *Journal of Personality and Social Psychology,* 1976, *33,* 25–35.

Lepper, M. R., Greene, D., & Nisbett, R. E. Undermining children's intrinsic interest with extrinsic rewards: A test of the "overjustification" hypothesis. *Journal of Personality and Social Psychology,* 1973, *28,* 129–137.

Lepper, M. R., Sagotsky G., & Greene, D. Overjustification effects following multiple-trial reinforcement procedures: Experimental evidence concerning the assessment of intrinsic interest. Unpublished manuscript, Stanford University, 1977. (a)

Lepper, M. R., Sagotsky, G., & Greene, D. Effects of a nominal contingency on children's subsequent intrinsic interest in "means" and "ends." Unpublished manuscript, Stanford University, 1977. (b)

Lepper, M. R., Sagotsky, G., & Greene, D. Effects of choice and self-imposed vs. externally-imposed contingencies on children's subsequent intrinsic motivation. In preparation, Stanford University, 1977. (c)

Lepper, M. R., Zanna, M. P., & Abelson, R. P. Cognitive irreversibility in a dissonance reduction situation. *Journal of Personality and Social Psychology,* 1970, *16,* 191–198.

Lewin, K., Dembo, T., Festinger, L., & Sears, P. W. Level of aspiration. In J. Hunt (Ed.), *Personality and the behavior disorders.* New York: Ronald Press, 1944.

Loftis, J., & Ross, L. Retrospective misattribution of a conditioned emotional response. *Journal of Personality and Social Psychology,* 1974, *30,* 683–687.

McGraw, K. O., & McCullers, J. C. Some detrimental effects of reward on laboratory task performance. Paper presented at the meeting of the American Psychological Association, Chicago, September, 1975.

McGraw, K. O., & McCullers, J. C. Monetary reward and water-jar task performance: Evidence of a detrimental effect of reward on problem solving. Paper presented at the meeting of the Southeastern Psychological Association, New Orleans, 1976.

Meichenbaum, D. H., Bowers, K. S., & Ross, R. R. Modification of classroom behavior of institutionalized female adolescent offenders. *Behaviour Research and Therapy,* 1968, *6,* 343–353.

Miller, G. A., Galanter, E., & Pribram, K. H. *Plans and the structure of behavior.* New York: Holt, Rinehart & Winston, 1960.

Mischel, W. Towards a cognitive social learning reconceptualization of personality. *Psychological Review,* 1973, *80,* 252–283.

Mischel, W., Ebbesen, E. B., & Zeiss, A. R. Cognitive and attentional mechanisms in delay of gratification. *Journal of Personality and Social Psychology,* 1972, *21,* 204–218.

Nuttin, J. R. Pleasure and reward in human motivation and learning. In D. E. Berlyne & K. B. Madsen (Eds.), *Pleasure, reward, preference.* New York: Academic Press, 1973.

O'Leary, K. D. Token reinforcement programs in the classroom. In T. Brigham & C. Catania (Eds.), *The analysis of behavior: Social and educational processes.* New York: Irvington–Naiburg/Wiley, in press.

O'Leary, K. D., & Drabman, R. Token reinforcement programs in the classroom: A review. *Psychological Bulletin,* 1971, *75,* 379–398.

O'Leary, K. D., Drabman, R. S., & Kass, R. E. Maintenance of appropriate behavior in a token program. *Journal of Abnormal Child Psychology,* 1973, *1,* 127–138.

O'Leary, K. D., Poulos, R. W., & Devine, V. T. Tangible reinforcers: Bonuses or bribes? *Journal of Consulting and Clinical Psychology,* 1972, *38,* 1–8.

Payne, J. W. Task complexity and contingent processing in decision making: An information search and protocol analysis. *Organizational Behavior and Human Performance,* 1976, *16,* 366–387.

Pepitone, A., McCauley, C., & Hammond, P. Change in attractiveness of forbidden toys as a function of severity of threat. *Journal of Experimental Social Psychology,* 1967, *3,* 221–229.

Piaget, J. *The moral judgment of the child.* New York: Free Press, 1965. (Original translation, London: Routledge & Kegan Paul, 1932.)

Pittman, T. S., Cooper, E. E., & Smith, T. W. Attribution of causality and the overjustification effect. *Personality and Social Psychology Bulletin,* 1977, *3,* 280–283.

Reiss, S., & Sushinsky, L. W. Overjustification, competing responses, and the acquisition of intrinsic interest. *Journal of Personality and Social Psychology,* 1975, *31,* 1116–1125.

Rosenhan, D. Some origins of concern for others. In P. A. Mussen, J. Langer, & M. Covington (Eds.), *Trends and issues in developmental psychology.* New York: Holt, Rinehart & Winston, 1969.

Ross, L. The intuitive psychologist and his shortcomings: Distortions in the attribution process. In L. Berkowitz (Ed.), *Advances in experimental social psychology* (Vol. 10). New York: Academic Press, 1977.

Ross, L., Lepper, M. R., Strack, F., & Steinmetz, J. Social explanation and social expectation: The effects of real and hypothetical explanations upon subjective likelihood. *Journal of Personality and Social Psychology,* 1977, *35,* 817–829.

Ross, M. Salience of reward and intrinsic motivation. *Journal of Personality and Social Psychology,* 1975, *32,* 245–254.

Ross, M. The self-perception of intrinsic motivation. In J. H. Harvey, W. J. Ickes, & R. F. Kidd (Eds.), *New directions in attribution research* (Vol. 1). Hillsdale, N.J.: Lawrence Erlbaum Associates, 1976.

Ross, M., Karniol, R., & Rothstein, M. Reward contingency and intrinsic motivation in children: A test of the delay of gratification hypothesis. *Journal of Personality and Social Psychology,* 1976, *33,* 442–447.

Ross, R., Meichenbaum, D., & Bowers, K. A brief summary of a case history of a correctional institution: Innovative treatment programs for delinquents. Unpublished manuscript, University of Waterloo, 1974.

Rumelhart, D. W., & Ortony, A. The representation of knowledge in memory. In R. C. Anderson, R. J. Spiro, & W. E. Montague (Eds.), *Schooling and the acquisition of knowledge.* Hillsdale, N.J.: Lawrence Erlbaum Associates, 1977.

Salancik, G. R. Interaction effects of performance and money on self-perception of intrinsic motivation. *Organizational Behavior and Human Performance,* 1975, *13,* 339–351.

Salancik, G. R. Extrinsic attribution and the use of behavioral information to infer attitudes. *Journal of Personality and Social Psychology,* 1976, *34,* 1302–1312.

Salancik, G. R., & Conway, M. Attitude inferences from salient and relevant cognitive content about behavior. *Journal of Personality and Social Psychology,* 1975, *32,* 829–840.

Schank, R. C., & Abelson, R. P. Scripts, plans, and knowledge. Paper presented at the 4th International Joint Conference on Artificial Intelligence, Tbilisi, U.S.S.R., 1975.

Seligman, M. E. P. *Helplessness.* San Francisco: W. H. Freeman and Company, 1975.

Shapira, Z. Expectancy determinants of intrinsically motivated behavior. *Journal of Personality and Social Psychology,* 1976, *34,* 1235–1244.

Shultz, T. R., & Butkowsky, I. Young children's use of the scheme for multiple sufficient causes in the attribution of real and hypothetical behavior. *Child Development,* 1977, *48,* 464–469.

Shultz, T. R., Butkowsky, I., Pearce, J. W., & Shanfield, H. Development of schemes for the attribution of multiple psychological causes. *Developmental Psychology,* 1975, *11,* 502–510.

Simon, H. A. *Models of man.* New York: John Wiley & Sons, 1957.

Simon, H. A. Motivational and emotional controls of cognition. *Psychological Review,* 1967, *74,* 29–39.

Smith, T. W., & Pittman, T. S. Reward, distraction, and the overjustification effect. *Journal of Personality and Social Psychology,* 1978, in press.

Smith, W. F. The effects of social and monetary rewards on intrinsic motivation. Unpublished doctoral dissertation, Cornell University, 1976.

Spence, J. T. The distracting effects of material reinforcers in the discrimination learning of lower- and middle-class children. *Child Development,* 1970, *41,* 103–111.

Staw, B. M. *Intrinsic and extrinsic motivation.* Morristown, N.J.: General Learning Press, 1976.

Swann, W. B., Jr., & Pittman, T. S. Initiating play activity of children: The moderating influence of verbal cues on intrinsic motivation. *Child Development,* 1977, *48,* 1125–1132.

Thorndike, E. L. *Animal intelligence.* New York: Macmillan, 1911.

Thorngate, W. Must we always think before we act? *Personality and Social Psychology Bulletin,* 1976, *2,* 31–35.

Tolman, E. C. *Purposive behavior in animals and men.* New York: Appleton–Century–Crofts, 1932.

Vroom, V. H. *Work and motivation.* New York: John Wiley and Sons, 1964.

Walker, H. M., & Buckley, N. K. Programming generalization and maintenance of treatment effects across time and across settings. *Journal of Applied Behavior Analysis,* 1972, *5,* 209–224.

Weiner, B. *Theories of motivation: From mechanism to cognition.* Chicago: Markham, 1972.

Weiner, B. (Ed.). *Achievement motivation and attribution theory.* Morristown, N.J.: General Learning Press, 1974.

White, R. W. Motivation reconsidered: The concept of competence. *Psychological Review,* 1959, *66,* 297–333.

Winett, R. A., & Winkler, R. C. Current behavior modification in the classroom: Be still, be quiet, be docile. *Journal of Applied Behavior Analysis,* 1972, *5,* 499–504.

Wixon, D. R., & Laird, J. D. Awareness and attitude change in the forced-compliance paradigm: The importance of when. *Journal of Personality and Social Psychology,* 1976, *34,* 376–384.

Wortman, C. B., & Brehm, J. W. Responses to uncontrollable outcomes: An integration of reactance theory and the learned helplessness model. In L. Berkowitz (Ed.), *Advances in experimental social psychology* (Vol. 8). New York: Academic Press, 1975.

Zanna, M. P., & Cooper, J. Dissonance and the attribution process. In J. H. Harvey, W. J. Ickes, & R. F. Kidd (Eds.), *New directions in attribution research* (Vol. 1). Hillsdale, N.J.: Lawrence Erlbaum Associates, 1976.

Zanna, M. P., Lepper, M. R., & Abelson, R. P. Attentional mechanisms in children's devaluation of a forbidden activity in a forced-compliance situation. *Journal of Personality and Social Psychology,* 1973, *28,* 355–359.

7

Cognitive Evaluation Theory and the Study of Human Motivation

Edward L. Deci
Joseph Porac
University of Rochester

INTRODUCTION

This book was conceived as an opportunity to bring together recent researches into the detrimental effects of extrinsic rewards on motivation and performance. Our work has been concerned only with motivation—indeed, primarily with intrinsic motivation. Further, although much of our work has shown that extrinsic rewards do have a detrimental effect on a person's intrinsic motivation, some results have indicated that rewards may leave unchanged or even enhance intrinsic motivation. Thus, we outline a series of studies that have investigated the effects of extrinsic rewards on intrinsic motivation, showing that under varying conditions, extrinsic rewards may enhance, diminish, or maintain intrinsic motivation.

We have not, however, been primarily concerned with the effects of rewards per se. Rather, our main focus has been on an explication of the psychological processes of intrinsic motivation and more generally on the psychological processes of human motivation. Therefore, this is primarily a chapter about intrinsic motivation that includes a discussion of the effects of rewards on intrinsic motivation and a discussion of the relation of intrinsic motivational processes to extrinsic motivational processes. There are three main sections to the chapter. First, we briefly discuss the nature of intrinsic motivation, conceptualizing it as being based in the human need to be competent and self-determining. Second, we review a series of our investigatons into the effects of extrinsic rewards on intrinsic motivation. In so doing we present cognitive evaluation theory (Deci, 1975) as a means of integrating the research findings. Finally, we outline a general information theoretic framework for the study of human motivation. We then show how cognitive evaluation theory operates within this general framework.

INTRINSIC MOTIVATION

An activity is generally said to be intrinsically motivated if there is no apparent external reward associated with the activity. In other words, the reward is said to be in the activity itself. There are both advantages and disadvantages to this definition. Because it is stated in terms of the presence or absence of an observable extrinsic reward, it is very useful as an operational definition for purposes of research. In our own work, we have used this operational definition. We have called it a free-choice measure, because people are left alone and are free to choose from two or more activities that have no external rewards dependent on them. The extent to which the people engage in the target activity is assumed to reflect their intrinsic motivation for that activity. This definition of intrinsic motivation satisfies the requirements of the research tradition in psychology, which demands that definitions be stated in terms of behaviors and observable variables. Finally, the definition does suggest that there is something about intrinsic motivation that is different from extrinsic motivation, since with intrinsic motivation the reward is said to be in the activity itself.

There are, however, serious disadvantages to defining intrinsic motivation in operational terms. It says nothing about psychological processes and therefore does little to further our understanding of intrinsic motivation. Thus, although the definition is quite useful for research purposes, it has little utility for theorizing. If this definition is logically correlated with a more meaningful theoretical definition, then it is quite appropriate to retain it as an operational definition while theorizing at a deeper psychological level. Further, because an operational definition focuses on behaviors, it facilitates the confusion of intrinsically motivated behaviors with behaviors motivated by extrinsic processes or affective processes. In a recent critique of our work by Scott (1975), this was done repeatedly.

The study of human motivation is the study of behavior which is emitted *in the service of human needs*. An understanding of intrinsic motivation will involve an understanding of such things as the human need that is its basis, the way in which the need initiates and energizes behavior, the way it relates to other types of needs, and the way it influences and is influenced by cognitive and affective processes. Thus, we have been interested in explicating the nature of people's intrinsic motivation and its relationship to extrinsic motivation by considering these kinds of questions.

At a physiological level, intrinsic and extrinsic motivation can be distinguished in part by the fact that intrinsic motivation is based in the needs of the central nervous system and has no appreciable effect on non-nervous-system tissues, whereas extrinsic motivation is based to a considerable extent in non-nervous-system tissues (Berlyne, 1971). Though this area is certainly quite fascinating, we do not deal with it here; instead we discuss the psychological basis of intrinsic motivation.

Intrinsic Motivation Defined

The human organism is in constant interaction with the environment. Humans are active in this process, operating on the environment and adapting to it. By nature, they strive to be competent and self-determining in these interactions, because competence and self-determination have important survival value. People need to feel effective, to feel like they can bring about desired outcomes. This need for competence and self-determination is the psychological basis of intrinsic motivation (deCharms, 1968; Deci, 1975; White, 1959). It is innate to the human organism and motivates such things as play, exploration, thinking, and the development of cognitive structures (Connolly & Bruner, 1974; Elkind, 1971; Piaget, 1952; White, 1959).

Intrinsic motivation underlies an ongoing cyclical pattern in which people *seek out and conquer challenges that are optimal for their capacities*. When people encounter challenges, they turn their attention to conquering the challenges. If there are no challenges appropriate for them, they seek challenges. These challenges must, however, be ones for which they are equipped. If the challenge is too difficult, they will avoid it until they have the capacity for dealing with it; if the challenge is too easy, they will seek more difficult ones. Of course people don't always know what challenges are optimal for them, so intrinsically motivated behavior often involves a good deal of trial and error. People aim to find challenges that are optimal, though sometimes the challenges turn out to be too easy or too hard. In these cases, people will either abandon the activity and move to a more appropriate one, or they will force themselves to continue. Children ask "why" questions out of intrinsic curiosity; yet when the answer is too complicated or too trivial, their attention wanders. Adults who engage in do-it-yourself activities either summon the aid of someone else or force themselves to continue when the challenges turn out not to be optimal.

The experience of finding and managing optimal challenges satisfies people's intrinsic need to be competent and self-determining. These challenges involve some incongruity between an internal standard (such as a value, an adaptation level, or an achievement) and a stimulus input to the central nervous system. Since the nature of the organism is one of activity, people are continually dealing with incongruities. These may take the form of overt action or internal cognitive activity. How long can one typically remain in a state of absolute congruity, for example, without beginning a new activity or attempting to solve some problem?

These are examples of intrinsic activities. When people are intrinsically motivated, they are dealing with some stimulus input and an internal standard such as a cognitive structure. For example, "How shall I integrate these new data (the stimulus input) into the theory with which they seem slightly discrepant (the cognitive structure)?" is an example of working to reduce an incongruity (or conquer a challenge). It is particularly interesting, however, that people not only try to integrate incongruities that they encounter but that they seek or create incongruities if there are none readily available to them. Psychologists may continue to extend their theories to new areas by finding incongruities and then working to reduce the incongruities by accommodating the theories to the new data.

Hunt (1965) has proposed that the psychological basis of intrinsic motivation is in the organism's need for maintaining an optimal amount of psychological incongruity. Although we believe that this optimal incongruity is an important aspect of intrinsic motivation, the notion of maintaining an optimal incongruity is a concept of equilibrium rather than a concept of an ongoing process. We hold that people seek situations that represent optimal incongruity (or challenge) not because they have a need to maintain that level, but rather because it is part of the active process of finding and reducing incongruities—of seeking and conquering challenges.

Others have attempted to deal with intrinsically motivated behavior in terms of reduction of cognitive dissonance, psychological incongruity, or uncertainty (Festinger, 1957; Kagan, 1972). This approach implies that inactivity or quiescence is the preferred state and that action is aimed at inaction. Indeed people do behave to reduce dissonance or incongruity, but the assertion that people prefer no incongruity misses the basic fact that action is the normal state of the organism. Action takes the form of seeking and reducing incongruities, and this action is motivated by the intrinsic need to feel competent and self-determining. Deci (1975) suggested that there are two classes of intrinsically motivated behaviors, the "seeking" behaviors and the "conquering" behaviors. That distinction of creating two classes was done to emphasize the inclusion of both kinds of processes—the seeking optimal incongruity and the reduction of incongruity, dissonance, or uncertainty. In fact, it is more appropriate simply to say that humans are active organisms who are engaged in an ongoing process of seeking and conquering challenges for which their knowledgc and capacities are appropriate.

Recently, Csikszentmihalyi (1975) has discussed the phenomenological experience involved in intrinsically motivated behavior. He talked of an "experience of flow" that is characterized by: (1) the merging of action and awareness; (2) the centering of attention; (3) the loss of ego or self-consciousness; (4) the sense of control of oneself and the environment; (5) coherent demands for action and unambiguous feedback from action; and finally (6) the fact that the purpose of the flow is to keep on flowing rather than to look for a goal or peak.

His approach to the question of intrinsic motivation is atypical for academic psychology in that his central focus is phenomenology. It is clear, however, that his approach and the approach to intrinsic motivation that focuses on the active organism needing to feel competent and self-determining bear considerable similarity and seem to be dealing with different aspects of the same general phenomenon.

Other Aspects of Intrinsic Motivation

Intrinsic motivation is innate to the human organism and begins as a basic, undifferentiated need for competence and self-determination (Deci, 1975). Hunt (1965) has outlined the epigenesis of intrinsic motivation, pointing out that it is sometime in the latter half of a child's 1st year that one can begin to observe intrinsically motivated behavior as we typically think of it. In other words, it is at about this time that the child begins to seek out novelty or challenge. As the child grows older, the basic need begins to differentiate into specific adult needs such as the need for achievement (McClelland, 1961), the need for self-actualization (Maslow, 1970), the need for power (McClelland, 1976), and so on. These various needs develop out of the basic, undifferentiated intrinsic motivation as a result of interactions with one's environment. For example, research has shown how certain child-rearing practices facilitate the development of achievement motivation (cf. Berkowitz, 1964); in other words, child-rearing practices influence how the basic intrinsic motivation becomes differentiated into the need for achievement. The way in which people's intrinsic motivation is evidenced depends both on their innate capacities and on their history of interactions with the environment. A child who is surrounded by artist–painters and is supported for engaging in various art endeavors is more likely to become intrinsically motivated toward art than is a person who has had no exposure to art until college. So the interplay of the child's need to be effective and self-determining with the environmental contingencies for doing art increases the likelihood that the child will experience intrinsically motivated activity in the realm of art. We wish to emphasize that this is not, however, simply an internalizing of the contingencies for doing art; nor is it a surfacing of an innate need for art. Rather, the process of differentiation occurs as the organism, with its innate capacities or native equipment (Woodworth, 1918), interacts with an environment full of contingencies.

We further believe that there is a high degree of correspondence between one's psychological health or well-being and one's being active in the sense of being intrinsically motivated. The intrinsic need for competence and self-determination must be satisfied for people to maintain natural, healthy functioning. White (1960) has used the term ''sense of competence'' to refer to one's history of efficacies and inefficacies. This sense of competence is a set with which people approach situations: A stronger sense of competence underlies greater psychological well-being, and a weaker sense of competence underlies lesser psychological well-being. Smith (1974) seemed to suggest the same thing when he stated that "the motivational core of competence is a cluster of attitudes toward the self as potent, efficacious, and worthy of being taken seriously by self and others [p. 250]." In other words, people who have a more positive attitude toward themselves will be more motivated to engage in new behaviors. Positive attitudes toward oneself result from success experiences, those experiences where one is able to match some inner standard of acceptability at an activity.

Experiences that leave people feeling noncompetent and non-self-determining, particularly when the experiences are prolonged or continual, cause people to be less psychologically healthy. Seligman (1975) has presented a wealth of data that indicates clearly that people who have been unable to effect desired changes in their environment display decreased motivation, impaired learning, and increased emotionality. Seligman refers to this state as *helplessness* and likens it to depression.

In our discussion thus far we have been concerned with some theoretical issues that we think are critical to a directed attempt at understanding intrinsic motivation. We turn now to specific research questions that seem to have both pragmatic and theoretical value. We shall focus primarily on the general topic of how people's intrinsic motivation changes over time. Because humans continuously seek out challenging opportunities from the environment, activities that at one time stimulated one's curiosity and elicited marked enthusiasm eventually lose their psychological appeal—becoming, in essence, mundane habits. What factors induce such a decline? Can one's intrinsic motivation for an activity be increased? If so, through what mechanisms? In the next section, we highlight the results of a program of research into the effects of extrinsic rewards on intrinsic motivation. In so doing, we discuss a set of theoretical propositions derived from the obtained evidence.

EFFECTS OF REWARDS ON INTRINSIC MOTIVATION

Learning theorists have long asserted that extrinsic reinforcements, when administered for the performance of a specific behavior, will increase the likelihood that the behavior will persist even after the rewards have been terminated. The rewards are said to strengthen the association between the stimulus and response, thereby increasing the likelihood of the response's being emitted. Studies with animals have repeatedly supported this point of view. With humans, however, a different interpretation of the effects of rewards seems more plausible, because people's cognitive activities have a direct, causal influence on their behavior. Rewards serve to establish or strengthen expectations that certain behaviors will lead to the rewards. Thus, people engage in the behaviors in order to attain the desired rewards. When the rewards are terminated, people will continue to respond if they still expect the reward; but they will cease to respond if they believe the reward will not follow. In other words, we are asserting that rewards affect behavior not through the mechanism of strengthening associative bonds but rather through the establishment or changing of expectations about attaining desired rewards.

Locus of Causality

If certain behaviors are seen by people to be instrumental for the attainment of specific extrinsic rewards, then those people will engage in the behaviors only when they want the rewards and when they believe the rewards will be forthcoming from the behavior. Thus, when people are extrinsically rewarded for an interesting activity, we would expect that they will begin to view the behavior as an instrument for achieving the external reward and will therefore emit the behavior only in the presence of reward contingencies. In other words, their intrinsic motivation will be decreased, and their persistence in the absence of extrinsic reward contingencies will be lessened.

DeCharms (1968) argued that performance of an activity in order to obtain an extrinsic reward eventually results in the belief that the reward is the "cause" of the behavior. Thus, the behavior will be dependent on the expectation of the extrinsic reward, and intrinsic motivation will wane. Drawing on the earlier work of Heider (1958), deCharms referred to this as a change in the perceived locus of causality for the behavior. When an individual is intrinsically motivated, the locus of causality is internal. The presence of a reward, which results in the perception that the reward is itself the "cause" of the behavior, implies that the perceived locus of causality has become external to the person; it is now in the reward. In other words, we might expect that salient extrinsic rewards will lead to the development of instrumentalities between the behavior and the rewards such that the rewards represent the reason for engaging in the activity. If the rewards are available, the subjects will engage in the activities, whereas if the rewards are unavailable they will not.

This process in which the administration of rewards for intrinsically motivated activities cause the behavior to become an instrumentality for the reward so that the perceived locus of causality changes from internal to external represents the first proposition of what Deci (1975) has called *cognitive evaluation theory*. The experiments reported below were designed to provide an empirical test of this speculation.

Monetary rewards. The first investigation (Deci, 1971) employed a three-session experimental paradigm to explore the effects of extrinsic monetary rewards on intrinsic motivation. During each of the three 1-hour sessions, subjects worked on an interesting block-construction puzzle called *Soma*. They were asked to construct four puzzle configurations in each session and were allowed

13 minutes per puzzle. If subjects were unable to complete a puzzle within this time, they were made aware of the solution in order to forestall the Zeigarnik (1927) effect. Both experimental and control subjects proceeded in identical fashion throughout the experiment, except that in the second session the treatment group received a payment of $1 for each configuration that they completed within the allotted time. Thus, the sole difference between the control and treatment groups was that the latter subjects were provided with extrinsic monetary rewards during the second puzzle-solving session.

Although the psychological substrate of intrinsic motivation is the human need to feel competent and self-determining in relation to the environment, the operational definition states that intrinsically motivated behaviors are ones that are performed for no apparent external reward. Thus, the dependent measure of intrinsic motivation was the amount of time spent by the subject working on the Soma puzzle in the absence of any external reward contingency. During each session, the experimenter left the laboratory for a period of 8 minutes, ostensibly to go to a computer terminal located in another room. The subjects were encouraged to do as they pleased during the experimenter's absence. They could have worked on the puzzles, read magazines, etc. The experimenter then positioned himself behind a one-way mirror and tabulated the amount of time each subject spent manipulating the puzzle pieces. It was hypothesized, based on the cognitive interpretation outlined above, that those subjects who were paid to construct puzzle configurations during the second session would evidence a decrease in intrinsic motivation from session 1 to session 3. On the other hand, no such decrease was expected for control subjects. The data did support this hypothesis. Statistical analyses revealed that there was a significant decrease in the measured intrinsic motivation for paid subjects relative to no-pay subjects from the first to the third session.

A field experiment was then done as a conceptual replication of the first study. The subjects were eight male undergraduates who, working in two four-member groups, staffed a corps of headline writers for a college newspaper. During four time periods encompassing a total of 12 weeks, each group was observed, and each member's performance—operationally measured by the average time required to write a headline—was recorded. The members of one group were paid $.50 for each headline written during the second session (a period of 3 weeks). The members of the second group were not paid at any time during the 12 weeks.

The prediction was simply that the four staff members in the experimental group would need more time to write headlines in the final observation period than the controls would, because it was expected that their intrinsic motivation to write headlines would be decreased. The data supported this hypothesis. Experimental group members took about the same amount of time on the average to write a headline in the latter part of the observation as in the early part, whereas control-group members improved their performance markedly during that time.

Extrinsic rewards seem to have interfered with the experimental subjects' motivation to perform the headline-writing activity.

In a later study, the finding that monetary rewards decrease intrinsic motivation was once again replicated using a one-session, "after-only" experimental design (Deci, 1972a). As in the earlier laboratory experiment, subjects worked on the Soma puzzle ostensibly as part of an investigation into styles of problem solving. The experimental subjects were paid $1 for each puzzle they solved within a 10-minute time period. Control subjects were told nothing about the possibility of receiving monetary payments. As before, the experimenter left the experimental setting for 8 minutes "in order to retrieve from the computer an appropriate post-experimental questionnaire." Through the clandestine use of a second experimenter (who was naive to both the experimental hypothesis and subject condition), the amount of time each subject spent working on the puzzle during the first experimenter's absence was recorded. As predicted, experimental subjects paid to solve the puzzles exhibited significantly less intrinsic motivation than control subjects. Once again, these data suggested that extrinsic monetary rewards contingently paid for performing an interesting activity significantly reduced an individual's intrinsic motivation for the rewarded activity.

From these three investigations, clear evidence exists attesting to the debilitating effects of extrinsic monetary rewards on intrinsic motivation. The studies have empirically demonstrated that when people are rewarded for working on an intrinsically interesting activity, there will be a reduction in behavioral persistence on the activity when the rewards are not present. Further, the results lend initial support to the proposition that instrumentalities develop between the activity and the reward, causing a change in subjects' perceived locus of causality. To test the proposition further, it is important to investigate the effects of other rewards. Presumably, rewards other than just monetary rewards should produce the same results if the change in perceived locus of causality is operative.

Threats of punishment. Deci and Cascio (1972) reasoned that rewards in the form of negative reinforcements (i. e., being rewarded for a behavior by the avoidance of punishment) should, like positive monetary rewards, decrease intrinsic motivation by changing the perceived locus of causality. They suggested that if people are made aware that they will experience an unpleasant event for not performing adequately on an intrinsically motivated activity, their intrinsic motivation will decrease. The people will begin to do the behaviors as a way of avoiding the punishment, so they will begin to perceive the avoidance of the punishment as the reason for their behavior. In other words, their perceived locus of causality for a given activity will change from internal to external when they are threatened with punishment for inadequate performance on the activity.

Subjects participated in a 1-hour puzzle-solving session and were requested to reproduce four puzzle configurations. Experimental subjects were informed that when the allotted time for each puzzle had elapsed, a buzzer would sound, indicating that they should cease work. A ½-second sample exposure to the buzzer made known to the subjects that it was a noxious stimulus. These subjects, then, were threatened with an aversive event contingent upon their failure to solve any one of the four puzzle configurations. This study parallels the earlier ones. Here the avoidance of punishment is the reward, and it is administered contingent upon adequate performance. The results showed that subjects who had been threatened for unsuccessful performance worked on the puzzle considerably less during the free-choice period than the nonthreatened controls. Threats of punishment for inadequate performance decreased subjects' intrinsic motivation, apparently by causing a change in their perceived locus of causality.

Undermining attitudes.   Benware and Deci (1975) provided a further test of the "change in perceived locus of causality" proposition. In their study, subjects were either paid or not paid for espousing a proattitudinal communication. The investigators reasoned that those subjects who were rewarded extrinsically for trying to convince others of something that they themselves believed would experience a change in perceived locus of causality from internal to external. They would come to believe that the cause or justification for their behavior was the money, so they would not need to hold to the attitudes to justify the behavior. Thus the attitudes are more vulnerable to being undermined. The authors reasoned further that people often seem to maintain an appropriate balance between a behavior and the justification for the behavior. Thus, in this situation where the money becomes the predominant justification for the communication, subjects will weaken their attitudes somewhat to restore the balance of behavior and attitudes.

The results of the Benware–Deci study indicated that payments for proattitudinal advocacy of student control of university course offerings did indeed weaken the subjects' attitudes. Although this study did not investigate intrinsic motivation, it did provide further support for the "change in perceived locus of causality" proposition of cognitive evaluation theory.

Contingency.   In the experiments discussed above, the rewards—whether money or the avoidance of an aversive stimulus—were administered to experimental subjects contingent upon their engaging in the activity as directed by the experimenter. It is now appropriate to ask whether the undermining of intrinsic motivation and attitudes was caused by the rewards per se or by the rewards made contingent upon specified performance. According to the change in perceived locus of causality proposition, rewards co-opt intrinsic motivation for an activity when the activity is perceived as an instrument for receiving the rewards. Thus, anything that facilitates the perception of the activity as an instrument for attaining a reward should facilitate the undermining of intrinsic motivation for the activity. If performance of the activity is not clearly tied to receiving the reward, the reward is less likely to diminish intrinsic motivation because it is less likely to be perceived as the cause of the activity.

Deci (1972b) reported an experiment that utilized the one-session paradigm outlined above. Experimental subjects were informed at the beginning of the experiment that they would be given $2 for participating in the experiment. This reward, unlike those in the earlier studies, was not made contingent upon their performing the activity; it was given to them for participating in the experiment. Accordingly, the reward should be less likely to decrease the subjects' intrinsic motivation as it is less likely to be seen as the cause of the activity. The results of the experiment indicated that the noncontingent payment of $2 had no effect on the intrinsic motivation of treatment subjects. It appears that rewards are more likely to interfere with people's intrinsic motivation for an activity when they are made clearly contingent upon performing the activity.

Competence and Self-Determination

Must all externally mediated rewards be detrimental to people's intrinsic motivation? Surely it is possible to conjure up in one's mind examples from daily experience in which rewards don't seem to "co-opt" intrinsic motivation, incidents in which rewards even seem to increase an individual's interest in an activity. To be cited for a heroic deed (extrinsic verbal reward) or to be paid a bonus for a job well done (extrinsic monetary reward) are just two of many situations in which people are likely to feel good about themselves, and might therefore become more intrinsically motivated.

We noted earlier in the chapter that intrinsically motivated activities are ones in which people engage to experience a sense of competence and self-determination—that is, to feel good about themselves as effective causal agents. This suggests that those extrinsic rewards that, when administered, increase people's sense of competence and self-determination should in turn increase their intrinsic motivation. The experimental investigations reviewed in this section were designed to examine this assertion.

Positive feedback.   Deci (1971) conducted a study utilizing the three-session paradigm described earlier. Verbal praise was administered as the reward to the experimental subjects, whereas the control subjects received no feedback. The subjects were undergraduate students who by chance turned out to be about 90% male.

Subjects worked on the Soma puzzles during three experimental meetings. The half that were rewarded verbally during the second session were told such things as, "That's very good; it's much better than average for this configuration," after each of the puzzle configurations that they reproduced. When subjects were unable to reconstruct a configuration correctly, they were told that it was one of the more difficult configurations and that most people were unable to reproduce it.

The dependent measure was the change in subjects' intrinsic motivation (as reflected by their free-choice persistence at the puzzle activity) from the first, pretreatment session to the third, posttreatment session. The results of the study indicated that positive-feedback subjects showed a significant increase in intrinsic motivation relative to no-feedback controls. Such evidence suggests that positive information may increase people's sense of efficacy, thereby strengthening their intrinsic motivation.

This led to the second proposition in Deci's (1975) cognitive evaluation theory: Intrinsic motivation can be affected by a change in feelings of competence and self-determination. If people's feelings of competence and self-determination are enhanced, their intrinsic motivation will increase. If their feelings of competence and self-determination are diminished, their intrinsic motivation will be decreased.

This proposition suggests a process through which intrinsic motivation may be either strengthened or weakened. The study just reported showed that positive feedback to the (male) subjects increased their intrinsic motivation, presumably by enhancing their sense of competence and self-determination. It now remains to be demonstrated that people's intrinsic motivation can be decreased by diminishing their sense of competence and self-determination.

Negative feedback.   Deci, Cascio, and Krusell (1973) investigated this, hypothesizing that negative feedback will reduce an individual's sense of efficacy and personal causation, resulting in decreased intrinsic motivation as evidenced by decreased behavioral persistence in the absence of the external contingencies.

Their study utilized the one-session paradigm in which male and female subjects were assigned to one of three conditions: control, negative verbal feedback, and negative feedback through failure. Subjects in the control and negative verbal feedback conditions were requested to assemble the same relatively easier configurations; those in the failure group were given more difficult puzzles that insured a high failure rate. The negative feedback for subjects in the verbal condition was administered by the experimenter who after each puzzle told them such things as, "You have done more poorly than average." The negative feedback in the failure condition was "self-administered"; subjects failed and were therefore aware that they were not very effective at this activity. An analysis of variance revealed that negative feedback—whether self-administered or administered verbally by the experimenter—adversely affected the intrinsic motivation of both male and female subjects.

Thus, we have seen that the "change in feelings of competence and self-determination" process seems quite reasonable as an underlying process for the increases in intrinsic motivation when (male) subjects receive positive information about their efficacy at an activity and for the decreases in intrinsic motivation when subjects receive negative information about their efficacy.

Praise and sex differences.   As we mentioned above, the subjects in the positive verbal feedback experiment (Deci, 1971) were, by chance, nearly all males. A replication experiment (Deci, 1972a) once again showed a significant increase in the intrinsic motivation of males who were given positive feedback; however, it also showed a marked decrease in the intrinsic motivation of the females who received positive feedback. This unexpected result led to another experiment that was designed to explore the effects of praise and its possible interaction with the sex of the praised or praiser. This experiment (Deci, Cascio, & Krusell, 1975) utilized both a male and a female experimenter. Half the subjects for each experimenter were male, and half were female. Finally, there were both a positive-feedback and a control condition crossed with the sex of experimenter and sex of subject. The paradigm was the standard one-session paradigm described earlier. The data revealed that female subjects provided with positive verbal feedback about performance spent less of the free-choice period working with the puzzles than did the controls. Positive-feedback males, on the other hand, worked considerably longer than their control counterparts. Furthermore, no experimenter effects emerged; the increase in the intrinsic motivation of male subjects and the decrease in the intrinsic motivation of female subjects occurred whether they were praised by a male or a female experimenter. How can we interpret this finding of the differential effects of praise on males and females?

First, it is important to recognize that the positive feedback was administered verbally by the experimenter. Thus, it was not simply an instance of information transmittal but was an interpersonal exchange in which the experimenter was praising the subject. It is useful therefore to think of the reward as praise, one component of which was positive information about competence and self-determination.

Utilizing the first two propositions of cognitive evaluation theory to account for the findings leads to the following interpretation: The reward of praise when administered to females initiates the "change in perceived locus of causality" process. Whereas initially they engaged in the puzzle activity for the intrinsic satisfaction it provided them, gradually, as they were praised, the praise became their reason for doing the puzzles. The activity became an instrumentality for the attainment of praise, and the perceived locus of causality became external. On the other hand, for males the praise seems to have been primarily informative about their efficacy; in other words, it initiated the "change in feelings of competence and self-determination" process, enhancing their feelings of efficacy, thereby increasing their intrinsic motivation.

The Dual Nature of Rewards

If the above interpretation of the sex difference is correct, it raises a very important question. Why does praise initiate one process for males and the other for females? Or, what is the crucial characteristic of a reward that determines the nature of its effect on intrinsic motivation? The key to answering these questions seems to lie in the fact that all rewards, whether they be money, praise, candy or promotions, have two aspects. Rewards have a *controlling aspect*—the aspect that controls or regiments behavior—and an *informational aspect*—the aspect that conveys positive or negative information about a person's competence and self-determination. These aspects, we assert, are present in all rewards, though the way in which rewards are used sometimes emphasizes one rather than the other.

To elaborate this point, let's consider the underlying rationales for the administration of rewards in our society today. First of all, rewards are very often utilized to "control" behavior. When plant managers take note of sagging production outcomes, they may institute lucrative incentive structures to improve their workers' performance. Parents generously administer rewards to their children in an attempt to improve their academic performance. The important point is that rewards are designed to change behavior, to control an individual's activities, to bring them into line with the expectations of the allocator.

Then again, the presence of extrinsic rewards may convey information to people about the quality of their performance. When, for example, an individual is awarded the gold medal for an excellent performance on the giant slalom, the prize is indicative of a superior level of competency at skiing. In such cases, the reward directly affects one's sense of personal efficacy; it represents evidence of one's competent interaction with the world.

The third proposition of cognitive evaluation theory is: All rewards have two aspects—a "controlling" aspect and an "information about one's efficacy" aspect. The relative salience of the two aspects determines which of the two hypothesized processes will be operative. If the controlling aspect is more salient, it will initiate the change in perceived locus of causality process. If the informational aspect is more salient, it will initiate the change in feelings of competence and self-determination process.

When we conceptualize rewards as being both controlling and informational in nature, it becomes a straightforward task to integrate the sex-difference data presented above. It appears to be the case that for females, the controlling nature of praise is more salient than the informational aspect, relative to the salience of the two for males. Thus, the relatively more salient controlling aspects of praise for females initiates the change in perceived locus of causality process, whereas the relatively more salient informational aspect of praise for males initiates the change in feelings of competence and self-determination process.

There are a number of considerations that argue for our interpretation of these

data. First, intuitively as well as empirically, we know that the traditional socialization process for boys and girls is quite different. Girls have generally been
socialized to be more aware of interpersonal matters, and they've been socialized
to be more dependent. Boys have, by contrast, been socialized to be strong,
independent, and achievement-oriented. Given this traditional picture—which
fortunately seems to be changing—one would expect the controlling aspect of
praise to be more salient for females than males. This is also compatible with the
findings reported by Alegre and Murray (1974) that females are more easily
conditioned by verbal statements than are males. Further, Feather (1966, 1968)
has reported finding that success experiences (and hence self-administered positive feedback) increases both the confidence and subsequent performance of
females as well as males. In other words, it seems to be the case that positive
information about performance increases the intrinsic motivation of females just
as it does for males; however, when it is administered interpersonally in the form
of praise, the information contained in the praise to females is overruled by the
controlling aspect of praise.

The relative salience.   We've suggested that the relative salience of the two
aspects of rewards determine whether the change in perceived locus of causality
or the change in feelings of competence and self-determination will be invoked.
What then are the factors that determine the relative salience to some particular
rewardee?

The first factor is individual differences, which derives in part from the
person's history of interactions with the environment. Therefore, if some aspect
of the environment affects one ''group of people'' differently from another, we
might expect to see average differences between these groups. It is precisely this
mechanism that we have suggested is responsible for the sex differences in the
effects of praise on males and females. Because of the differences in treatment of
males and females, they tend to interpret praise differently.

There may also be temporal fluctuations with each person, so that factors
such as the need for information could influence the perceived purpose of the
reward. If, for example, the recipient faces some type of decision based on his or
her competency at the rewarded activity, the informational value of the reward
may be enhanced.

These factors—individual differences and situational fluctuations—are both
related to the rewardees and the way they interpret rewards. There are also
factors related to the rewarder and the way rewards are administered that could
highlight either the informational or controlling aspect of the reward. If the
rewarder's purpose is to control people's behavior, then the controlling aspect
will probably be more salient. Teachers who use rewards to try to make the kids
do what they (the teachers) want them to do will surely affect the kids differently
from the teachers who use rewards to communicate that the kids are behaving
efficaciously.

We have just begun to explore these concerns in various laboratory and field settings. Our first pilot study has provided encouraging results. In this unpublished study we attempted to substantiate our hunch that when allocators overtly express an attitude that the reward is designed to communicate information, the salience of its informational aspect is likely to be greater and will affect intrinsic motivation accordingly. In this study, which utilized the standard one-session paradigm, subjects in two groups were rewarded with monetary payments of $.50 for each of four puzzles they were able to solve within the limit of 10 minutes. Subjects in one group were simply rewarded with $.50 each time they solved a puzzle. Subjects in the other group were made aware that they were being rewarded as an indication that they had done well on the activity. Initially, the experimenter told them that they would receive $.50 if they solved the puzzle faster than 80% of the previous people; that they would receive $.25 if they solved the puzzle faster than 50%; and that they'd not receive a payment if they were in the bottom 50%. In fact, they received $.50 each time they solved a puzzle, just as was the case in the other group. Our aim in this manipulation was to make differentially salient the two aspects of the monetary reward. Those paid subjects for whom the positive information was made salient were expected to evidence greater intrinsic motivation than those for whom the informational aspect was not made salient. Although the results were only preliminary and therefore not unequivocal, there was a significant difference in the intrinsic motivation of the two payment groups. Those for whom the informational aspects of the reward was emphasized spent more time in the free-choice period working with the puzzles than did the subjects in the other payment group. Monetary rewards seem to have a different effect on intrinsic motivation, depending on whether the controlling or the informational aspect of the rewards is more salient.

Contingency revisited.   Earlier we pointed out that when rewards are made contingent upon engaging in the task, they are more likely to undermine intrinsic motivation than rewards that are independent of engaging in the task. It is useful to differentiate two types of reward contingencies: The first requires only doing the task (task-contingent rewards), whereas the second requires a specific level of proficiency at the task (quality-contingent rewards). Task-contingent rewards have been shown to undermine intrinsic motivation (cf. Lepper & Greene, Chapter 6) as have performance-contingent rewards (Deci, 1971, 1972a). The use of performance-contingent rewards raises an interesting point, namely that being contingent upon some level of quality has potential for increasing either the controlling aspect or the informational aspect of rewards. They emphasize that the activity is instrumental for attaining rewards, but they also indicate that people have done well enough to receive them. Thus, it is clear that the fact of contingency in and of itself is not the determiner of whether quality-contingent rewards will decrease intrinsic motivation by changing the locus of causality or increase intrinsic motivation by bolstering one's feelings of competence and self-determination; rather the determiner is whether the way in which the performance-contingent rewards are administered emphasizes the controlling aspect or the informational aspect of the reward. For example, piece-rate payments and bonuses are both quality contingent; yet the former is more controlling and the latter more informational.

A FRAMEWORK FOR THE STUDY OF MOTIVATION

Cognitive evaluation theory, which has just been outlined, is one aspect of a more comprehensive cognitive/affective framework for the study of human motivation. The framework assumes that behavior (except for reflex behavior) is voluntary; in other words, people decide how to behave. These decisions are assumed to be lawful and understandable and are based on people's expectations about satisfying some need(s). Decisions may be conflicted in that the behavior that is expected to satisfy one or more need may block the satisfaction of other needs or have dysfunctional consequences. Still, the decisions are assumed to be based in the processing of information that is salient to the people and is interpreted by them (cf. Mandler, 1975). In other words, the meaning of a stimulus is different for different people, and we assume that it is the meaning of a stimulus to the person rather than the stimulus in an objective sense which is a determiner of behavior. People process information and decide on behaviors that they expect will lead to the satisfaction of needs that are salient for them at that time. Thus, we are concerned with needs and their satisfaction and with the ways in which people choose behaviors they expect to render the desired satisfaction.

The needs that motivate behavior may either be intrinsic needs or extrinsic needs, and the behavior may be aimed at the satisfaction of either or both of these types of needs. Therefore, although we have been emphasizing the difference between intrinsic and extrinsic motivation throughout this chapter, we now emphasize the similarity. As Robert White (personal communication) has pointed out, both kinds of motivation are really intrinsic in the sense that they occur in the person and are based in the person's needs, whether for competence, hunger, sex, or approval. Further, of course, external factors in the environment are almost always involved, because needing ''to have an effect on the environment requires an environment.'' Thus, both intrinsic and extrinsic motivation involve needs of the organism that lead people to choose behaviors aimed at satisfying one or more of these needs.

This framework for studying motivation is cognitive in that we assume people decide how to behave by processing the information that is salient to them in an attempt to achieve some desired end state. This aspect of the framework derives out of the early work of Lewin (1938) and Tolman (1932) and the more recent work of people such as Atkinson (1964), Vroom (1964), Irwin (1971), and Kagan (1972).

A cognitive approach to motivation treats motives as cognitive representations of desired future states.

The framework is affective in that we assume that people are motivated to achieve internal satisfaction that has affective components. Thus, we assume that people choose the behaviors they expect to lead to the ultimate achievement of internal satisfaction and to the intermediate achievement of certain behavioral goals that are calculated to result in the desired satisfaction. Accordingly, our definition of a motive is a cognitive representation of a future, internal condition that the organism will experience as satisfying. Another way of saying it is that a motive is an ''awareness of potential satisfaction.''

This framework is a means of analyzing a sequence of motivated behaviors into meaningful elements. By ''sequence of motivated behavior'' we simply mean a piece of behavior that is initiated, directed, and terminated.

Overview

A sequence begins with information that is processed by the central nervous system to form a motive. A motive, as we said, is an awareness of some future condition that is internally satisfying. Thus, people are motivated to achieve the internal satisfaction of which they became aware by processing informational inputs. For example, information such as gastric motility, the time of day, and a picture of a steak dinner in a magazine might create in someone a motive (generally called *hunger*), which is an awareness of the satisfaction that could be experienced from ingesting various substances.

People may at any time have several motives, some of which will be more salient than others. People attend more to the more salient motive(s); and this salience is a function of both the condition of the organism (e.g., their blood-sugar level) and the environmental stimuli that are present.

People decide what behaviors to engage in based on their expectations about satisfying salient motives. A behavior might be aimed at satisfying one motive or many motives. Once people have chosen a behavior, they perform the behavior with the expectation that completion of the behavior will lead to the desired satisfaction.

The Framework Elaborated

The elements of the system appear schematically in Figure 7.1. Information comes to the central processor from three sources: the environment, memory, and the physiology of the organism. This information blends together to create in people an awareness of potential satisfaction. The level of one's blood sugar and the level of one's excitation are examples of physiological conditions that provide information for motive formation. Information also comes from a person's memory. Remembering that 7 o'clock is dinner time, recalling an idyllic experi-

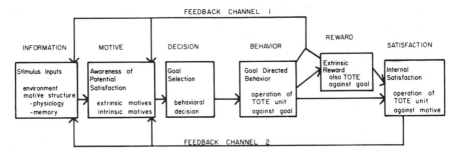

FIG. 7.1.   A schematic representation of a cognitive/affective framework for the study of human motivation.

ence of watching the sun set over the Pacific, remembering an upsetting experience with a certain person—all are pieces of information that are stored in memory and may be processed as part of the motive formation. Finally, information is always available in the environment and also plays a part in determining what motive(s) will be salient.

A motive is a transitory awareness of the possibility of achieving some internal satisfaction. It is a cognitive representation of a future organismic condition the individual expects to be satisfying. Thus, the referent of a motive is a state of the organism and not a behavior. For example, ''wanting to eat a hot fudge sundae'' is *not* a motive. The motive is the awareness that one could satisfy (to speak loosely) one's hunger and/or one's craving for sugar. ''Eating a hot fudge sundae'' may be the behavior one chooses to satisfy the motive, but the motive itself is independent of specific behaviors.

Although a motive is a transitory awareness, one's motive structure or need structure is an enduring aspect of the person. By motive structure, we mean the amalgam of people's physiology and memory that provides part of the information that creates motives (i.e., awarenesses of potential satisfaction). People have needs for achievement and needs for affiliation of varying strengths, and these enduring characteristics are aspects of their motive structure that exist in their memory and physiology and provide inputs to the central processor for the formation of motives.

People may have only one motive or they may have several motives in their awareness at any given time. Often there will be several salient motives, though in times of homeostatic crisis or poignant environmental stimulation there may be only one. When there are several, they may vary in salience as a function of the motive structure and the stimuli in the environment. When there is a motive (or motives) salient for people, they choose to behave in ways that they expect to lead to satisfaction of the motive(s). Thus, the third element in a sequence of motivated behavior is the choosing of particular behaviors; it is the selection of a pathway to the desired internal satisfaction, the awareness of which constitutes the motives.

Goal Selection

The process of deciding how to behave is often referred to as *goal selection* and is a central concern for cognitive theories of motivation (e. g., Atkinson, 1964; Vroom, 1964). Goals refer to behaviors and rewards. One might have a goal of passing a test, eating a hot fudge sundae, earning $10, or solving a puzzle. These are all pathways to desired satisfaction that the person has chosen because of his or her expectation that the paths, if successfully traversed, will result in the satisfaction of one or more motives. Let us reiterate the difference between goals and motives. Goals are selected in an attempt to satisfy motives; they are pathways that are expected to lead to internal satisfaction. Motives are awarenesses of potential satisfaction; in other words, cognitive representations of desired states of the organism.

Behaviors that are primarily extrinsically motivated have extrinsic rewards as their goal: earning money, achieving status, or getting an A in a course. Behaviors that are primarily intrinsically motivated have behavioral completion as their goal: reaching the top of Mount Everest, dancing, or playing music. Of course, any behavior may be either intrinsically motivated or extrinsically motivated; that depends on a person's motive structure. The point is simply that a goal may be either the completion of a set of behaviors or an extrinsic reward. At any rate, a goal is selected by people because of their expectations that the goal, if achieved, will yield desired satisfaction. In cases where the goal is an extrinsic reward, then the decision making involves choosing both the goal and the instrumental behaviors.

Goals are selected by processing information. Relevant pieces of information include one's motives and their valence or psychological value, one's expectations (or probability estimations) that various behavioral alternatives will satisfy one or more salient motives, the costs incurred in the various behaviors, and so on. It is a process of selecting behavioral goals in an attempt to maximize motive satisfaction at the minimum psychological cost.

Cognitive theories of motivation have tended to concentrate on the behavioral-selection aspect of motivated behavior. Most of them have postulated that one's motivation to behave is some function of the psychological value of the outcomes to which the behavior might lead, multiplied by the subjective probability that the behavior will actually lead to those outcomes (e.g., Atkinson, 1964; Lewin, 1938; Tolman, 1932; Vroom, 1964).

From our perspective, the valence (or psychological value) of an outcome derives from the outcome's potential for providing the internal satisfaction of motives. When the goal is an extrinsic reward, behaviors are selected in an attempt to achieve the reward that has valence because of its potential for the satisfaction of extrinsic motives. When the goal is the completion of a set of behaviors without an extrinsic reward, the goal has valence because of its potential for satisfaction of intrinsic motives. In real situations, of course, a behavior may be motivated by several motives, so the analysis would not be so clean; yet it is essentially the same.

Some of the cognitive theories of motivation relate primarily to extrinsic needs and others to intrinsic needs. We discuss two particular expectancy–valence theories—one of which highlights extrinsic aspects of goal selection (Vroom, 1964) and the other, which highlights intrinsic aspects of goal selection (Atkinson, 1964; Atkinson & Raynor, 1974).

The most important common element in the two theories is the assertion that one's motivation to do a given behavior is a function of the valence of the various outcomes to which the behavior might lead multiplied by the subjective probability that the outcomes will actually follow the behavior. The primary difference between the two theories centers around the way in which valence accrues to various outcomes. For Atkinson, the desirability of achievement-related outcomes is largely a matter of the difficulty of attaining the outcomes, whereas for Vroom the desirability of outcomes depends on the instrumentality of those outcomes for attaining other outcomes.

In Atkinson's theory, valence comes largely from the satisfaction of one's need for achievement, which is an intrinsic need to match a standard of excellence. Since the accomplishment of more difficult activities can be reasonably assumed to provide greater satisfaction, Atkinson suggested that the valence of completing an activity is a function of the difficulty of the activity (namely, 1 minus the Probability of Success). Thus, when the valence factor is multiplied by the expectancy factor (namely, Probability of Success), motivation is maximized when the subjective probability of success at the activity is .5. In other words, according to Atkinson's theory, people will be most motivated to engage in moderately difficult tasks, and their goal will be the satisfactory completion of the moderately difficult tasks.

By contrast, Vroom's theory is largely an extrinsic theory. Outcomes are said to be valent in accord with the other outcomes to which they lead. The Goal is an outcome such as a monetary reward to which a behavior will lead, rather than just the satisfactory completion of the behavior. Thus, people select behaviors based on their expectations of the valued outcomes to which they will lead; the outcomes in turn hold value, because they lead to still other outcomes. Money has valence because it is instrumental for obtaining food, exercising power, or attaining other desired outcomes. Utilizing this approach, valence is assumed to be independent of the difficulty of the task.

As a corollary of the fact that valence accrues differently for the two theories, we've seen that the theories make different predictions about the level of task difficulty that will be most motivating or most preferred. In Atkinson's theory, the valence of outcomes is equal to 1 minus the probability of success on the activity; so motivation (which is a function of valence times probability of success) is maximized when the difficulty of the task is .5. In Vroom's theory, the difficulty of the activity has no effect on the valence of outcomes but figures into motivation because it directly affects the probability of success (or expectancy). Thus, according to Vroom's theory, people are hypothesized to prefer the easiest tasks that lead to the desired outcomes.

One study from our laboratory (Shapira, 1976) was designed to investigate whether the difference in the hypothesized relationship between difficulty and valence is understandable in light of the predominantly extrinsic versus intrinsic orientations of the Vroom versus Atkinson models. If the same monetary rewards are offered to people for solving puzzles of varying difficulties, one might expect them to select the easiest task as a path to the desired reward. On the other hand, if there are no extrinsic rewards offered to people for solving puzzles, one might expect them to select harder tasks, which would afford them greater intrinsic satisfaction. Shapira also investigated whether in the absence of extrinsic rewards moderately difficult activities (where the probability of success is .5) are actually the most intrinsically preferred tasks, as Atkinson proposed.

Shapira asked subjects to choose one from among seven different puzzle problems. The probability of success for the different puzzles ranged from 3% (very difficult) to 97% (very easy) and was prominently displayed on each puzzle drawing. Subjects in one group were asked to choose one puzzle to work on and were told that they'd receive $2.50 if they were able to solve the puzzle within 15 minutes. Subjects in the other group were asked to choose one to work on, but there was no mention of money.

The prediction was that subjects offered money would select the task with the greatest expectancy for receiving the highly valent reward. This prediction, of course, is consistent with Vroom's theory. It was further predicted that subjects offered no money would choose more difficult puzzles (perhaps with a .5 probability of success as Atkinson asserted or with an even lower probability of success).

The results showed that extrinsically motivated subjects chose relatively easy tasks, though not the easiest, as one would expect from Vroom's theory. Thus, an extrinsically oriented theory such as Vroom's seems to predict quite well when there are valent extrinsic rewards; however, even then subjects have a tendency to choose more challenging tasks.

In the no-money condition, subjects chose relatively difficult tasks, with the median probability of success being 21%. This, of course, is a much lower probability of success than the 50% that was predicted from Atkinson's theory. Interpreting these results within an expectancy–valence framework, Shapira suggested that when no external rewards are available, people choose activities that could be most accurately described by an intrinsic valence function that is a positively accelerated function of task difficulty. Thus, intrinsic valence would be represented as follows:

$$V_{\text{intrinsic}} = c(1 - Ps)^k$$

where V stands for valence, c is a constant, Ps represents probability of success, and k is an exponential parameter. This equation represents a family of functions, some one of which describes any person's intrinsic valence function. Valence will be maximized for a person when $Ps = 1/(K + 1)$. This function is positively accelerated, thereby indicating that a given increment in task difficulty increases the intrinsic valence more for relatively difficult tasks than for easier tasks. The function describes an individual's intrinsic valence function and could also describe a population by using an average value for k.

A more complete instrumentality–valence function that will predict an individual's goal selection will of course need to include both intrinsic and extrinsic components, though Shapira was concerned only with valence determinants of intrinsic motivation.

Having considered the goal-selection aspect of the motivational framework, we proceed to the next step, which is the behavior itself.

Purposive Behavior

In the preceding step, people set goals for themselves. A goal is either the satisfactory completion of a set of behaviors (intrinsic) or the attainment of some reward (extrinsic). Goals are chosen because people expect the goals to result in desired internal satisfaction. Having set goals, people begin behaving in an attempt to achieve the goals. As they behave, they will use the goal as a standard against which to compare their behaviors to determine whether they have completed the desired behaviors, and if not, to know what they need to do to reach the goal. Another way of saying this is that their behavior will be governed by a feedback loop, which Miller, Galanter, and Pribram (1960) have called the TOTE unit. This is a central element for an information-processing approach to behavior in which people are assumed to be operating or behaving so as to try to achieve some standard, solve some problem, or reach some goal. Miller et al. suggested that the process can be conceptualized as one in which people *Test* where they are against where they aim to be; if there is a discrepancy, they *Operate* to reduce the discrepancy; then once again, they *Test* for discrepancy; and if there is none, they *Exit*. We are suggesting that this is precisely the mechanism that directs behavior in our framework; people, once they have set a goal, operate to reach the goal, continuously testing to determine if they have achieved it. Once they have, this phase of the sequence of motivated behavior will be terminated. The person will have accomplished the set of behaviors that constitute his or her goal.

We know, of course, that people do not always persist at an activity until they reach their goal. As new information about valence or expectancy becomes available to them, they may change their goals. Further, people sometimes engage in cognitive distortion or dissonance reduction (Festinger, 1957) as a means of reducing the discrepancy between their current state and their goal. The question of when people will continue to reduce discrepancies and when they will engage in cognitive distortion to reduce them is quite fascinating and deserves attention.

Performance variations. So far, we have suggested that people will perform in an attempt to achieve their goals and that this process will be governed by the operation of the TOTE unit. It is now important to note that there will be wide variations in people's performance, which can be addressed at this phase of the framework. For example, Locke (1968) has reported that the type of goal affects people's performance; more difficult goals rather than easy ones lead to better performance, as do specific rather than vague goals.

Researchers have also found that performance decrements may be caused by the introduction of extrinsic rewards (see McGraw, Chapter 3, for a review). Their research has shown that when people are rewarded for doing an interesting activity which requires some creativity and resourcefulness, their performance is less effective than when they do the same activity for no reward. Why might one expect such results? There are several possible explanations, a few of which are mentioned briefly to demonstrate how they might be handled within this framework. The introduction of an extrinsic reward may direct part of one's attention away from the activity toward the reward, thereby making one more restricted in considering the problem elements. Extrinsic rewards might also arouse people's anxiety, thereby directing their attention to the management of or reduction of the anxiety. Lepper and Greene (Chapter 6) have suggested further that when extrinsic rewards are administered by another person, the performer may be unsure about the specific behaviors the rewarder requires; so the performer may have to try out several behaviors before finding the required one.

Rewards and Satisfaction

People select goals because they expect them to lead to the satisfaction that was recognized as a potential in their motive. If their expectations were correct, the desired satisfaction will follow the achievement of their goals. This satisfaction may accrue directly from the behavior as in the case of intrinsic satisfaction, or it may be mediated by an extrinsic reward. An example of the latter is that people may do something to get praise, which will lead them to feel satisfaction; here the reward of praise mediates between the behavior and the satisfaction. In either case, the satisfaction represents the ultimate aim of the behavior and is therefore the final element in the sequence; when people attain the desired satisfaction, the sequence terminates.

There is always some uncertainty about whether the satisfaction will actually accrue when the goal is reached. If the expectations the people had in setting the goal were correct, the satisfaction will follow; if not, it won't. Therefore, this aspect of the framework is also governed by the operation of a TOTE feedback loop. The standard of comparison is the potential satisfaction comprising people's motives. They plan a goal in hopes of achieving the satisfaction. Upon goal attainment they will test their state of satisfaction against the standard; if they have not reached the desired satisfaction, they operate—which in this case means setting a new goal aimed at the satisfaction and behaving to achieve the goal. If when they test they have matched the standard of comparison (i.e., the desired satisfaction), then of course they exit from the TOTE feedback loop, which also means they terminate the sequence of motivated behavior.

As with the feedback loop that governed the goal-directed behavior, people do not always operate to reduce the discrepancy between their current state and their standard of comparison; sometimes they distort their cognitions so as to believe there is congruity. Again the question of when they will behave to reduce the discrepancy and when they will distort cognitions to reduce it is an interesting question. In one study (Deci, Reis, Johnston, & Smith, 1977), we found that the degree of ambiguity about the discrepancy mediated between behaving versus cognitive distortion as a mechanism for reducing the incongruity. When a discrepancy was portrayed as being ambiguous, subjects changed their attitudes to achieve congruence, whereas when the very same discrepancy was not said to be ambiguous, subjects engaged in behaviors to reduce the discrepancy. Thus, it appears that subjects are more likely to distort their cognitions to achieve congruence when less distortion is required.

To recapitulate the general framework, people's motivated behavior is hypothesized to be governed by two TOTE feedback loops, one operating within the other. The more global one uses the motive (i.e., the potential satisfaction) as a standard against which to compare their satisfaction. Within this is another feedback loop that uses the goals as a standard against which to compare one's behavioral state. These processes are shown schematically in Figure 7.1.

Cognitive Evaluation Theory

The final point about the framework that we make here is that there are a variety of feedback channels involved. These should not be confused with the two TOTE feedback *loops* mentioned above. The TOTE feedback loops govern the operation or termination of elements in the sequence of motivated behavior. Feedback channels are additional mechanisms through which people's experiences can modify their motives or motive structures. Two feedback channels represent the two processes of cognitive evaluation theory, which was discussed earlier.

The first feedback channel begins in the linkage between behavior and extrinsic rewards and feeds back to the motives, motive structure, and goal selection. This feedback channel represents the process called *change in perceived locus of causality*. Here an instrumentality develops, so the behavior becomes a means to a specific extrinsic reward—thereby undermining the person's intrinsic motivation for the activity. The person's goal changes from the behavior to the reward, and the person becomes less motivated by intrinsic motives.

The second feedback channel of interest begins with a person's satisfaction and feeds back to the motives, motive structure, and goal selection. This is the change in feelings of competence and self-determination process through which people's success and failure experiences affect their intrinsic motivation. The experiences of intrinsic satisfaction or dissatisfaction may either enhance or diminish their feelings of competence and self-determination, which in turn strengthens or weakens their intrinsic motivation.

The question of precisely how intrinsic motivation is undermined is a fascinating one. We offer only the most general speculation. One interpretation is that people learn (i.e., store information in their memories) that the particular activity is not one they engage in for intrinsic satisfaction. Thus, in our general framework, feedback would be stored in people's memories, and when they are selecting behaviors to satisfy their intrinsic motives, they would know not to select the activity for which their intrinsic motivation has been undermined.

It is quite likely, however, that in real-life situations, the impact is more pervasive. We suspect that with continual exposure to controlling rewards and negative information about one's efficacy, one's overall level of intrinsic motivation becomes undermined. People would then be generally less active, would be less likely to have what Csikszentmihalyi (1975) has called the *flow experience,* have less of a sense of competence (White, 1959), and experience themselves less as causal agents (deCharms, 1968). If this were so, then people's motive structure would be affected in more major ways. The key question is whether— as the first interpretation implies—the undermining of people's intrinsic motivation for an activity simply means that they won't choose that activity as a means to intrinsic satisfaction or whether it means that their overall intrinsic motivation will tend to decrease in addition to their decreased interest in the one activity. The experimental results have not yet provided a definitive answer to this question; however, they seem to imply that the second interpretation is correct. With repeated exposures to controlling rewards and negative feedback, people's general level of intrinsic motivation seems to decrease. Seligman (1975) has reported that when organisms are unable to affect their contingencies (i.e., are unable to satisfy their need for competence and self-determination), they lose motivation, become lethargic, are less able to learn, and display other symptoms associated with depression. In a similar vein, deCharms (1976) has found that when school children are treated as self-determining causal agents, they generally act like causal agents; whereas if they are treated as pawns and controlled with rewards, they fail to act like causal agents. In short, it is becoming clearer that continual exposure to negative feedback about one's competence and self-determination and continual receipt of controlling extrinsic rewards will have a significant impact on people by generally undermining their intrinsic motivation and sense of well-being (Deci, 1978).

If this is so, how might it happen? According to our framework, feedback would affect one's motive structure. Thus, people would store messages in their memory such as: they're not intrinsically motivated; they shouldn't do things unless they get rewarded; there's no use in trying this type of activity because they're so bad at it; and so on. In short, people retain various kinds of information that interferes with their intrinsic motivation. Further, it is possible, as Reich (1960) and others have suggested, that experiences such as repeated failures and continual negative feedback actually modify people's physiology in such a way as to block intrinsic motivation. Thus, changes in such things as muscle structures or glandular operation may also be involved in the undermining of people's intrinsic motivation.

We are merely speculating about the possible ways in which rewards and feedback actually affect one's intrinsic motivation. The question presents many fascinating research possibilities, as does the whole area of human motivation that is now emerging.

ACKNOWLEDGMENTS

Preparation of this chapter was facilitated by research grant MH 28600-01 from the National Institute of Mental Health to the first author.

REFERENCES

Alegre, C., & Murray, E. J. Locus of control, behavioral intention, and verbal conditioning. *Journal of Personality*, 1974, *42*, 668–681.

Atkinson, J. W. *An introduction to motivation.* Princeton, N.J.: Van Nostrand, 1964.

Atkinson, J. W., & Raynor, J. W. (Eds.). *Motivation and achievement*, Washington, D.C.: Winston, 1974.

Benware, C., & Deci, E. L. Attitude change as a function of the inducement for espousing a pro-attitudinal communication. *Journal of Experimental Social Psychology*, 1975, *11*, 271–278.

Berkowitz, L. *The development of motives and values in the child.* New York: Basic Books, 1964.

Berlyne, D. E. *Aesthetics and psychobiology.* Englewood Cliffs, N.J.: Prentice–Hall, 1971.

Connolly, K. J., & Bruner, J. S. (Eds.). *The growth of competence.* New York: Academic Press, 1974.

Csikszentmihalyi, M. *Beyond boredom and anxiety.* San Francisco: Jossey–Bass, 1975.

deCharms, R. *Personal causation: The internal affective determinants of behavior.* New York: Academic Press, 1968.

deCharms, R. *Enhancing motivation: Change in the classroom.* New York: Irvington, 1976.

Deci, E. L. Effects of externally mediated rewards on intrinsic motivation. *Journal of Personality and Social Psychology*, 1971, *18*, 105–115.

Deci, E. L. Intrinsic motivation, extrinsic reinforcement, and inequity. *Journal of Personality and Social Psychology*, 1972, *22*, 113–120. (a)

Deci, E. L. The effects of contingent and non-contingent rewards and controls on intrinsic motivation. *Organizational Behavior and Human Performance*, 1972, *8*, 217–229. (b)

Deci, E. L. *Intrinsic motivation.* New York: Plenum Publishing Corp., 1975.

Deci, E. L. *Motivation, will, and well-being.* Unpublished manuscript, 1978.

Deci, E. L., & Cascio, W. F. Changes in intrinsic motivation as a function of negative feedback and threats. Paper presented at the meeting of the Eastern Psychological Association, Boston, 1972.

Deci, E. L., Cascio, W. F., & Krusell, J. Sex differences, positive feedback, and intrinsic motivation. Paper presented at the meeting of the Eastern Psychological Association, Washington, D.C., May 1973.

Deci, E. L., Cascio, W. F., & Krusell, J. Cognitive evaluation theory and some comments on the Calder and Staw critique. *Journal of Personality and Social Psychology*, 1975, *31*, 81–85.

Deci, E. L., Reis, H. T., Johnston, E. J., & Smith, R. Toward reconciling equity theory and insufficient justification. *Personality and Social Psychology Bulletin*, 1977, *3*, 224–227.

Elkind, D. Cognitive growth cycles in mental development. In J. K. Cole (Ed.), *Nebraska Symposium on Motivation* (Vol. 19). Lincoln: University of Nebraska Press, 1971.

Feather, N. T. Effects of prior success and failure on expectations of success and subsequent performance. *Journal of Personality and Social Psychology*, 1966, *3*, 287–298.

Feather, N. T. Change in confidence following success or failure as a predictor of subsequent performance. *Journal of Personality and Social Psychology*, 1968, *9*, 38–46.

Festinger, L. *A theory of cognitive dissonance*. Evanston, Ill.: Row, Peterson, 1957.

Heider, F. *The psychology of interpersonal relations*. New York: Wiley, 1958.

Hunt, J. McV. Intrinsic motivation and its role in psychological development. *Nebraska Symposium on Motivation*, (Vol. 13). Lincoln, University of Nebraska Press, 1965.

Irwin, F. W. *Intentional behavior and motivation*. Philadelphia: Lippincott, 1971.

Kagan, J. Motives and development. *Journal of Personality and Social Psychology*, 1972, *22*, 51–66.

Lewin, K. *The conceptual representation and measurement of psychological forces*. Durham, N. C.: Duke University Press, 1938.

Locke, E. A. Toward a theory of task and motivation incentives. *Organizational Behavior and Human Performance*, 1968, *3*, 157–189.

Mandler, G. *Mind and emotion*. New York: Wiley, 1975.

Maslow, A. H. *Motivation and personality* (2nd ed.). New York: Harper and Row, 1970.

McClelland, D. C. *The achieving society*. Princeton, N.J.: Van Nostrand, 1961.

McClelland, D. C. *Power: The inner experience*. New York: Irvington, 1976.

Miller, G. A., Galanter, E., & Pribram, K. H. *Plans and the structure of behavior*. New York: Holt, Rinehart, and Winston, 1960.

Piaget, J. *The origins of intelligence in children*. New York: International Universities Press, 1952.

Reich, W. *Selected writings: An introduction to orgonomy*. New York: Farrar, Strauss, and Giroux, 1960.

Scott, W. E. The effects of extrinsic rewards on "intrinsic motivation": A critique. *Organizational Behavior and Human Performance*, 1975, *15*, 117–129.

Seligman, M. E. P. *Helplessness*. San Francisco: Freeman, 1975.

Shapira, Z. Expectancy determinants of intrinsically motivated behavior. *Journal of Personality and Social Psychology*, 1976, *34*, 1235–1244.

Smith, M. B. *Humanizing social psychology*. San Francisco: Jossey–Bass, 1974.

Tolman, E. C. *Purposive behavior in animals and men*. New York: Century, 1932.

Vroom, V. H. *Work and motivation*. New York: Wiley, 1964.

White, R. W. Motivation reconsidered: The concept of competence. *Psychological Review*, 1959, *66*, 297–333.

White, R. W. Competence and the psychosexual stages of development. In M. R. Jones (Ed.), *Nebraska Symposium on Motivation* (Vol. 8). Lincoln: University of Nebraska Press, 1960.

Woodworth, R. S. *Dynamic psychology*. New York: Columbia University Press, 1918.

Zeigarnik, B. Das behalten erledingter und unerledigter handlungen. *Psychologische Forschung*, 1927, *9*, 1–18.

III
DISCUSSION

In light of the pervasive influence of explicit reward systems throughout our lives, research demonstrating that there may be unintentional "costs" associated in some circumstances with the use of rewards inevitably provokes discussion of the potential social implications of these findings. Particularly given the demonstrable benefits that have been shown to result from the use of systematic reinforcement programs in a variety of contexts, the issue of boundary conditions and the domain in which detrimental effects may occur becomes critical. Likewise, if rewards may simultaneously produce detrimental effects on some aspects of performance and beneficial effects on others in a given context, how are these competing forces to be weighed against each other?

In this final section, several contributors present their views concerning the possible implications and limitations of the data presented in this volume. Though differences in approach among authors are apparent, it seems clear in each of these accounts that questions of practical implications cannot be answered except with reference to one's goals and values and often to one's theoretical presuppositions as well.

Condry (Chapter 8) discusses the implications of the study of "hidden costs" for the socialization process. Treating the internalization of basic societal values and the preservation of individual initiative and curiosity as complementary goals of socialization, he examines the role that incentive systems may play, at home and in school, in facilitating or impeding the attainment of these goals.

Deci (Chapter 9) examines broadly the possible implications of the data in this volume for a variety of settings in which systematic incentive systems are commonly employed. Weighing potential costs versus benefits of a particular program in any of these contexts, he argues, must involve a clear specification of one's goals and values in instituting and evaluating the program.

Csikszentmihalyi (Chapter 10) argues the position that, within a wide range, rewards and tasks are what you make of them, that the boundary between them is frequently the result of arbitrary, self-imposed distinctions or culturally shared definitions. Recognition of the potential for enjoyment and effectance in a variety of activities, he suggests, may allow individuals to find greater satisfaction in the mundane events of everyday life, as well as the glamorous.

Lepper and Greene (Chapter 11) conclude the volume with a discussion of the divergent approaches to the study of rewards exemplified by the contributors to this volume on one hand and by investigators concerned with the application of reinforcement principles to applied settings on the other. In this discussion, they argue that paradigmatic differences in goals and theoretical presuppositions between these two divergent traditions have lead to different experimental procedures, different results, and different conclusions. As a result, they suggest that considerable caution may be required in extrapolations from either approach to new settings that are not easily assimilated to situations in which the two approaches have been investigated.

8 The Role of Incentives in Socialization

John Condry
Cornell University

There are two faces to the research described in this book. One face is the effects of a variety of task-extrinsic incentives—rewards, surveillance, social feedback—on learning, development, and performance. Because most of the effects are seen as "undermining" ongoing intrinsically motivated behavior, we have termed this face the "hidden costs of rewards." The other face of the same coin is the character of intrinsic motivation as it is revealed by the same research. Whenever we study the effects of reward, the actions of the "no-reward" groups may be scrutinized to determine the nature of exploratory or "intrinsically" motivated behavior.

The question we seek to answer is this: What does the research summarized in this book tell us about the use of task-extrinsic incentives in the socialization process, particularly in child rearing and education? To answer a question like this we must first posit what socialization is and observe when incentives seem to be used in the process. Socialization is acquiring the rules, roles, and basic modes of behavior required of the individual in order to fit comfortably into the niches available in the society in which he or she will live. I speak of these "rules and roles" as being represented in the person as a set of *skills* that are acquired in the process of growing up in a particular society. The extent to which these skills are used by adults is another matter and one that does not concern us here.

These skills exist at several levels in the human being. There are skills of action and behavior, there are skills of perception and cognition, and there may be skills of emotion and empathy. A cognitive–perceptual skill would be, for example, the ability to extract a rule in an ambiguous situation (or simply a situation in which the "rules" are unknown) by observing the *actions* of others. Young children are frequently seen to laugh at jokes they could not possibly "understand." The laughter is occasioned not by what was said but by what was done in response to what was said. Children recognize, even before they can understand the words or their "cognitive" meanings, that certain things are "funny" when a number of people laugh at them. Kelley (1973) calls this the criterion of "consensus" in his attributional analysis, and children are not born with the knowledge of how to apply it. They must learn when to apply it and when not to. The "developed capacity" to apply this rule I would call a *skill*—a skill of social perception. A behavioral skill, would be, for example, the ability to play a specific role in such a way that the performance is recognized as competent by the other members of society. Thus, a young child caught holding a doll by the feet and dragging its head bumping and bouncing over the ground is often told, "That's no way to treat a baby!" In doing so, we are communicating to the child a small fact about the skill of parenthood, a role he or she may play in the society. As I see it, the acquisition, internalization, and integration of this multitude of skills—including cognitive, behavioral, and emotional aspects—is the main purpose of the socialization process.

Broadly speaking, children must first learn to explore the world in which they live and to discover what the culture affords. These affordances are contained in the informational arrays of the environment. In the social environment, for example, we observe the attitudes, institutions, and social displays of the other members of society. I think we should call the skills needed to accomplish this task "exploratory skills" and note that they are "intrinsically motivated" but must be developed and refined within a particular culture. That is, the constituents of exploratory skills—the attraction to novel information, the inborn patterns of manipulative action, and the other characteristics of the process of exploration—are found in the organism due to "internal, prefunctional factors" (Bruner, 1974a, p. 170). They appear at a certain stage of development as a consequence of both maturation and experience. But the "application to external stimulus conditions . . ." (Schiller, 1952) must be accomplished within a particular real environment. The components of the skills are found at birth, because they were adaptive to niches in the evolutionary past of the organism. Those that survived were useful, but they must be accommodated to the demands of the particular environment in which the child grows. Thus, both the degree to which exploration is encouraged and the characteristics of the environment available for the child to explore are critical items of information about the socialization process. As we have seen, most research in this volume is directed to the first of these considerations, what might be loosely called the atmosphere of learning. Little if any attention has been devoted to the second consideration, and this is a point to which we shall return.

Once these exploratory skills are developed and functional, the child will use them to explore as much of the real world as is possible, with the aim of becoming competent within it (White, 1959). With this view in mind, we can study the socialization process and see where rewards, particularly task-extrinsic rewards, are used to "motivate" or train children.

At least through childhood, there are two broad contexts in which rewards and incentives may be used and typically are used to motivate and train children: the home and the school. Rewards are also used for control, as Deci (1975) notes, in childhood to achieve compliance to demands and in adolescence and adulthood to compensate individuals for their labors. I will focus my attention on the use of rewards to motivate learning and to control behavior in childhood.

THE HOME

In the home, rewards and incentives are used less systematically than in schools. But in the study of child rearing, it is possible to speak of the intensity and type of pressure exerted to bring about obedience to some rule or norm and the attitude structure or "atmosphere" of the home in which that pressure is exerted. In the home, the use of extrinsic incentives encompasses not only commands, punishments, and rewards but also a way of thinking about the importance of such incentives. In particular, these attitudes involve the concept of "control" and the degree to which the child's impulses need to be controlled. Many people believe that it is necessary to "train" children and to expose them early in life to physical discipline and the withdrawal of what are thought to be rewarding interactions in order to compel obedience, in order to induce "respect for authority." I suggest that these actions are comparable to the "extrinsic motivational context" (created by the offer and use of extrinsic incentives) described by the research in this book.

On the other hand, the "intrinsic context" is represented in child rearing not by a complete absence of rewards but rather by the attitude that children can and often do learn on their own without the effort of explicit training, and without constant oversight and direction by adults. The suggestion is twofold—first, that the "intrinsic" atmosphere in the home is associated not with an absence of reward and praise but with a use comparable to the "unanticipated-reward" condition described in the research by Lepper, Greene, and Nisbett (1973). That is, in some homes, when praise, rewards, and punishments are dispensed, they are not usually "contracted for" in the sense of being offered in advance but are occasionally "given" in response to something done. Second, control is valued and is a central concept in these homes, also, but it is self-control rather than external control.

The use of rewards and incentives to train children often comes part and parcel with a set of notions about how and why children should be trained. A common belief is that to respond to a child while he/she is crying is to "spoil" the child by rewarding the cry with the parent's presence. In fact, parents used to be warned against any display of affection in the face of the "tantrums" by the child. Thus, the father of behaviorism, J. B. Watson (1928), cautioned parents:

> Let your behavior always be objective and kindly firm. Never hug and kiss them, never let them sit in your lap. If you must, kiss them once on the forehead when

you say goodnight. Shake hands with them in the morning. Give them a pat on the head if they have made an extraordinarily good job of a difficult task. Try it out. In a week's time you will find how easy it is to be perfectly objective with your child and at the same time kindly. You will be utterly ashamed of the mawkish sentimental way you have been handling it [pp. 73–74].

Nor is this attitude so much a part of past history as one might imagine. Two modern-day behaviorists (Blackham & Silberman, 1971) describe first how a disturbed child was treated (by closing his bedroom door, a painful and anxiety-arousing event) in order to "reinforce" the desired behavior, and they go on to suggest:

With a little ingenuity, this basic procedure can be modified and used with most bedtime problems. While opening and closing a door will work, a light or a child's favorite blanket may be used. That is, a light in the child's room is either left on or turned off according to the behavior he exhibits; or the child's favorite blanket—or toy or teddy bear—can be removed until he behaves properly. It can be seen that this method utilizes negative reinforcement as well as response-contingent withdrawal of reinforcement. An aversive stimulus is removed (the door is opened) when the child exhibits the specified behavior: negative reinforcement is being used. When a favorite blanket or toy is removed because an undesirable behavior is exhibited, response-contingent withdrawal of reinforcement of being used [p. 162].

We might compare this attitude, this approach to child rearing, with a less pressured approach to "control" a specific behavior. Bell and Ainsworth (1972) studied the incidence of crying by children who either were not responded to (thus not "reinforced") or who were immediately responded to by parents. They found that high-responsive mothers, ones they called "sensitive," had children who cried less than mothers who were less responsive (Ainsworth, Bell, & Stayton, 1974). If one conceptualizes parental response as a reward and the failure to make this response as "response-contingent withdrawal of reinforcement," then the effects observed are the opposite of those suggested by a "behaviorist" analysis. The more infants are "punished" by the failure of the parent to respond to their crying, the more they cry.[1] Not only that, but a vicious

---

[1] It is interesting to note how the failure to respond to children in order to avoid "spoiling" them is based on a false conception of what the child is doing, and it fails in part for that reason. The assumption is that children who make "demands" and who are reinforced for those demands by parental responsiveness will become spoiled and demanding. This may be true; the flaw in the reasoning is that little children are not "making demands" when they cry—they are engaging in communication in the only way available. This becomes clear when one observes what happens to the original "cry" as it is responded to. First it becomes a coo and later the words "ma-ma." In short, early vocalization, including cries, are the first step in the process of acquiring language, and few people would advocate the "punishment" of language. This analysis reveals one of the difficulties with the use of extrinsic rewards and training—it is necessary to be *accurate* about what the child is doing *precisely;* or the training will falter, the wrong things will be reinforced, and the wrong things punished.

cycle is established by the end of the 1st year. "Babies whose cries have been ignored tend to cry more frequently and persistently, which further reduces prompt responsiveness" (Ainsworth, Bell, & Stayton, 1974, p. 111).

Substantially the same thing was found by Stayton, Hogan, and Ainsworth (1971) for obedience and "training." The infant's compliance to commands and internalized control was studied as these behavioral skills related to maternal sensitivity. They found that a "disposition" toward obedience emerges in a responsive, accommodating social environment without extrinsic training, discipline, or other massive attempts to shape the infant's course of development. Mothers who did the *least* "training" of their children and who relied more on the child's ability to learn from observation than from the application of "incentives" had the most obedient children who had most internalized controls over their behavior.

These two studies suggest that the *less* the pressure from the social world for "training" and compliance, the greater the internalization of behavioral and cognitive skills, especially exploratory skills. Further support for this suggestion is found in a series of experimental studies by social psychologists. In "forbidden-toy" experiments (Aronson & Carlsmith, 1963; Carlsmith, Ebbesen, Lepper, Zanna, Joncas, & Abelson, 1969; Freedman, 1965; Pepitone, McCauley, & Hammond, 1967; Zanna, Lepper, & Abelson, 1973), two levels of prohibition (mild and severe) are compared in terms of a child's subsequent liking for and willingness to play with a forbidden toy. Typical findings are that children like the toy less when forbidden to play with it under the mild threat as opposed to severe threat, and in some studies they play with it less several weeks after the prohibition. Once again, it would appear that *low* environmental demand is associated with internalization and self-control. It is notable that the behavioral skill under study in the forbidden-toy experiment is the internalization of a prohibition. In the home, most incentives are used for this purpose.[2]

From this evidence, we can see that the hidden costs of rewards in the home are twofold. First, the desire to explore the world is reduced by too much of a demand to attend to outside factors and forces. This may reduce the "activity" of the organism. Second, the stronger incentives are shown to have the weakest effects when it comes to the degree of internalization of the prohibition, both measured attitudinally and behaviorally. The human being, from infancy on, is born with adequate, preformed mechanisms for learning about the world—for

---

[2]There are social class differences in the use of incentives in the home (Baumrind, 1966, 1967; Crandall, Katovsky, & Preston, 1962; Sears, Maccoby, & Levin, 1957). The atmosphere of intrinsic motivation—with low pressure for obedience and training is more commonly found in upper-income families; the "extrinsic context" is more common in lower-income homes. An important consequence of this fact is that the interface between the home and the school must be studied, especially if we are to understand the effectiveness of the use of incentives in school. It may be difficult for children who are accustomed to one style in the home to adapt to the use of a different style in the school, although I know of no finished research on this topic. We are investigating this interrelationship now at Cornell (Boykin, Note 1).

exploring it, manipulating it, and for understanding it—if these mechanisms are allowed to develop and function. They appear to do so best when external pressure for compliance and obedience are *least*. It is possible to train the human child to do things with the use of selected rewards and punishments for the performance of a specific behavior, but it is not necessarily the most efficient and effective way to do so.

It must be stressed here that I am not opposed to the use of rewards and punishments; both are effective in certain circumstances and in some version essential to child rearing, as any parent knows. The issue is not whether rewards should be used, but *how* and for what purpose. I am concerned that we come to an accurate understanding of the human organism, particularly when it is immature, and that we use whatever training procedures we deem necessary within the confines of that understanding. Inevitably, there will arise among practitioners differences of opinion about what aspects of the socialization process should be given particular attention and value. I stated my own position at the outset, but let me expand on it now. I believe the most important characteristics to be developed in children during the period from birth to maturity are skills that allow the children to actively manipulate and control the world around them and themselves within it. I believe this control is characterized by the ability to anticipate outcomes that are predictable and to manipulate other outcomes that are obtainable with the proper action. This control, and the sense of mastery and competence that arise from it, is the most important, single outcome of the socialization process. Fully developed, control is vested in the human being in the form of skills such as those mentioned at the beginning of this chapter. I believe it is to the development and internalization of skilled control that all socialization processes should be directed.

Within the confines of this particular value system, I believe that any procedure for training the immature organism that undermines or detracts from the development of mastery and control is "bad" and any procedure that facilitates the development of mastery is "good." I have tried to illustrate, by the use of selective examples, how the use of incentives in the home reflects different conceptions of the human organism. If one views the child as impulsive, chaotic, and in need of much early training and supervision, this conception of the child may lead to intrusive techniques that will undermine the child's natural curiosity. In addition, the use of strong incentives when mild ones are sufficient is often counterproductive when long-term, "internalized" behavior patterns are what is desired.

I have argued for a different conception of the child and thus a different conception of the role of incentives in the process. I have suggested that the child is neither passive nor chaotic but rather possesses adequate, preformed motivation to act and the cognitive competence to observe and comprehend the consequences of that action. This is "intrinsic motivation" in its most basic form. It is best expressed when the environment is not threatening and when the body's needs have been satisfied. It takes its strength from the early attachment to the parents and wanes greatly when they are not available for this purpose (Harlow, 1962; Skeels, 1966; Spitz, 1962).

I believe the use of incentives in the home should come part and parcel with a conception of how to work with what is already there. They should be used to *enhance* intrinsic motivation whenever this is possible and to work in concert with the organism's natural capacity for learning. They should serve the goal of competence. This can be done using extrinsic incentives including rewards, but we must never lose sight of the fact that it is the organism's own control and mastery that is at the heart of the endeavor. With this thought in mind, let us turn to the question of how and why incentives are used in the schools.

SCHOOLS

In schools, the problem of the use of incentives is more complicated than in the home. For one thing, the most common use of incentives in the home is to produce an inhibition or induce compliance to a demand for obedience; whereas in the schools, by far the most common use is to motivate learning. In addition, schools use incentives more systematically than do parents; and within the system of schools, in the United States at least, there is less variation in the use of incentives than in homes.

Finally, there has been a powerful trend in schooling to "modularize" learning, to break down a skill—say, reading—into its component parts and teach the abstract parts. This gives rise to a problem of motivation not usually found in the home. What we will do is to look at what the schools are attempting to accomplish with the use of incentives, at why "motivation" is such a problem, and then see if the research outlined in this book and elsewhere has a bearing on this problem.

If one views education through the historian's inverted telescope, what one sees from the past leading up to the present is a steady and unswerving increase in "abstract" learning and a steady decrease in the learning of specific skills in a context in which they are meaningful. Of course, most skills in life are still learned by either practice or observation of a skilled model, as we have noted; but in school this paradigm has been abandoned in favor of early abstraction and modularization. This is a problem identified by Bruner (1974b) as the *decontextualization* of knowledge. Abstract skills are taught that are recognized to have wide application, but these skills are taught in circumstances far removed from those in which they will be used and by persons with whom the "student" typically has little relationship. Although these changes in schooling may have readied much of the population for technological changes, they have come at a high cost. The central problem in a system of decontextualized education is "motivation." To see this problem in perspective, let us look at motivation in the acquisition of skills in everyday life and then contrast these circumstances with what happens in scbools.

The acquisition of skills in concrete (real-life) situations, as we have seen, is motivated partly by the basic human drive to explore, manipulate, and master the environment (Berlyne, 1966; Deci, 1975; Hunt, 1965) and partly by an awareness of the utility of these skills to the society in which one lives (Bruner, 1966). A child in a hunter–gatherer society, for example, is aware of the consequences both to himself and to his society of his developing skill as a competent, spear-throwing hunter. At least part of the motivation for developing that skill as far as he does is his knowledge of the long-range consequences of the activity. Moreover, this same child is able to monitor his progress in the process of "play" without much in the way of reinforcement from the adults around him, although their availability as models is clearly necessary. In fact, after reviewing "tens of thousands of feet" of film of the !Kung Bushmen (a modern-day hunter–gatherer tribe), Bruner (1974b) comments: "One virtually never finds an instance of teaching taking place outside the situation where the behavior to be learned is relevant. Nobody teaches away from the scene, as in a school setting. Indeed, there is nothing like a school [p. 31]."

In short, when skills are learned "in context," in the environmental niche in which they are relevant, the motivation for acquisition is "intrinsic," i.e., a primitive desire to explore and master the world of one's immediate surroundings. Skills so learned are sharpened by a desire for competence (White, 1959). The level of excellence finally achieved is at least partly a function of the social demands made for competence (in a specific skill) within the part of society in which one lives. The competence with which one uses spoken grammar, for example, is related primarily to the demands of the social group to which one is adapted, as G. B. Shaw noted in *Pygmalion*. It is not as if we *cannot* exert a tighter control over most of the skills we exercise; it is that we *need* not do so given the level of demand. Again, this appears to be true for most skills learned today, when they are learned out of school. When skills are modularized, however, when they are taken out of the context in which they are relevant, they lose these "intrinsically" motivating characteristics. It is often difficult to see the utility, relevance, or instrumentality of such abstract learning to one's life, and *motivation* then becomes a problem.

For the last century (cf. Cremin, 1961), educators have reacted to this problem by providing extrinsic incentives to supplant the usual intrinsic incentives of context-relevant learning. Fear (of the birch) was an early motivator, later to be replaced by rewards, or "positive" incentives. This represented an increase in freedom and was a radical departure and improvement over earlier, more brutal methods, yet motivation remains a central problem in our schools. Part of the reason for this concerns changes that have occurred in society in regard to the sheer numbers in school and the degree of acceptance of school authority. These are not discussed here except in passing. Another part of the reason for the failure of positive incentives to "motivate" school work, however, concerns the way these task-extrinsic incentives function in the learning process.

A great deal of evidence described in this book is relevant to the use of incentives in schools. Most of it focuses upon using rewards to encourage learning or school-type performance, and the evidence is not encouraging. Two broad classes of findings are described in other chapters: effects on "undermining" interest and effects on undermining the process and products of learning.

Within the context of school activity, the "lowering of interest" found in most of the early research on this topic has meaning. If we take the purpose of the educational system to be the internalization of intellectual skills, then the evidence cited throughout this book raises serious questions about the wisdom of using task-extrinsic rewards to accomplish this purpose. It is true that much of this research was done in laboratory settings, but there is confirming evidence from the school system where token economics have been in use for some time.

In fact, a token economy was introduced into the New York City school system in the 1820s by the Society for Progressive Education. The society objected to the use of corporal punishment to motivate and control behavior, so a system of rewards and fines was introduced and used for several years. The system was abandoned in the 1830s, because the trustees of the society came to feel these extrinsic incentives: "fostered a mercenary spirit" and were "more often rewarding the cunning that the meritorious" (Ravitch, 1974).

Recent experience is not much more encouraging. Kazdin and Bootzin (1972), in a review of the token economy literature, report that generalization of treatment effects is often not found: "Generally, removal of token reinforcements results in decrements in desirable responses and a return to baseline or near baseline levels of performance [p. 359]." David Greene's (1974) thesis (Greene, Sternberg, & Lepper, 1976) bears out this contention and establishes a link between the token economy literature and the literature described in this book on the hidden costs of reward. Garbarino (1975) also conducted a field study of cross-age tutoring and found the offer of a reward had "undermining" effects on the interaction between the tutor and the tutee, making the interaction more negative and resulting in poorer performance on a learning task for the tutee in the "reward" condition (see Condry & Chambers, Chapter 4).

Although most of these studies were conducted within schools, they do not usually compare *alternative* conceptions of how learning might proceed if rewards were not used. One such study comparing achievement in high school chemistry under a "directed" vs. "nondirected" program was done by Rainey (1965); the results are instructive. The subjects were 124 high school seniors randomly assigned to "directed" and "nondirected" labs in a chemistry class. One group conducted laboratory experiments "on their own" with no direction other than test material and notes from class discussion; the other group performed the same 16 experiments with "detailed instructions and direction." Both groups attended the same class lectures and discussions. The dependent variables included conventional written tests of achievement and performance in laboratory tasks. No differences were found between the two groups on the conventional written tests (none were expected because both groups took the same lectures and discussion groups), but significant differences favoring the nondirected groups were found on a test of laboratory performance. In addition to the measurable factors, Rainey reports the following observations:

1. Students in the nondirected group consistently produced better write-ups of experiments than those in the directed group.
2. The nondirected group took longer to adjust to the style (which is hardly surprising given the "directed" nature of most other school work), but this initial resistance gave way to "considerable pride in being able to carry through with this sort of procedure."
3. Although the nondirected group started in an unsystematic and chaotic way, often looking for shortcut methods, " . . . by the end of the year it became necessary to hurry them along. On occasion they were spending extra laboratory periods checking results that could have been accepted without extra work" (Rainey, 1965, p. 11).

These studies, taken together with the other research presented in this book, lead us to conclude that the use of extrinsic rewards to motivate learning or to train children may have a variety of undesirable side effects. In the home, powerful extrinsic demands appear to undermine the development of exploratory skills when compared to conditions of less extrinsic pressure. In the schools, these same extrinsic incentives do not have the expected effect of motivating learning. Instead, they seem to produce a superficial interaction with the task and less subsequent interest in pursuing it. If we are to utilize these findings to improve education, however, much more information is needed about how to develop an alternative system. The research presented in this book suggests we should encourage the use of exploratory or intrinsic motivation as much as possible in the schools as an alternative to the system of task-extrinsic rewards now utilized. It is clear, however, that this is not enough. If children are to be able to use their inherent abilities to manipulate and explore the world, the schools will have to make available interesting and coherent worlds for them to explore. In short, what is needed is not just more "freedom" from control but a different conception of how it might be accomplished in the school context.

The method of teaching that "encourages" by demanding attention and grading performance, the system of motivating by the use of task-extrinsic rewards and incentives, is simply not an efficient way to teach the human being. Human beings have evolved more complex and subtle forms of learning that are more and far better internalized than that which is obtained in extrinsic demand contexts by "training" and direction. What is learned when learning is abstracted, modularized, and motivated by grades is not well learned in the sense of being internalized; and it is often *alienated* from the self, because it is so little related to the willful actions of the self. To turn these facts around, we will need to take a greater interest in the way in which people take active control over what they do and in the way mastery and competence develop in the human being. Clearly this is a concept of primary concern in the schools. James Coleman, for example, in a massive study of factors affecting schooling, found that self-concept and a feeling of control account for more variance in performance in grades 9 through 12 than any other family background or school characteristic (Coleman, Campbell, Hobson, McPartland, Mood, Weinfeld, and York, 1966). Regardless of what techniques of instruction we develop for the schools, it is clear they should not detract from these feelings of control and mastery. We need to ask what institutions can do to take advantage of intrinsic motivation in its variety of forms; and before we can do that, we need to discuss what other learning processes exist and are utilized by the human being.

I have presented only a very small part of the picture here. Rather than tally up research in which rewards have and have not been used, I have tried to make several points about the way any system of incentives should function, given basic organismic needs and capacities. I have suggested that even from the first moment of life, the human being does not need to be trained or motivated from without in order to learn. What is needed is a contingent and responsive social environment in which growth and development may take place. We need to be able to act in the world and to observe the relationship between our actions and our outcomes. We need to develop preexisting exploratory skills. This is the beginning of active control and mastery. As the child grows older, direct experience in learning is joined by observational learning (Bruner, 1974b), or modelling (Bandura & Walters, 1963). That is, eventually we become capable of learning by simply seeing another person *do,* without the intervention of environmental outcomes directed toward ourselves. I suspect this new form of learning greatly expands the range of adaptation that we may accomplish, and it appears to be relatively unique to primates and man. Finally, we learn by hearing another person tell us how to do something or by reading about it, and this set of (linguistic) skills *is* unique to human beings. At least we seem to have taken it to rather unique extremes. It is also the most advanced form of learning and the most dependent upon acquired (as opposed to preexisting) skills. It may be noted that this last form of learning offers the widest possible adaptation; once it is developed, it is possible to learn from what people may tell us of their experience without having to observe them encountering that experience and without doing it ourselves. For this reason, I have called it the most advanced form of learning. It is a higher order capacity appearing late in the evolutionary scheme that allows a very great range of adaptive behavior.

These three forms of competency—exploratory learning, observational learning, and linguistic learning—exhaust, I believe, the basic learning capacities of the human organism. Each capacity undoubtedly flourishes in some environments, as we saw with exploratory skills, and does poorly when the environment is insensitive to the organism's basic needs and abilities. Most of what we have discussed in this chapter bears on the first of these forms of competency. In fact, most of the research in this book focuses on direct learning and direct environmental feedback. What additional prerequisites may be needed to learn by observation and language I have not discussed; but I do suggest that the role of self-directed activity and feelings of control are much the same, regardless of the type of learning under consideration. The role of the environment in providing feedback is also unspecified in this discussion except in general terms, and a substantial additional analysis is required to be complete.

Such a detailed analysis of the environment is beyond the limitations of this chapter, but a word of warning is in order. Discussions of the detrimental effects of rewards often lead to the erroneous conclusion that no feedback (or only positive feedback) from the environment is what is required for development to proceed "naturally." Nothing could be further from the truth. Growing up in an environment where no feedback follows a response can lead the human being to become just as helpless as growing up in an environment where the feedback is rigidly programmed and intense. What we must keep dead center in our minds is that it is the child's developing *control* of the world that must be encouraged and promoted, and any system of incentives that does not undermine this control is acceptable within the value system I have outlined.

I have argued that what the human being must acquire in the course of development are basic learning skills. These involve skills of exploration, observation, and language. For these skills to be useful, they must be "internalized." That is, they must be under the active direction and control of the individual. The research in this book speaks to the ways in which systems of rewards, in some uses, undermine the internalization of skills primarily by undermining the perception of control and efficacy. But this research is not enough, as I have indicated. Before these findings are applicable, we need to know a great deal more about the basic learning capacities of the human being and how these capacities interact with what is available in the environment.

To answer the question of "how" we will educate our young, either in the home or the school, I believe we will need to state the problem differently than we have in the past. For the last century we have conceptualized the problem of how to teach by looking for ways of "motivating" individuals. As we have seen, this issue in turn derives from the way we have chosen to abstract and "modularize" learning, especially in schools. But if children, as this chapter suggests, have adequate mechanisms of "motivation," then the problem of education becomes: How do we best arrange a coherent, intelligent, and responsive *environment* in which discovery and learning may occur?

We may not be able to assure that each individual becomes "competent," given the difficulty of attaining this goal; but at the very least, we should not make people *helpless* by the use of well-intentioned procedures designed to motivate them.

I think we should worry less about whether our children are motivated to learn, in both the home and the school, and worry more about what kind of a world we are making available for them to learn about. If it is not interesting, coherent, stimulating, and useful, then we cannot expect much to be learned from it, no matter how hard we try to motivate or what incentives we try to use. The most important focus of our attention must be on how we can facilitate the development of basic skills while at the same time encouraging the development of feelings of control and efficacy that lie at the heart of intrinsic motivation.

ACKNOWLEDGMENTS

The author gratefully acknowledges permission to quote from Blackman & Silberman (1971) on p. 182 of this volume.

REFERENCES

Ainsworth, M. D. S., Bell, S. M., & Stayton, D. J. Infant–mother attachment and social development: Socialization as a product of reciprocal responsiveness to signals. In Martin P. M. Richards, (Ed.), *The integration of the child into a social world.* London: Cambridge University Press, 1974.

Aronson, E., & Carlsmith, J. M. Effect of the severity of threat on the valuation of forbidden behavior. *Journal of Abnormal and Social Psychology,* 1963, *66,* 584–588.

Bandura, A. and Walters, R. H. *Social learning and personality development.* New York· Holt, Rinehart, & Winston 1963

Baumrind, D. Effects of authoritative parental control on child behavior. *Child Development,* 1966, *37,* 888–907.

Baumrind, D. Child care preactices anteceding three patterns of preschool behavior. *Genetic Psychology Monographs,* 1967, *4*(1), 43–88.

Bell, S. M., & Ainsworth, M. D. S. Infant crying and maternal responsiveness. *Child Development,* 1972, *43,* 1171–1190.

Berlyne, D. F. Curiosity and exploration. *Science,* 1966, *153,* 25–33.

Blackham, G. J., & Silberman, A. *Modification of child behavior.* California: Wadsworth, 1971.

Boykin, A. W. Experimental psychology from a black perspective: Issues and examples. *Journal of Black Studies,* in press.

Bruner, J. S. *Toward a theory of instruction.* Cambridge: Harvard University Press, 1966.

Bruner, J. S. The organization of early skilled action. In Martin P. M. Richards (Ed.), *The integration of the child into a social world.* London: Cambridge University Press, 1974. (a)

Bruner, J. S. Nature and uses of immaturity. In K. Connally & J. S. Bruner (Eds), *The growth of competence.* New York: Academic Press, 1974. (b)

Carlsmith, J. M., Ebbesen, E. B., Lepper, M. R., Zanna, M. P., Joncas, A. J., & Abelson, R. P. Dissonance reduction following forced attention to the dissonance. *Proceedings of the American Psychological Association,* 1969, *4,* 321–322.

Coleman, J. S., Campbell, E. Q., Hobson, C.J., McPartland, J., Mood, A. M., Weinfeld, F. D., and

York, R. L. *Equality of educational opportunity.* Washington, D.C.: U.S. Department of Health, Education and Welfare, Office of Education, 1966.

Crandall, V. J., Katkovsky, W., & Preston, A. Motivational and ability determinants of young children's intellectual achievement behaviors. *Child Development,* 1962, *33,* 643–661.

Cremin, L. A. *The transformation of the school.* New York: Vintage Books (Random House), 1961.

Deci, E. L. *Intrinsic motivation.* New York: Plenum, 1975.

Freedman, J. L. Long-term behavioral effects of cognitive dissonance. *Journal of Experimental Social Psychology,* 1965, *1,* 145–155.

Garbarino, J. The impact of anticipated rewards on cross-age tutoring. *Journal of Personality and Social Psychology,* 1975, *32,* 421–428.

Greene, D., Sternberg, B., & Lepper, M. Overjustification in a token economy. *Journal of Personality and Social Psychology,* 1976, *34,* 1219–1234.

Harlow, H. F. The heterosexual affectional system in monkeys. *American Psychologist,* 1962, *17,* 1–9.

Hunt, J. McV. Intrinsic motivation and its role in psychological development. *Nebraska Symposium on Motivation,* 1965, *13,* 89–282.

Kazdin, A. E., & Bootzin, R. R. The token economy: An evaluative review. *Journal of Applied Behavior Analysis,* 1972, *5,* 343–372.

Kelley, H. H. The processes of causal attribution. *American Psychologist,* 1973, *28,* 107–128.

Lepper, M. R., Greene, D., & Nisbett, R. E. Undermining children's intrinsic interest with extrinsic rewards: A test of the overjustification hypothesis. *Journal of Personality and Social Psychology,* 1973, *28.* 129–137.

Pepitone, A., McCauley, C., & Hammond, P. Change in attractiveness of forbidden toys as a function of severity of threat. *Journal of Experimental Social Psychology,* 1967, *3,* 221–229.

Rainey, R. G. The effects of directed vs. non-directed laboratory work on high school chemistry achievement. *Journal of Research in Science Teaching,* 1965, *3,* 286–292.

Ravitch, D. *The great school wars.* New York: Basic Books, 1974.

Schiller, P. H. Innate constituents of complex responses in primates. *Psychological Review,* 1952, *59,* 177–191.

Sears, R. R., Maccoby, E., & Levin, H. *Patterns of child rearing.* New York: Harper, 1975.

Skeels, H. M. Adult status of children with contrasting early life experiences. *Monograph for Social Research in Child Development,* 1966, *31,* 3.

Spitz, R. A. Hospitalism: An inquiry into the genesis of psychiatric conditions in early childhood. In R. S. Eissler, (Eds.), *The psychoanalytic study of the child* (3rd ed., Vol. 1). New York: International University Press, 1962.

Stayton, D. J., Hogan, R. T., & Ainsworth, M. D. S. Infant obedience and maternal behavior: The origins of socialization reconsidered. *Child Development,* 1971, *42,* 1057–1069.

Watson, J. B. *Psychological care of infant and child.* New York: W. W. Norton, 1928.

White, R. W. Motivation reconsidered: The concept of competence. *Psychological Review,* 1959, *66,* 297–333.

Zanna, M. P., Lepper, M. R., & Abelson, R. P. Attentional mechanisms in children's devaluation of a forbidden activity in a forced compliance situation. *Journal of Personality and Social Psychology,* 1973, *3,* 355–359.

9 Applications of Research on the Effects of Rewards

Edward L. Deci
University of Rochester

When psychologists step out of their ivory towers to make prescriptive statements about the best way to do something, there is considerable potential for debate, confusion, and emotionality. Some topics will create more of this, others will create less. Statements about the utility or disutility of extrinsic rewards and controls are—for a variety of reasons—likely to create more rather than less.

We are all concerned about *controlling* others: controlling our children so they'll behave themselves; controlling our students so they'll learn what we think they should learn; controlling our workers so they'll produce more and we'll make more profits; controlling our legislators so they'll vote in ways we want. It is not surprising therefore that information about the use of rewards for controlling or motivating behavior is of interest to most people.

THE APPLICATION OF RESEARCH FINDINGS

The research and theorizing that are presented in the previous section of this book point to the conclusion that extrinsic rewards, whether money, praise, good player awards, or gold stars—under varying circumstances—have deleterious effects on the intrinsic motivation and performance of the rewardee. In this chapter I consider the possible implications and applications of this conclusion for prescriptions about education, managerial motivation, child-rearing practices, and psychotherapy.

It has very important implications. It suggests, for example, that many of the widespread practices and many of the widely espoused prescriptions for using extrinsic rewards to motivate people don't work the way the practitioners and prescribers expect them to. This does not mean that rewards don't motivate behavior nor that they should not be used in certain situations; it simply means that there are certain unintended consequences to the use of extrinsic rewards that deserve consideration. Whether or not rewards should be used is a complex question, as the use of rewards has both advantages and disadvantages. A decision about whether to use rewards necessitates an understanding of the trade-offs that come into play and an evaluation of these trade-offs in light of one's values.

VALUES AND ASSUMPTIONS

When psychologists do venture into the arena of prescribing, they carry with them two bags, the contents of which are inextricably related to each other. The first bag contains empirical findings (which were gathered using scientific methodology) and theories (which must conform to criteria such as logical consistency). The other bag contains their own values and assumptions, which may or may not be clear to them. The first bag usually gets emphasized, and often people think that prescriptions are simply logical derivations from research and theory. They are not. Psychologists' values and assumptions come into play in ways that are much more important than is typically recognized.

Underlying Assumptions

Theory and research in psychology derives in part from a set of basic assumptions about human nature. These assumptions play a critical role both in the interpretation of data and subsequently in the formulation of prescriptions. For example, many psychologists assume that there is no such thing as intrinsic motivation and that all behavior is caused by reinforcements and environmental contingencies. I, on the other hand, assume that there is such a thing as intrinsic motivation and that behavior is caused by motivational, affective, and cognitive processes within the person. Thus, when I observed that subjects who were rewarded extrinsically for working on an interesting puzzle activity spent less of their free-choice time working on the activity than did subjects who had done the activity for no reward, I interpreted the result as evidence that extrinsic rewards decreased the subject's intrinsic motivation for working with the puzzle activity. I then offered a prescription for decreasing reward contingencies so that people would be freer to pursue activities out of intrinsic interest. Other psychologists have criticized both the interpretation and the prescription (cf. Scott, 1976), because they begin with the assumption that there is no such thing as intrinsic motivation. These psychologists explain the decreased responding by saying that another response that competes or interferes with the puzzle activity was inadvertently reinforced, and they offer prescriptions for restructuring the reinforcement contingencies. Both the theoretical interpretations and the prescriptions are profoundly affected by starting with different philosophical assumptions.

Personal Values

Psychologists' *values* also affect the prescriptions they make. To prescribe that one way is the *best* way to do something requires that the word *best* have some meaning; that meaning derives from people's values.

When a prescription (such as for the use or nonuse of certain extrinsic-reward systems) is instituted, there are likely to be a variety of ramifications, which form the basis for evaluating the prescription. In other words, the manipulation of an independent variable is evaluated by considering the consequent changes in relevant dependent variables. First, one must decide whether each dependent change is preferred or dispreferred. There is often considerable disagreement on whether specific dependent changes are desirable, and this disagreement is a reflection of different underlying values. For example, the research reported in this book points to the conclusion that rewarding children for engaging in interesting activities such as playing or learning will decrease their intrinsic motivation for those activities. Using these findings to prescribe, for example, that schools should put less emphasis on the use of extrinsic rewards depends on how much people value intrinsic motivation. Whereas I place very high value on the creativity, spontaneity, and vitality that are involved with intrinsic motivation, others find such concerns to be frivolous and annoying. Our values are different, so we judge the importance of intrinsic motivation differently.

Because there are usually several different ramifications to any given prescriptive change, values also play a critical role in combining the evaluations of each dependent change. Some dependent changes will be desired, others not desired. Thus, there are trade-offs between various outcomes, and the judgment of these trade-offs depends on people's values.

Consider this anecdote. For centuries artists of the Middle and Far East have been hand-weaving oriental rugs. They have done this in traditional ways that reflect the beauty of their heritage and of themselves as individuals. In the late 19th century and increasingly up to the present, the Western consumers and business people have used money and other controls to exert influence on the rug weavers. Wool is now being spun by machine rather than by hand; rugs are more uniform in color, design, and size; chemical processes are used to treat the color and sheen of the rugs. Weavers have become more extrinsically oriented, and the rugs are very different. It has been said that modern rugs seem to come from the *hands* of the weavers, whereas the older rugs seem to have come from the *hearts* of the weavers. New rugs are more suited to the modern, interior decorating requirements of wealthy consumers, but they have lost much of their beauty, depth, and individuality.

As the orientation of the weavers has changed from intrinsic to extrinsic, the nature of the output has changed. On one hand, the rugs are now more uniform and are produced more quickly. On these grounds many people would rejoice over the way that extrinsic rewards have affected rug production. But I'm quite disappointed by these changes. The old rugs are far more pleasing to me, and I deeply regret the way in which the extrinsic influences have affected the output. The experiences of the weavers also seem to be different; whereas they used to be more involved in the experience of creating works of art, they now have jobs of producing rugs. Thus, we have isolated several changes: greater uniformity, different colors, less individuality, quicker production, and so on. Each change can be evaluated and the evaluations combined. Some people's values lead them to favor the overall change in the procedures, for even if they don't like some of the dependent changes, there are trade-offs that they are willing to accept. I don't like the procedural changes, because I evaluate most of the ramifications negatively. I would prescribe reverting to earlier methods and trade off quicker production, which is the only dependent change that I evaluate positively.

Personal experience.   In evaluating prescriptions, the dependent changes that receive most attention are output variables, whereas personal experience variables tend to receive relatively little attention. Recently, Csikszentmihalyi (1975) has discussed in detail the phenomenological experience of intrinsically versus extrinsically motivated people. Intrinsically motivated people seem to experience an inner "flow," a highly pleasurable sensation in which they experience a loss of self-consciousness and their attention is focused on the immediate interchange between them and the activity. In May's (1967) terms, they are experiencing themselves as subjects rather than objects. I place high value on the *personal experience* of being intrinsically motivated. It is an experience that I think is important to find in education, in organizations, in social interactions, in play. It is, I believe, important for psychological well-being. Yet many people fail to pay attention to it in their evaluations of educational programs or work settings. Schools are generally said to be good if students do well on achievement tests; no mention is made of whether they enjoy the learning or experience themselves as competent, self-determining, or excited by school. Industrial organizations are generally said to be good if the shareholders make large profits; no mention is made of whether the workers are alienated or whether they are able to experience a sense of accomplishment from their work (cf. Chapter 10).

I think the personal experience of students and workers should be given greater attention. It is part of the trade-off system that has generally been traded off with scarcely a second thought. Only when people's experiences are given much greater attention will we be able to structure institutions that stand a good chance of yielding both satisfying experiences and good performance.

The use of data.   Values also affect the types of data we use in making prescriptions. Criteria must be established that are used in deciding whether some piece of knowledge has been established. As scientists we place central importance on data and on replicability of experimental findings. Doing so, however, has led to our ignoring much valuable data because our methods of collection are still crude. Intrinsic motivation is an area in which the price for strict experimental standards has been high, because personal experience, psychological well-being, and willfulness (or self-determination) are integrally related to intrinsic motivation; yet the still imprecise experimental methodologies and the values of scientists have tended to keep these important matters in the background. In short, I'm suggesting that offering prescriptions related to intrinsic motivation may have important ramifications that we as psychologists have still tended to ignore because of difficulties in collecting relevant data. Thus, the prescriptions are likely to be more value laden and affectively toned than those in many other areas of psychology.

THE FINDINGS AND THEIR APPLICATIONS

The research reported in the preceding chapters has established that:

1. Extrinsic rewards that are salient and contingent upon performing an activity tend to decrease people's intrinsic motivation for doing interesting activities (cf. Chapters 6 and 7).
2. However, when extrinsic rewards are used so that they primarily convey information that a person is competent and self-determining and they aren't intended as controllers of behavior, they tend to enhance rather than undermine intrinsic motivation (cf. Chapter 7).
3. Extrinsic rewards tend to impair people's performance on open-ended activities such as problem solving (cf. Chapters 3 and 4).
4. However, extrinsic rewards tend to improve performance on routine, well-learned activities (cf. Chapter 3).

In addition to these findings, people have speculated that rewards hinder the experience of being intrinsically motivated (Csikszentmihalyi, 1975), that they may impair one's sense of willfulness and well-being if one has no control over the contingencies (Deci, 1978; Seligman, 1975), and that they could awaken people's intrinsic motivation for an activity if they lead people to activities they had never tried or if they help people to develop a level of competence necessary to enjoy the activity (Lepper, Greene, & Nisbett, 1973).

We see therefore that rewards have uses and disuses. Knowing the above effects of rewards, one might readily prescribe the use or nonuse of rewards for a specific person in a specific situation. To get a person to do an uninteresting task now, extrinsic rewards will surely help. To maintain a child's curiosity, don't attempt to control learning with contingent extrinsic rewards. Difficulties in prescribing occur, however, because prescriptions generally apply to many people, often in varying situations, and so many ramifications are involved.

For example, most people value having children be intrinsically motivated to learn. Yet, when students are learning out of intrinsic motivation, they will be learning at their own speed and they will be learning the things that interest them—perhaps poetry, carpentry, or history. Intrinsically motivated learning will involve trial and error, following one's curiosity, feeling free to learn what interests one, developing one's potential as one experiences it. When teachers and parents decide what things children must learn and at what pace they must learn them, this is fundamentally at contradiction with the idea of having children be intrinsically motivated to learn. Intrinsic motivation implies self-direction; thus, if people think that the directing must be done largely by the teachers, then they are placing other values above the value of having children be intrinsically motivated to learn. Trade-offs must be made in these multidimensional situations, and values determine who trades off what. I place high value on intrinsic motivation and self-direction. One of my central goals in teaching and doing therapy is for the people with whom I work to experience an increase in choice and autonomy and to enhance their sense of self-determination. Thus, for me, this value would override my desire for more standardized (and easier to manage) education.

The matter of prescribing procedures based on the experimental findings is clearly quite complex; still, I should like to make a few summary statements and to look briefly at the intrinsically oriented versus extrinsically oriented methods that have been tried in education, management, and psychotherapy.

First, extrinsic rewards do have potential for motivating people to do many things. They won't always work, as people sometimes react against constraints or opt for paths that provide more freedom and less extrinsic pay-off. Still, rewards do often serve to control behavior. Further, they can often make situations more uniform and manageable, because rewards can be administered selectively. However, though performance may be facilitated on routine or well-learned tasks, it tends to be impaired on open-ended problems that require creativity and resourcefulness (cf. Chapter 3). In addition, rewards tend to undermine people's intrinsic motivation for the rewarded activity (cf. Chapters 6 and 7).

To use an intrinsically oriented system—whether for education, management, or whatever—the people must be intrinsically motivated to do the target activity. Hence, rewarding people for doing dull, boring activities will have fewer costs than rewarding them for doing interesting and challenging activities as there is less intrinsic motivation to be undermined. In fact, rewards will generally be necessary to motivate people to engage in an uninteresting activity unless the situation can be restructured to make it more interesting.

Although extrinsic rewards generally decrease intrinsic motivation, this need not be so if rewards are used simply as carriers of positive information about one's effectance rather than as controllers of behavior. Rewards carry information about people's competence and self-determination, and if this aspect of rewards is more salient than the controlling aspect, intrinsic motivation may be maintained or enhanced rather than undermined (cf. Chapter 7). Generally, I suspect that rewards are intended as controls rather than as sources of information, yet reward systems which emphasize feedback and are responsive to competence and self-determination will work quite differently from more authoritarian reward systems.

Within the various applied areas, people have proposed systems that are extrinsically oriented and others that are intrinsically oriented. I now outline these systems very briefly and then consider the implications of the research in this volume for these various areas.

Education.   Traditionally, schools have been very extrinsically oriented. Teachers and administrators decide what should be taught, at what speed it should be taught, how the children should demonstrate that they've learned it, and so on. Further, the schools employ a wide range of extrinsic-control systems: grades, gold stars, detention, rankings. They have neither recognized nor encouraged the children's natural curiosity.

· There have, however, been some people who have called for systems that are more intrinsically oriented. The Summerhill school in England (Neill, 1960) has been in existence for several decades and is the archetype of the free or progressive school. The assumption underlying Neill's approach to education is that people are intrinsically curious and will be motivated to learn if they are in a system that is supportive and encourages them to try what interests them. This freedom for exploration allows them to trust and strengthen their own inner direction and responsiveness. Other critics of traditional education (e.g., Bruner, 1962; Holt, 1964; Montessori, 1967) have also asserted that extrinsic rewards may destroy the love of learning or convey that the material is not worth learning for its own sake. Much of the research presented in this book is in agreement with these assertions. Rewards have been shown to hinder performance on interesting activities such as problem solving. Further, unless they are used primarily to convey information, they undermine children's intrinsic motivation for the rewarded activity.

The approach to education that focuses systematically on extrinsic rewards is the token economy program. Here children are rewarded with tokens whenever they emit target behaviors. The tokens may in turn be cashed in for desired rewards such as candy. This approach, which has developed out of operant conditioning, is aimed at bringing desired behaviors under the functional control of rewards. However, Greene, Sternberg, and Lepper (1976) found that when they employed a token economy program with children in a math program, many of the rewarded children tended to lose intrinsic motivation for math activities.

Frequently, token economies are used in very disruptive classrooms—ones where little learning is going on anyway. In these situations some programs have succeeded in making classes more orderly. This is no small achievement in its own right. However, these immediate improvements typically don't generalize to other situations (Meichenbaum, Bowers, & Ross, 1968), and when the tokens are no longer operative the target behaviors usually return to baseline or may drop below baseline (Johnson, Bolstad, & Lobitz, 1976).

In most classes disruption and unruliness are not predominant problems. Further, in some cases the disruption that exists may be a response to the over-control of the system. The more normal, less disruptive classrooms are well suited to methods that are more intrinsically and less extrinsically oriented. Children will be taking greater part in their own learning, they will be doing better on creative problem solving, and they will be maintaining or strengthening their natural curiosity. Further, I suspect that there will be less disruption, because the children will have the opportunity to pursue what interests them.

Work organizations.   American industry has also been very extrinsically oriented. In early years, slaves were owned, and other employees—though not actually owned—might as well have been. Employers saw fit to prescribe how their employees should behave on and off the job, and they used extrinsic rewards to assure the required behavior. In this tradition, Taylor (1911) developed a system called *scientific management,* which has had a profound impact on work organizations. This approach is very extrinsic in its orientation. It assumes that workers are passive—even lazy and indolent—and that the only way to get effective performance is through tightly controlled reward systems. This is typically operationalized by piece-rate payment plans in which people's weekly wages depend directly on how many units of output they produced that week. Other reward structures in the world of work that have developed out of the same philosophy include sales commissions and bonus plans—the idea being to improve performance through the use of extrinsic rewards which are contingent on performance.

In the last two decades, managerial theorizing has begun to change. There has been a recognition that intrinsic motivation exists and can have important ramifications for the effectiveness of an organization. *Participative* or *Theory Y management* has evolved as a basis for understanding the management process (McGregor, 1960). This approach focuses on structuring the work situation so that employees will motivate themselves out of a desire to be competent and self-determining. There is an attempt to combine rather than separate the planning of a job and the doing of that job. In other words, workers are given much greater participation in making decisions that directly affect them, because it is clear that people become more involved with and committed to decisions they've helped to make than they do to decisions that are made by superiors and with which they are expected to comply.

The design of jobs has also been the focus of considerable attention in the literature of organizational behavior. Jobs are being redesigned to be enriched or enlarged (Myers, 1970) so that employees not only have greater autonomy but also more variety in the tasks they undertake. Research has indicated that the newer approaches to management that pay greater attention to intrinsic motivation are generally more successful (Likert, 1967) in that employee morale is higher and performance of the organization is more effective. Of course, all situations do not lend themselves to intrinsically oriented systems, because many jobs are uninteresting and difficult to redesign. In these situations, controlling reward systems can work effectively, particularly when they are used to reflect efficacy.

Psychotherapy.   The concept and conclusions we have discussed so far also have direct relevance to the field of psychotherapy. The aim of psychotherapy is of course different, depending on both the treatment approach and the individual therapist; yet all approaches seem to be working toward having the patient or client behave more adaptively. This means creating behavior changes that persist outside the therapy session and continue following termination of the treatment.

For me, that aim translates into "fostering self-determination and self-responsibility." Some approaches to therapy would not, however, accept that translation. The aim of behavior therapy (or behavior modification) is generally stated simply as "to produce desired behaviors." Behavior modification, having developed largely out of a reinforcement paradigm, is concerned with establishing reinforcement contingencies that will elicit the desired behaviors. It is at this point that the research reported in this book becomes directly relevant. When rewards or other extrinsic controls are relied on to produce behavior change, there is a high probability that the behavior will become dependent on those rewards and will not persist in the absence of rewards. Thus, it is critical that the therapeutic process involve a minimum of extrinsic rewards or controls in order to encourage the patients or clients to take the responsibility for their behavior and to act in ways that allow them to achieve their desired outcomes.

Dienstbier and Leak (1976) reported a study with obese subjects who were either rewarded or not rewarded with monetary payments for losing weight. Following the experimental period, subjects were observed for a 5-month period in which the investigators reported that the paid subjects gained weight, whereas the nonpaid subjects continued to lose. These differences confirm the finding that extrinsic rewards tend to undermine internal control so that when the rewards are no longer present, the desired behaviors cease. Here the paid subjects not only did not continue to lose weight; they were even unable to maintain the losses they had achieved during the treatment phase. This study, therefore, lends further support to the conclusion that the therapeutic process will be most effective when the desired behaviors are achieved with the least possible use of external rewards and controls.

This of course does not mean that behavior modification is inappropriate in all situations. As with token economies, it can be very effective with people who have little intrinsic motivation when treatment begins. Further, behavior modification will be more useful when the monitoring is done by the person being reinforced. The important point is that care should be used in such programs so as not to use rewards in a way that will undermine the desired effect.

In discussing education, management, and therapy, I have briefly mentioned general approaches that focus on intrinsic versus extrinsic aspects of motivation. No system works best in all situations; and in fact, any situation might use aspects of both general approaches. That involves structuring situations to elicit intrinsic responding whenever possible. And rewards should be used primarily to convey competence information. In education and psychotherapy, rewards should be kept at the minimum level that will ensure the needed responding; whenever possible the target person should participate in establishing the contingencies, and when rewards are removed they should be withdrawn gradually so the people can develop internal controls to replace the external ones being removed.

Society.   The general conclusion that extrinsic rewards can undermine intrinsic motivation and internal control may have implications that are broader even than those I've been discussing. People in our society have lost much of their sense of inner direction; there is widespread alienation, and people seem to be striving unendingly for more status, power, and wealth than they realistically need. I interpret these behaviors as motivated by *substitute needs* that develop as replacement needs when people lose touch with the intrinsic satisfaction of competence and self-determination. From an early age, people's behaviors are so strongly governed by extrinsic rewards and controls that behavior becomes largely a pathway to extrinsic rewards rather than a means of satisfying interest or curiosity. I suspect that as rewards continue to co-opt intrinsic motivation and preclude intrinsic satisfaction, the extrinsic needs—for money, for power, for status—become stronger in themselves. Thus, people develop stronger extrinsic needs as substitutes for more basic, unsatisfied needs. Then they develop strong linkages between their behaviors and these needs, so they end up behaving as if they were addicted to extrinsic rewards (cf. Chapter 10).

I would like to see people become much more aware of intrinsic needs, to work toward the kind of inner peace that, I think, results from enhanced feelings of competence and self-determination and that makes the compulsive pushing (always to do more and accumulate more) fade in importance. While all this is speculation, it seems to me to be an extremely critical matter and one that deserves an enormous amount of attention.

REFERENCES

Bruner, J. *On knowing: Essays for the left hand.* Cambridge, Mass.: Harvard University Press, 1962.
Csikszentmihalyi, M. *Beyond boredom and anxiety.* San Francisco: Jossey–Bass, 1975.

Deci, E. L. Motivation, will, and well-being. Unpublished manuscript, 1978.

Dienstbier, R. A., & Leak, G. Effects of monetary reward on maintenance of weight loss: An extension of the overjustification effect. Paper presented at the meeting of the American Psychological Association, Washington, D.C., 1976.

Greene, D., Sternberg, B., & Lepper, M. R. Overjustification in a token economy. *Journal of Personality and Social Psychology,* 1976, *34,* 1219–1234.

Holt, J. *How children fail.* New York: Dell, 1964.

Johnson, S. M., Bolstad, O. D., & Lobitz, G. K. Generalization and contrast phenomena in behavior modification with children. In E. J. Marsh, L. A. Hamerlynck, & L. C. Handy (Eds.), *Behavior modification and families.* New York: Brunner/Mazel, 1976.

Lepper, M. R., Greene, D., & Nisbett, R. E. Undermining children's intrinsic interest with extrinsic rewards: A test of the "overjustification" hypothesis. *Journal of Personality and Social Psychology,* 1973, *28,* 129–137.

Likert, R. *The human organization.* New York: McGraw–Hill, 1967.

May, R. *Psychology and the human dilemma.* New York: VanNostrand & Reinhold, 1967.

McGregor, D. *The human side of enterprise.* New York: McGraw–Hill, 1960.

Meichenbaum, D. H., Bowers, K. S., & Ross, R. R. Modification of classroom behavior of institutionalized female adolescent offenders. *Behavior Research and Theory,* 1968, *6,* 343–353.

Montessori, M. *The discovery of the child.* New York: Ballantine, 1967.

Myers, M. S. *Every employee a manager.* New York: McGraw–Hill, 1970.

Neill, A. S. *Summerhill: A radical approach to child rearing.* New York: Hart, 1960.

Scott, W. E. The effects of extrinsic rewards on "intrinsic motivation": A critique. *Organizational Behavior and Human Performance,* 1976, *15,* 117–129.

Seligman, M. E. P. *Helplessness.* San Francisco: Freeman, 1975.

Taylor, F. W. *Principles of scientific management.* New York: Harper, 1911.

10 Intrinsic Rewards and Emergent Motivation

Mihaly Csikszentmihalyi
University of Chicago

In the 1930s, a famous American psychologist was quoted as saying that he didn't understand why people were interested in motivation when it was so obvious that money was the source of all incentive. His opinion has the ring of truth, it is generally supported by experience, and it has the pragmatic directness that makes much sense in a culture based on pragmatic assumptions. No wonder most people would agree that the long and the short of the matter is that men and women will or won't do things depending on the money—or other extrinsic rewards or punishments—they get. Our social institutions, from nursery schools to jobs, are built on this belief. It is also the assumption underlying the main psychological theories currently in use.

There is no doubt that this assumption corresponds to reality. Extrinsic rewards and punishments do motivate people to act. Yet the fact that extrinsic rewards are motivating is not in itself enough to satisfy a scientist's curiosity, famous psychologists and popular opinion notwithstanding. To use the analogy of a case where the truth appears to be similarly clear-cut, it is true that no matter how often we look around us, the surface of the earth will appear to be lying on a plane. The flat-earth assumption is "true" for almost all conditions of observation; it corresponds to common sense and is perfectly adequate for building houses, roads, cities, and most bridges. Or let us take another example, closer to the topic we are discussing. Ever since mankind has existed, it seems, group disputes beyond a certain threshold have degenerated into violence. From this fact it has been inferred, among other things, that people are aggressive by nature, that war is inevitable, that martial behavior is good for the community, and so forth. Only recently have some people begun to question the inevitability of these truths: Perhaps if people were to remove themselves to some higher vantage point, the necessity of war would seem just as illusory as the flatness of the earth.

Returning to the issue of motivation and extrinsic rewards, scientific curiosity suggests a few questions about their apparently so obvious relationship. The first one, which the other authors in this volume have addressed, is: Do extrinsic rewards always increase performance, or do they sometimes serve to inhibit certain behaviors? This is a revolutionary question, long overdue, and one that will certainly have a strong impact on the future of psychology. In this context, however, I wish to raise some other issues that, although related to the central thesis of this book, may open up some new problems and new implications. Some of these questions are: Do people have to learn to respond to extrinsic rewards, or are we biologically programmed to obey them? If the response is learned, how flexible is the range of rewards that are rewarding? What are the sociocultural conditions that emphasize motivation through external rewards? What are the ones that deemphasize them?

And perhaps the central issue, which is: Why do we keep talking about rewards? Do people really behave to maximize rewards and minimize punishment? Should "reward" be our main motivational construct?

The most influential motivational theories—both those based on the concept of biological drive like the ones of Hull and Freud and the more cognitive perspectives of Tolman, Murray, or McClelland—assume that performance is directed to achieve some external state, either through reinforcement, habit, or the anticipation of a future "goal." For instance, the achievement motive is defined as a predisposition to compete against an internalized standard of excellence (McClelland, Atkinson, Clark, & Lowell, 1953), and the power motive is held to be a concern over controlling the means of influencing the behavior of another person (Veroff, 1975). Performance is always seen to be motivated by an external, future goal state—such as meeting a standard of excellence or getting control over other people. These models assume that the individual has stored somewhere a mental picture of a desirable goal state and that he or she will behave in relation to this internalized picture. The same assumption underlies the more recent cybernetic models of behavior (Miller, Galanter, & Pribram, 1960; Simon, 1967).

EMERGENT GOALS AND FIXED GOALS

Research on intrinsic motivation, however, suggests a somewhat different model. It reveals that a considerable proportion of behavior cannot be explained in terms of anticipated goals or rewards but rather in terms of goals and rewards that arise out of direct involvement with an ongoing activity. My argument here is that one of the hidden costs of reward has been a cost at the metatheoretical level: The obviousness of extrinsic rewards has made us assume that they are more prevalent and powerful than they really are, thereby blinding us to the existence of less visible causal factors in behavior. In the long run, however, these may be more important than extrinsic rewards are for understanding what man does now and what he could be doing in the future.

Research on intrinsic motivation has alerted us to the fact that people will work at tasks that offer nothing beyond the completion of the task itself. Even rats (Montgomery, 1954) and monkeys (Harlow, 1953) can sustain behavior motivated only by the solution of a puzzle. Children spend much of their time finding challenges and then trying to cope with them (de Charms, 1968; Piaget, 1957; White, 1959). The same is true for adults (Csikszentmihalyi, 1975b).

It is possible, of course, to say that all these behaviors fit the traditional models of motivation, because there must be rewards hidden in the activity itself. The only difference is that instead of coming after the completion of the activity, the rewards are much closer to the behavior itself; the feedback loops might be shorter, but there is no qualitative distinction between intrinsic and extrinsic rewards.

Yet it is also possible that "explaining away" intrinsic rewards in this fashion distorts their real nature. It is worth considering the possibility that a new model might be necessary to explain their existence.

In the first place, intrinsic motivation suggests an *open* model of the human (and primate) organism. In other words, much of what is intrinsically motivating cannot be predicted from known biological needs and drives or from socially learned reinforcement schedules. It is easy to explain why a person will respond to food or sex when deprived of them or why someone will work to obtain money or avoid pain. These extrinsic rewards operate within a *closed* system of positive and negative stimuli whose impact on the individual are biologically and socially overdetermined. But in addition to responding to these strongly programmed external signals, the organism is constantly busy defining neutral stimuli as rewarding. A large part of everyday behavior is directed toward goals that are not visualized as goals before the individual has completed his or her involvement with the task. Such behavior is usually not followed by any of the fixed rewards derived from a *closed* system, nor does it make much sense to claim that it is the association with previous rewards that sustains the behavior.

For instance, when small children begin to play with building blocks, they rarely have a plan or a goal to guide their actions. They will place the blocks more or less randomly next to or on top of each other until some combination of shapes suggests a particular form that the children will then seek to approximate—at this point we might say that they have a "goal" or plan to direct their actions. This goal will typically change with every new block they place along the others, as new possibilities are suggested by the developing structure. The reward that keeps the children going is the feedback that tells how closely they are able to match what they do with what they want to do. What is essential to keep in mind is that neither the goal nor the rewards could be specified in advance, because both emerge out of the interaction. In such a situation, we are in an *open* setting, and this is where intrinsic motivation becomes a powerful causal factor.

By simplifying the picture somewhat, one could say that a person's actions are always determined by two sets of motives. On one hand, he or she will act in terms of fixed goals and rewards, which are either programmed in the genotype (like food or sex) or are programmed in the reward structure of the culture into which he or she is socialized. Extrinsic rewards are motivating because one already knows that the stimulus one is about to get is supposed to be rewarding. "Viscerogenic" needs are something one cannot do much about; their satisfaction is rewarding because evolution has planned for us to experience them as such. Money, praise, status, and power have been defined as satisfying by society. To the extent one works for them, one submits to the determining forces in the environment. People who respond exclusively to extrinsic rewards spend their life energies in getting things they did not themselves decide they should want. On the other hand, one is also always involved in discovering new goals and rewards through interaction with subsets of the environment. When one acts in terms of these, we speak of intrinsic motivation. Intrinsic rewards work because a person decides, more or less autonomously, that a certain goal or stimulus *is* rewarding. These do not derive their motivating power from genetic evolution or social conditioning, but rather from what to the actor appears to be "free will"—that is, his or her decision that a certain outcome is worth striving for. The discovery of new goals and rewards introduces a qualitatively different element in behavior: It defines the *emergent* state of the organism, which in its extreme forms leads to what we usually call creativity.

In a recently concluded longitudinal study of painters and sculptors, for instance, we found that young artists who usually knew what they wanted to do before they started to work ended up producing art that was considerably less original than the paintings made by artists who approached each canvas without knowing in advance what they were going to do. This latter group, who succeeded in becoming recognized as artists, typically discovered their goal in any given painting only after they had become involved with the painting itself. Their emotions and thoughts coalesced into a plan of work only after they had seen the results of their initially almost random and tentative brush strokes. In fact, original artists usually discovered the plan of their work after the work itself was half over. Less original artists, by contrast, have an aesthetic plan from the very beginning: They know how the finished picture will look (Getzels & Csikszentmihalyi, 1976). In the first case, the approach is *emergent*: The goal arises out of a unique interaction between person and environment. In the second case, it is programmed by cultural conventions. The same relationship holds as far as rewards are concerned. The conventional artist is rewarded when the painting matches recognized criteria of style. The original artist must discover his or her own rewards. Because the goal he or she sets has never quite existed before, it is difficult to know whether it has been achieved; in fact, only the artist can know.

In the case of creative artists and scientists, it is easy to see how intrinsic rewards are discovered and how they motivate behavior. It is also relatively easy to see it in the case of people who spend much of their life in activities like chess, rock climbing, and music, where extrinsic rewards are absent or minimal; yet the activities themselves are thoroughly enjoyable (Csikszentmihalyi, 1975a, 1975b, 1976). But what is the implication of such emergent rewards for those of us who lead average lives?

EMERGENT REWARDS IN EVERYDAY LIFE

Preliminary research—as well as common sense—indicates that a large proportion of what people do every day is not consciously directed to any goal, rational or otherwise. We spend a lot of time chatting with acquaintances, daydreaming, smoking cigarettes, leafing through magazines, drumming with fingertips on tabletops, and so on and on throughout the day. There is no evidence that any of these actions is goal directed in the sense required by existing motivational models. One does not start to daydream or smoke a cigarette in order to achieve a goal state. These behaviors start almost automatically, often without any *conscious* decision having been made, and what sustains them are stimuli inherent in the activity rather than incentives derived from a goal. Yet these inconspicuous, self-generated, behavior sequences are very important, because when people try to do without them, they get tense and irritable and their performance on necessary goal-directed tasks begins to suffer; in general, it looks as if their grasp on sanity begins to slip (Csikszentmihalyi, 1974, 1975b).

What this suggests is that potentially present in everyday life there are innumerable sources of reward that, if discovered, can serve to motivate behavior and provide enjoyment. If true, the implications of this finding are immensely important. It would mean that instead of resigning ourselves to the use of fixed rewards that are in limited supply, we could begin to develop the use of much more readily available, neutral stimuli to make life more rewarding. The parallel to the energy crisis is compelling. We are now trying to emancipate ourselves from the limited sources of energy that can be derived from oil and coal and hope to harness the potentially inexhaustible supply of the sun, the winds, and the tides. Similarly we must begin to concern ourselves with the exhaustion of rewards based on material gratification and learn how to use rewards that satisfy without the steep costs inherent in extrinsic rewards. As long as people will be motivated to act only when they get money, status, or power for their action, the spiral of exploitation will continue to escalate in even faster cycles. We have to learn how to derive enjoyment from life itself; we have to learn how to structure experience so as to make it rewarding without taxing the closed reward system that has been kept artificially limited through ignorance or political design.

The task is difficult but not impossible. The research on intrinsic motivation suggests that one can indeed find rewards in almost any situation. The central requirement seems to be that the situation should *provide information to the person that his or her actions are meeting a set of challenges in the environment.*

When this condition is present, any activity can become enjoyable and hence rewarding. From this it follows that the task of managing our motivational resources consists in restructuring normal life activities and situations so as to provide such information.

At present, most people are conditioned to use only a few channels of information to know whether their actions are up to par. Children find out from their grades if their schoolwork is successful, adults count their income to see what their life has been worth. Then there are other channels with a more limited band: One's tennis skills, golf score, car model, or success as a lover provide additional information about one's effectiveness as a person. Yet these channels of information are few and therefore crowded; there is great competition, and only the strongest signals get through. Why this should be so is not too difficult to explain. As long as we are conditioned to respond to only a few cues, our behavior will be more predictable and hence easier to control. Having money, status, and power as standard rewards makes the control of human behavior a more manageable task. The more universally accepted such incentives are, the easier it is to get the masses to respond the way they ought to—or the way some individuals or groups feel they ought to. In principle there is nothing wrong with this unification of purpose achieved through conditioning to a limited set of rewarding information. In fact, great power can be released by harnessing the motivation of entire societies this way. The danger is that if people forget how to derive rewarding information from other sources, they will devour each other and the resources of the planet in their drive to find satisfaction from the few rewards they are conditioned to recognize.

Therefore, research into intrinsic motivation must sooner or later enter a dangerous ground where powerful social and political forces are loose. To deemphasize conventional rewards threatens the existing power structure. If one raises the possibility that factory jobs may be restructured to provide greater intrinsic rewards to the worker, one immediately incurs the suspicion, not to say hostility, of both unions and management. Union officials fear, with some reason, that if the workers learn to derive rewarding information from their jobs, then their concern with pay and fringe benefits may become less exclusive. And since union officials' power derives from their ability to provide increases in extrinsic rewards, they are afraid that their power will become eroded in proportion to the increase in the force of intrinsic motivation. Management is adverse to intrinsic rewards because they are messy and unknown. Managers can deal with financial incentives: They know, more or less, how much effort their money will buy. But what if workers will now demand to get their rewards in other forms? Better not get involved in such potentially expensive and troublesome situations.

To take another example from a very different sphere of life—there are equally entrenched rewards in the area of interpersonal relations. We have been conditioned to expect, for instance, that the main thing a man can get out of a relationship with a woman is sexual satisfaction. The biological, social, and political reasons for the overemphasis of this simple set of rewards in this case are too complex even to begin deciphering. It is enough to point out the obvious: There is an almost infinite number of rewards potentially present in such an interaction, provided the persons involved learn the skills required. The satisfactions one can derive from matching perceptions, sensations, emotions, and thoughts between two persons who thereby stimulate and develop each other's range of experiences are powerful, but demand patience and discipline like any other skill.

The whole issue of intrinsic rewards eventually boils down to this—the acquisition of skills. Only by having a set of skills is it possible to produce feedback that conveys information about how one has met challenges. A person who has not learned how to mix pigments cannot enjoy painting for long; he or she will not be able to match goals with actions. A person who has not learned to listen, who is not able to share another's moods, insights, or thoughts, cannot derive rewards from that level of interaction.

The problem is that we tend to consider skills as purely means to ends. We admire the skills of a surgeon because they save lives. We admire the skills of a businessman because they make money. This means ds attitude is in some ways very functional, and it is easy to see how it has been established through evolution. But it also results in what we have called earlier a *closed* motivational system, in which only a few outcomes really count.

If we want to maintain the open flexibility of human behavior   the flexibility that is so precious in evolution—and if we want to avoid destroying the environment in search for those few rewards we have become conditioned to recognize, we must start learning new skills . . . and relearn some old ones that are almost lost.

We shall have to accept the fact that the exercise of any skill is an end in itself. It is justified first in terms of its own "aesthetics"—whatever structural difficulty is implied by the challenges the skill attempts to overcome. The skill of the javelin thrower is no longer functional, but we can still experience the beauty of a good throw when we know how difficult and rare it is. Second, a skill is justified because it provides information about the actor: By exercising his or her skills, a person discovers who he or she is, and this is the main reward of an open interactive system. Even the best surgeon or soprano is a limited human being if the only skills they have are those of their profession. Finally, a skill is justified, because variation is the first requirement for evolution. If the only skills we emphasize are the currently adaptive ones, we will end up being unable to respond creatively to the new challenges that will have to be overcome if the human race is to take the next step in its development.

Hence the study of intrinsic rewards suggests one must *multiply the contexts in which skills can be exercised*. Thereby, dependence on a limited set of rewards will be diminished, because the use of any skill in an appropriately structured setting provides its own rewards. To have a context for skills means first of all to have more or less clear set of challenges that are recognized and about which something can be done. Second, there should be a set of skills appropriate to meet these challenges. Music is a good example: The symbolic structure of music provides a language that allows one to meet an infinite range of challenges involved in the combination of sounds; musical tradition preserves forms within which the language can be used to confront particular challenges. The practice of music provides standards of excellence against which one's skills in the medium can be measured. All structured activities that provide intrinsic rewards have the same characteristics: from sports to mathematics, from craft hobbies to dance, from astronomical investigation to yoga and Zen.

But in order to have an activity that is a meaningful context for skills, there must be at least some people who care about that activity. Challenges acquire reality in part from other people's concern with them. If nobody paid any attention to music, the language of musical notation would probably not be sufficient to get children interested enough to develop their musical skills. Music as a medium of expression, as an activity with powerful intrinsic rewards, would then cease to be a viable option. Such losses have occurred before. For instance, a very important human skill in the past has involved the exercise of memory. Many activities were based on this skill, ranging from recitation of poetry to games of competitive recollection. By all accounts, such disciplined use of memory provided rich rewards to participants and audiences alike. Perhaps unfortunately, with the advent of literacy and other systems of record keeping, memory has seemed to be less and less "functional;" and hence mnemonic skills were held to be of decreasing usefulness. As a result people cared less about it, and by now in technological societies there is practically no way for a person to exercise such a skill and get feedback from it. A meaningful context is of course necessary also for extrinsic rewards to be effective. It is only because people have tacitly agreed that gold or diamonds are valuable that they act as motivators. The various status distinctions are rewarding only because they are accepted by a relevant sector of the population.

This dependence on a meaningful context accounts for the fragility of intrinsic rewards. But this is also what makes it possible for us to strengthen rewarding activities and to introduce new ones. "Fixed" rewards are rigidly implanted in the programmed needs of our bodies and have therefore become means rather than ends, however, the "emergent" rewards that come from mastering new challenges in the environment are enormously flexible. Therefore, it is in principle possible for us to constantly increase human satisfaction, to make life more and more rewarding. This is the great contribution that the study of intrinsic rewards brings to psychology. The old models of man assume that the sources of reward are few, finite, and must be bitterly contested. The study of intrinsic rewards suggests that we can enjoy a much broader range of experiences than the closed model allows for. And it points the way toward how to proceed.

INTRINSIC REWARDS AND THE FLOW EXPERIENCE

We have said earlier that any activity can become rewarding if it provides information about a person's ability to meet a set of challenges. This implies that the activity is one with rules of performance that can be evaluated at least by the actor. We have then added a further condition: That the activity must take place in a meaningful context, where other people's concern for the performance of the activity will lend reality to its challenges. The research we have conducted thus far suggests the following further requirements.

1. The activity should be structured so that the actor can increase or decrease the level of challenges being faced in order to match exactly his or her skills with the requirements for action.
2. It should be easy to isolate the activity at least at the perceptual level from other stimuli—external or internal—that might interfere with involvement in it.
3. There should be clear criteria for performance; one should be able to evaluate how well or how poorly one is doing at any time.
4. The activity should provide concrete feedback to the actor so that one can tell how well one is meeting the criteria of performance.
5. The activity ought to have a broad range of challenges and possibly several qualitatively different ranges of challenge, so that the actor may obtain increasingly complex information about different aspects of the self.

An activity that has these characteristics is bound to be intrinsically rewarding. This can be demonstrated in two ways: First, objectively one can show that an activity having such characteristics will be continued even in the absence of external rewards. Second, subjectively, because the person involved will describe the activity as satisfying, enjoyable, rewarding, "fun." It is presumably the subjective feeling of enjoyment that is responsible for the continuation of the activity; it is this feeling that constitutes the intrinsic reward.

I have tried to describe elsewhere this experience of enjoyment. When a person is involved in doing a thing that has the characteristics outlined above, he or she will experience a contraction of the perceptual field, a heightened concentration on the task at hand, a feeling of control leading to elation and finally to a loss of self-awareness that sometimes results in a feeling of transcendence, or a merging with the activity and the environment. This experience we call *flow*, and it seems to be the subjective experiential counterpart of what happens to the organism when it is involved in an activity that is structured in a way that approximates the model described above (Csikszentmihalyi, 1974, 1975a, 1975b, 1976).

It is the flow experience that people see as the reward in activities that have none of the fixed rewards. Flow occurs most often in settings that are not considered part of "real" life: games, sports, rituals, meditative states, aesthetic experiences. Yet it seems clear that any form of interaction can generate flow. The implication is that any form of interaction, from marriage to work, can be made more rewarding by the application of these principles.

For the sake of concreteness, let us take as an example a simple activity with which everyone is familiar—mowing a lawn. Now there are few things, in my experience, that can be as devastatingly boring as mowing lawns. One needs strong extrinsic incentives to engage in such an activity. Yet it is possible, if one is stuck with it, to make even this chore intrinsically rewarding. First, one needs to learn the information potential inherent in the activity: Can the speed at which I mow the yard or a part of it provide feedback to my actions? Can I tell how neatly I do this job in comparison to other times? Is it possible to develop rules about how to proceed—for instance by following a circular path, or a zigzag pattern? Or do I rather want to develop rules for my physical movements as I walk behind the machine? Or do I want to feel the freshness of the breeze or follow a certain chain of thought or fantasy? All of these are potentials for action that provide more or less clearly structured opportunities or challenges. In a real-life situation, one presumably will choose more than one of these "action frames." The next step consists of paying attention to the stimuli that appear in the frame and avoiding the rest. Once the relevant stimuli are isolated, it becomes easy to concentrate on them. One can then begin to "read" the feedback. Supposing I decide that I want to cut parallel swaths in the grass, making a U-turn at the end of each run without overlapping any of the runs, getting as close to the trees as possible without nicking the bark. As soon as I set up these tacit rules, they define what stimuli will be relevant for me to watch for. They also define what will be negative and positive feedback under the rules. When this is done, I am ready to go; and mowing grass becomes a moderately enjoyable activity with its own set of intrinsic rewards.

Of course most things we have to do, like mowing the lawn, have not enough challenges to be entirely self-sustaining in terms of intrinsic rewards. Perhaps there will always have to be an element of extrinsic reward, or coercion, necessary to get people to do them. But the more we learn about how enjoyment can be built into even the most boring routines, the less dependent we shall become on the limited range of closed rewards. And many activities that now are intolerable except as a means to an external reward could be entirely emancipated by transforming them into patterns of involvement people will freely choose because they are satisfying. This is the potential disclosed by the study of intrinsic rewards, and it is one that needs to be thoroughly explored for the sake of human survival.

There is one last point that needs to be stressed. Intrinsic rewards do not necessarily have a positive value. In this sense also they are like physical energy: Both are powerful, both are neutral. They are valuable because they do work for us, because they reduce the effort needed to accomplish a job. But it is possible to attach intrinsic rewards to destructive activities, just as energy can be channeled for destructive ends.

Flow is often experienced in zero-sum activities, which are structured appropriately. For instance, gambling and prize fighting are ideally suited to produce intrinsic rewards. So is torturing people and waging warfare: Many frontline veterans will admit that never have they felt as alive as they did while in the trenches, where every move was a response to clear challenges, concentration was intense, goals were unambiguous, feedback immediate, and control over the situation possible. Many a burglar has confessed that he would stop stealing if only he could find something as enjoyable to do as sneaking through a dark apartment without waking up the owners and riffling drawers to find the elusive jewelry.

In other words, intrinsic rewards are not an ultimate standard to strive for. One still must ask: *What are the consequences of this particular activity?* Only when that answer is evaluated does one know whether one should increase or decrease the intrinsic rewards it contains. Presumably we would not want to make robbery more enjoyable, for instance.

In the vast areas of everyday life that are more synergistic than destructive, however, understanding intrinsic motivation should allow us to expand enjoyment and at the same time to prolong the survival of mankind. The more one learns about these issues, the more intimately they appear to be linked. It is as if the surest road to survival and evolution leads through behavior that is most enjoyable. Whether we will be able to follow that course or not remains to be seen.

REFERENCES

Csikszentmihalyi, M. *Flow: Studies of enjoyment.* Chicago: PHS Research Report, 1974.

Csikszentmihalyi, M., Play and intrinsic rewards. *Journal of Humanistic Psychology,* 1975, *15,* 41–63. (a)

Csikszentmihalyi, M. *Beyond boredom and anxiety.* San Francisco: Jossey–Bass, 1975. (b)

Csikszentmihalyi, M. What play says about behavior. *Ontario Psychologist,* 1976, *8,* 5–11.

deCharms, R. *Personal causation.* New York: Academic Press, 1968.

Getzels, J. W., & Csikszentmihalyi, M. *The creative vision: A longitudinal study of problem-finding in art.* New York: Wiley Interscience, 1976.

Harlow, H. F. Mice, monkeys, men and motives. *Psychological Review,* 1953, *60,* 23–32.

McClelland, D. C., Atkinson, J. A., Clark, R. A., & Lowell, E. *The achievement motive.* New York: Appleton, 1953.

Miller, G. A., Galanter, E., & Pribram, K. H. *Plans and the structure of behavior.* New York: Holt, Rinehart and Winston, 1960.

Montgomery, D. C. The role of exploratory drive in learning. *Journal of Comparative Physiological Psychology,* 1954, *47,* 60–64.

Piaget, J. *Play, dreams, and imitation in childhood.* New York: Norton, 1957.

Simon, H. A. Motivational and emotional contróls of cognition. *Psychological Review*, 1967, *74*, 29–39.

Veroff, J. Development and validation of a projective measure of power motivation. *Journal of Abnormal and Social Psychology*, 1957, *54*, 1–8.

White, R. W. Motivation reconsidered: The concept of competence. *Psychological Review, 1959, 66*, 297–333.

11

Divergent Approaches to the Study of Rewards

Mark R. Lepper
Stanford University

David Greene
SRI International

INTRODUCTION

The title of this volume, *The Hidden Costs of Reward,* conveys a theme that links together several otherwise disparate streams of research and theory found in the preceding chapters. Despite rather obvious intramural differences in background, theoretical perspective, and research style, the contributors to this volume have all come to the conclusion that there are potentially significant "costs" associated with the indiscriminate use of tangible rewards to control human behavior. Moreover, the contributors are in agreement that these potential costs have remained largely hidden, having received far too little theoretical or empirical attention.

There are good reasons why the detrimental effects of rewards have remained hidden for so long. At one level, the data demonstrating these deleterious effects seem to be contradicted by the extensive literature documenting the beneficial outcomes of systematic reward programs in applied settings (e.g., Kazdin, 1975a, 1975b). At another level, the cognitive, contextualist orientation of the investigators in this area represents a significant departure from both operant and associationist or mechanistic models of motivational processes (cf. Jenkins, 1974; Mischel, 1977). In this final chapter, then, we compare the approach to the study of rewards that has yielded evidence of potential detrimental effects with more traditional approaches to the study of reinforcement processes and examine the fundamental differences between these divergent approaches in terms of their respective goals, presuppositions, and typical methods of research. These differences, we will argue, have contributed to the mutual isolation of the two lines of investigation and hence to the continued "invisibility" of the potential costs of rewards.

Our analysis focuses on two basic sources of divergence in approach. The first and more obvious source derives from an important difference in priorities between investigators in the two research traditions. The actual conduct of any research is profoundly influenced by whether one is primarily interested in the development of effective clinical techniques or primarily interested in general theoretical issues and only secondarily in the immediate application of research findings. The difference between a clinical and a theoretical focus of a research program is likely to dictate an investigator's choices on matters as fundamental as subjects, tasks, rewards, dependent measures, and experimental designs (cf. Cronbach, 1957; London, 1972).

The second and less palpable source of divergence stems from the conflict between the basic paradigms underlying the two approaches and the difficulties inherent in any attempt to accommodate to each other sets of findings derived from competing models of human behavior. Scientists' judgments about the merit and import of each other's work are inevitably made within a "disciplinary matrix" of shared assumptions, beliefs, and values that define both the domain of questions that may legitimately be asked and the range of answers that will prove acceptable (Kuhn, 1970; Mahoney, 1976). Thus, proponents of competing paradigms, as a function of the incommensurability of their respective disciplinary matrices, may literally "practice their trades in different worlds" (Kuhn, 1970, p. 150).

Krantz (1971) has used this perspective to describe the "separate worlds" of operant and nonoperant psychology. In doing so, he focused on three interrelated aspects of the disciplinary matrix of operant psychology: an assumption that variability in behavior is caused by variability in the environment; a preference for explanation via empirical, functional relationships between reinforcers and their effects; and the use of within-subject experimental designs to establish such functional relationships. These elements, he suggested, form a mutually interdependent and consistent approach to psychological questions within the framework of a "Skinnerian" analysis of behavior (cf. McCullers, Chapter 1). Conversely, in the nonoperant world, the belief that psychological explanations must make reference to states within the organism and that the interaction of man with the environment comprises a bidirectional process is frequently coupled with a preference for between-group designs and process-oriented models of human behavior.

In following sections we examine the consequences of these divergent goals and paradigms for the conduct and results of research undertaken within each approach. In the process, we hope to clarify the boundary conditions under which both positive and negative effects of particular reward procedures should be likely to occur.

OVERVIEW OF THE PRECEDING CHAPTERS

The preceding chapters share a concern for the ways in which an individual's engagement in, learning from, and subsequent interest in activities are affected by the immediate presence or prior imposition of salient extrinsic constraints. In different ways, each of the contributors has emphasized the differences in performance and subsequent behavior that may result when the same activity is undertaken in the presence vs. the absence of such constraints. This distinction, between extrinsic and intrinsic motivation, is woven throughout the preceding chapters in two complementary threads.

The Concept of "Competence"

The concept of competence can be traced to attempts by White (1959) and others (e.g., Berlyne, 1960; Koch, 1956; Woodworth, 1958) to identify significant classes of behavior that could not be adequately conceptualized within traditional models of motivation derived from laboratory investigations of external rewards and punishments. Mechanistic models of motivation, grounded in drive reduction or response-strengthening postulates, were held to be insufficient to account for the prevalence and persistence of behaviors like exploration, manipulation, and curiosity. These behaviors, it seemed, were directed more toward the exercise of effectance or control over the environment than toward the attainment of specific extrinsic goals or the reduction of specific drive states. As a result, the maintenance of such responses appeared relatively independent of the particular reinforcement schedules to which the organism had been subjected. Instead, they seemed to depend on reciprocal interaction and feedback between the organism and its environment—a dynamic process governed by the "match" between the organism's competencies and the demands and responsiveness of its environment (cf. Hunt, 1961, 1965). In this sense, exploration, curiosity, and related response patterns were postulated to be inherently or intrinsically motivated.

In the present volume, these concepts of competence and control are developed in two complementary directions. On one hand, the effects of extrinsic rewards on performance of a particular task are shown to differ as a function of both the nature of the task itself (e.g., its complexity, open-endedness, or "heuristic" quality) and the nature of the match between the subject's abilities or interests and the demands imposed by the task (e.g., the perceived difficulty or attractiveness of the task for the subject) (McGraw, Chapter 3; Condry & Chambers, Chapter 4, Csikszentmihalyi, Chapter 10). On the other hand, the observed effects of the imposition of extrinsic rewards on tasks that are open-ended, complex, or initially attractive to the subject are shown to vary systematically as a function of the specific performance measures obtained. A particular reward procedure may have simultaneous but different effects on qualitative vs. quantitative performance measures, central vs. incidental learning, etc. (McGraw, Chapter 3; Kruglanski, Chapter 5; Lepper & Greene, Chapter 6). Therefore, evaluation of the relative costs or benefits of extrinsic rewards necessarily depends on the particular character of the activity, the specific contingencies imposed on performance, and the criteria by which performance is judged.

"Internalization" vs. "Compliance"

The second historical thread, although conceptually related to the first, derives from the social-psychological distinction between internally and externally governed behavior or, in Kelman's (1958) terms, between "internalization" and "compliance." Whether described as a difference between free vs. restricted behavior (Brehm, 1966; Lewin, Lippett, & White, 1939), private vs. public behavior (Hovland, Janis, & Kelley, 1953), internalization vs. compliance (Kelman, 1961; Rosenhan, 1969), dispositional vs. situational control (Heider, 1958), or internal vs. external control (Bem, 1972; deCharms, 1968; Kelley, 1973), social psychologists have traditionally attempted to distinguish between behavior that is seen as a function of obvious, powerful, and clear contingencies in the person's environment and behavior that occurs in the seeming absence of clear, external contingencies and that is inferred to reflect structures or states within the organism (cf. Kruglanski, Chapter 2).

Though developed within different experimental domains, these distinctions share a common set of theoretical assumptions concerning the control of human behavior. First, they assume that social behavior is a joint function of a person's perceptions of salient environmental contingencies and his or her active, cognitive structuring of the situation in terms of previously acquired values, attitudes, expectancies, stereotypes, etc. Second, these distinctions imply that the conditions most effective in producing immediate compliance will not necessarily be those most likely to promote subsequent internalization. For example, highly coercive techniques for inducing compliance in the presence of an agent of authority may prove counterproductive in producing later "compliance" in the absence of that agent (Lepper, 1973; Rosenhan, 1969; Sears, Whiting, Nowlis, & Sears, 1953). Hence, these distinctions carry a further implicit presumption concerning the generality of these two sorts of influences on behavior. Perceived environmental contingencies are assumed to produce largely situation-specific control of behavior that is not likely to transfer to other situations unless those same contingencies are apparent. By contrast, internalized values or attitudes are assumed to have a relatively more situation-free or transsituational influence on the individual's behavior.

The present volume adds further weight to this historically significant distinction between internalization and compliance. In several independent programs of research (Condry & Chambers, Chapter 4; Kruglanski, Chapter 5; Lepper &

Greene, Chapter 6; Deci and Porac, Chapter 7), the provision of extrinsic rewards for performance of an activity—an effective means of increasing the
probability of engagement in the activity in the presence of these rewards—has
also been shown to produce detrimental effects on subjects' attitudes toward the
activity and on the probability that subjects will choose to engage in the task in
subsequent situations when these extrinsic contingencies are no longer applicable.

Similarities and Differences Among Contributors

Although various chapters in this volume have clearly placed differential emphasis on these two historical threads, there are a number of conceptual
similarities in general approach that characterize the contributors to this book and
differentiate them from researchers in the operant and associationist traditions.
Most basic is the presupposition that it is useful to distinguish intrinsic from
extrinsic motivation and possible to design measures that embody and reflect this
distinction. In addition, there are several assumptions implicit in this approach
concerning the appropriate procedures and level of analysis suited to the study of
the "hidden costs" of reward. For example, the preceding chapters share: (a) a
cognitive orientation in which behavior is viewed as a function of the manner in
which an individual perceives, codes, and interprets cues provided by the external environment; (b) an interactive and contextual model of behavior in which
these cognitive responses both influence and are influenced by the subject's
behavior and the circumstances in which it occurs; and (c) a fundamentally
theoretical approach, marked by a concern with understanding the processes by
which detrimental effects of rewards may occur.

Consequently, the experimental evidence presented in this volume derives
primarily from laboratory studies of the *relative* effects of reward procedures
(assessed against theoretically relevant control conditions) on qualitative performance measures or measures of subsequent engagement in complex, typically
interactive tasks of initial interest and intrinsic value to subjects. The models
presented to deal with these data are concerned primarily with cognitive variables
(e.g., expectations, goals, attributions, perceptions of control or competence,
labeling of activities); more particularly, they deal with the manner in which
these cognitive variables may be affected by the presence of salient extrinsic
rewards, and may in turn affect subjects' overt behavior.

Beyond these general similarities in conception and methodology, however,
lie important differences among contributors that deserve at least brief mention.
At the root of these differences lies the problem of defining intrinsic motivation.
Some contributors prefer to define this concept in terms of some specific theoretical construct—equating intrinsic motivation, for example, with perceptions of
control, feelings of competence and efficacy, or the structural interaction of task
demands with subject abilities. Other contributors choose to define intrinsic

motivation in operational terms—assuming that a variety of component processes that may not be reducible to a single construct may contribute to intrinsic interest. As a result, different contributors have focused on different stages of the process whereby subjects select, undertake, and complete activities. Similarly, various chapters have dealt rather differently with the complex theoretical and empirical question of the relationship between performance in the immediate presence and the subsequent absence of salient constraints. Finally, the present contributors differ markedly in their willingness to generalize their findings to situations that lie beyond the immediate purview of the experimental research described in this book.

These distinctions will no doubt be pursued and reflected in future research. In the present context, however, these differences in approach appear relatively small, compared to the larger and more fundamental divergence that exists between these cognitive models taken together and the operant model that underlies the use of systematic, tangible reinforcement programs (such as the token economy) to produce behavior change in applied settings.

OVERVIEW OF TOKEN ECONOMIES

In terms of their historical antecedents outlined above, the findings reported in this volume might be viewed as an interesting but modest extension of previous lines of research. Yet the considerable discussion occasioned by these findings (Bornstein & Hamilton, 1975; Calder & Staw, 1975a; Deci, 1975; Feingold & Mahoney, 1975; Ford & Foster, 1976; Greene, 1975; Hoppe, 1975; Lepper & Greene, 1976; Levine & Fasnacht, 1974, 1976; Reiss & Sushinsky, 1975a, 1975b; Scott, 1975) suggests the inadequacy of such a characterization. Instead, it would seem that the combination of traditions represented in this volume has provided data that strike a particularly dissonant chord for many researchers concerned with the application of reinforcement principles to natural settings. Significantly, it seems less the data themselves that are problematic than the implications of these data for the conceptual framework within which applied reinforcement programs such as the token economy have developed.

In the face of the several hundred token economy programs that have now been reported in the 15 years or so since Ayllon and Azrin's (1965) pioneering project (Kazdin, 1975a, 1975b; Kazdin & Bootzin, 1972; O'Leary, in press; O'Leary & Drabman, 1971), it is difficult to realize that the token economy is a relatively recent phenomenon. Yet it is only within the last decade that the attempt to modify complex social behavior through the creation of an artificial economy, in which tangible rewards or privileges are made explicitly contingent upon demonstrable increases in appropriate behavior patterns, has become a central focus of research. Some conception of even this brief history and of the operant tradition in which this paradigm has had its roots, however, is essential to a fuller understanding of both the dramatic successes and the possible limitations of this approach.

Goals and Philosophy

Let us begin with the goals of a token economy program. From a clinical perspective, the aim of such a program is clear: to modify behavior patterns that have proved maladaptive to a particular person or persons. From this perspective, the token economy literature can be seen as having an applied (in the best sense of the word) rather than a theoretical focus. Token economies were designed to deal with people in distress and to offer a method to help these individuals overcome some of their difficulties. It is not surprising, therefore, that many token economy programs deal with small and highly selected samples; nor is it surprising that such programs often involve treatment packages tailored to the specific needs and preferences of individuals in the program. The ultimate test of a token program's effectiveness is indeed one of clinical, rather than merely statistical, signficance.

Historically, token economies were begun as a procedure of last resort with selected, and typically institutionalized, populations for whom a variety of alternative and inferentially less powerful therapeutic techniques had proven unsuccessful. In its earliest applications, the token economy methodology was employed to change the behavior of chronic psychotics (Ayllon & Azrin, 1965, 1968), of severely retarded individuals (Birnbrauer & Lawler, 1964), and of persistent delinquents (Burchard & Tyler, 1965). Only more recently, after investigators had been "rewarded" by the striking success of these earlier programs with extreme clinical populations, did token economies come to be applied to less and less severely disturbed populations (e.g., O'Leary & Becker, 1967) as well as to "normal" children in everyday classrooms (e.g., Barrish, Saunders, & Wolf, 1969; Betancourt & Zeiler, 1971; Bushell, Wrobel, & Michaelis, 1968; McLaughlin & Malaby, 1972). Moreover, despite the current trend to consider token economy programs as a potential "method of choice" rather than a "method of last resort"—apparent in numerous "modify-it-yourself" handbooks aimed at parents and teachers (e.g., Becker, 1971; Krumboltz & Krumboltz, 1972; Zifferblatt, 1970)—it is still the case that the vast majority of experimental *research* on token economies continues to involve intervention into the lives of clinical populations selected for their maladaptive pretreatment behavior patterns.

From an operational rather than a clinical perspective, however, the goal of a token economy can be stated differently: to produce and demonstrate functional control over some class of behaviors exhibited by the subjects of the program. It is in this sense that the intellectual genealogy of the token economy movement and its roots in the tradition of an operant "Skinnerian" analysis of behavior are apparent. The important consequence of this lineage is that (with a few notable exceptions discussed later) the token economy approach shares with a Skinnerian analysis a set of fundamental philosophical presuppositions. Thus, it is assumed that:

1. Behavior is best conceptualized as a function of an individual's environment and the consequences an individual's actions have in that external environment.
2. As a result, causal analysis is best restricted to the search for empirical functional relationships between observable antecedents, behaviors, and consequences.
3. Variability in an individual's behavior necessarily implies variability in the environment that controls and maintains his or her behavior.

Functional Control

Traditionally, therefore, proponents of token economy programs have had as their aim not only the production of behavior changes beneficial to their clients, but also the demonstration of the effectiveness of their manipulation of environmental contingencies in controlling the behavior of their subjects. The natural methodological result of these theoretical presuppositions and the applied focus of token programs has been the use of intrasubject replication designs. In virtually all of the earlier token economy demonstrations, the behavior of individual subjects was monitored successively as the controlling environmental contingencies were altered. From a practical standpoint, of course, such a design makes eminent good sense for applied research, dealing with small samples and real-world settings that make random assignment in between-subjects designs extremely difficult. Intrasubject designs also allow a clear and often dramatic demonstration of the clinical significance of gains obtained through reinforcement programs.

More fundamental to the choice of designs than the practical exigencies of field research, however, is the philosophical or presuppositional rejection of alternative designs as insufficient for a functional analysis of human behavior (Kazdin, 1973b; Krantz, 1971; Sidman, 1960). Sidman (1960) provides the most extreme form of this argument, starting with the assumption that control and understanding of behavior are isomorphic. From such a viewpoint, between-group experimental designs, which assume unexplained intersubject variability, can only obscure the lawful effects of variables on behavior (Sidman, 1960). As a result, the modal and by far most common paradigm employed in the evaluation of token economy programs has been the ABAB or reversal design (Baer, Wolf, & Risley, 1968; Kazdin, 1973b), in which a subject's behavior is observed first during a pretreatment baseline period and then following the subsequent introduction, withdrawal, and reintroduction of the token program in a given setting.

Significantly, by these criteria of clinical effectiveness and of demonstrable functional control over behavior, the history of token economies has, as recent reviews attest (Kazdin, 1975a; O'Leary, in press), been one of virtually unmitigated success. Across a wide variety of subject populations (chronic psychotic inpatients, mentally retarded individuals, delinquents, children with emotional or learning problems, normal children, etc.), target behaviors (personal grooming habits, classroom deportment, aggression, work productivity, self-care behaviors, etc.), "back-up" reinforcers for which tokens may be exchanged (food, money, canteen articles, free-play time, special privileges, privacy, etc.), and specific procedures for administering the program, investigators have been able to produce dramatic increases in desired behavior patterns and to demonstrate that these behavior changes vary systematically with the presence or absence of the token program. Sufficiently powerful tangible rewards, systematically applied, can often be effective in producing major behavior change even in the most traditionally recalcitrant subject populations (Kazdin, 1975a).

Maintenance and Generalization

In terms of the establishment of immediate functional control, both the magnitude of effects produced by token economy procedures and the range of situations in which such programs have been applied are impressive. Potentially more germane to the concerns of this volume, however, are data concerning the maintenance and/or generalization of gains produced by these procedures. On this score the data seem considerably more mixed.

In two scholarly reviews of the token economy literature through the early seventies, O'Leary and Drabman (1971) and Kazdin and Bootzin (1972) considered the data concerning the maintenance of treatment gains following the withdrawal of token programs and the generalization of treatment gains to other settings in which tokens had not been administered. The general conclusion in both cases was clear. In a vast majority of studies, removal of the token program led to a rapid return to baseline rates of response. Similarly, examinations of the effects of the imposition of a token economy in one setting on behavior in a different setting typically indicated that behavior outside of the immediate setting remained unaffected by the program. As Kazdin and Bootzin (1972) summarized the situation:

> The generalization of treatment effects to stimulus conditions in which token reinforcement is not given might be expected to be the *raison d'être* of token economies. An examination of the literature leads to a different conclusion. There are numerous reports of token programs showing behavior change only while contingent token reinforcement is being delivered. Generally, removal of token reinforcement results in decrements in desirable responses to baseline or near-baseline levels of performance [p. 359].

There are, of course, a number of possible reasons for these initial conclusions. In part, the lack of attention to the question of generalization in these early studies was a natural result of the relative novelty of token programs and their applied focus. One wishes to document fully the immediate benefits of a new therapeutic regimen before turning to less pressing and more subtle questions such as generalization. At the same time, the relative lack of attention to issues of maintenance and generalization seems also to stem from conflicts inherent in the use of intrasubject reversal designs, in which the persistence of experimental effects over time becomes not merely an issue of lesser importance but an actual impediment to the demonstration of functional control (Kazdin, 1973b).

Significantly, although these early studies typically provided no evidence of gains in performance outside of the immediate setting in which the token program had been implemented, neither did they demonstrate detrimental effects of these programs on immediate performance or behavior in other subsequent settings. By far the modal outcome in these programs has been a return of behavior to baseline levels following the withdrawal of the token program and a lack of impact of the program in other settings where the token program was not in effect (cf. Kazdin, 1975a; O'Leary, in press).

In recent years, however, increasing attention has been paid to issues of maintenance and generalization in token economies. As a result, a number of more recent programs have been successful in producing at least some evidence of persistent or generalized gains through the use of either systematic programming of the posttreatment environment or the use of intermittent, naturally occurring, or self-managed reinforcement systems (e.g., Drabman, Spitalnik, & O'Leary, 1973; Jones & Kazdin, 1975; Kazdin & Polster, 1973; Kent & O'Leary, 1976; Medland & Stachnik, 1972; O'Leary, Drabman, & Kass, 1973; Rosenbaum, O'Leary, & Jacob, 1975; Turkewitz, O'Leary, & Ironsmith, 1975; Walker & Buckley, 1972). Conversely, observable detrimental effects of reasonably long-term token programs have remained relatively infrequent (Brownell, Colletti, Ersner–Hershfield, Hershfield, & Wilson, 1977; Colvin, 1971; Greene, Sternberg, & Lepper, 1976; Johnson, Bolstad, & Lobitz, 1976; Meichenbaum, Bowers, & Ross, 1968; Ross, Meichenbaum, & Bowers, 1974).

COMPARISONS BETWEEN DIVERGENT APPROACHES

The clinical success of these procedures contrasts sharply with the reports of detrimental effects of rewards contained in this volume. To understand why such seemingly conflicting results and conclusions have been obtained within these divergent research domains requires attention to a number of specific differences in the manner in which research is carried out in these two traditions.

Selection of Subjects and Target Behaviors

Consider, first, the selection of subjects and target behaviors. In the applied reinforcement literature, these decisions are generally dictated by the existence of recognized dysfunctional behavior patterns. Subjects tend to be selected on the basis of a low incidence of appropriate or socially approved behavior during preexperimental observations, or on the basis of obvious deficits in social or academic skills. Consequently, subjects in these programs are frequently drawn from disturbed, disruptive, or institutionalized populations, and the behaviors targeted for reinforcement are typically those that subjects find of low initial value or interest, relative to the behavioral alternatives available to them. Furthermore, to provide unambiguous behavioral measures, target behaviors are generally selected for the ease with which successful adherence to an imposed contingency can be clearly discriminated by subjects and observers. The result has been a focus, in much of the early work, on classroom deportment (Winett & Winkler, 1972), or, in some of the more recent work, the completion of specific academic tasks (O'Leary, in press).

By contrast, choices concerning subject populations and target behaviors are made quite differently in the research reported in this volume. To allow investigation of the effects of reward on intrinsic motivation, subjects and target activities are selected to insure that the activity will be of *high* initial interest or inherent value to the subjects. Typically, these studies have employed "normal" subjects, for whom activities of initial interest are selected on the basis of either preexperimental attitude measures or high base rate levels of spontaneous choice of the activity. As a result, the target behaviors assessed in these studies tend to have a very different character from those used in applied programs. These investigations are more likely to examine complex response patterns, that are appropriate to complex and open-ended tasks for which a variety of self-imposed and externally imposed performance criteria may be employed (cf. Condry & Chambers, Chapter 4; Csikszentmihalyi, Chapter 10; McCullers, Chapter 1; McGraw, Chapter 3). Consequently, these tasks lend themselves to qualitative analysis of a sort that is frequently not applicable to the kinds of target behaviors commonly employed in token programs. Measures of originality or excellence, for example, seem sensible in the context of artistic endeavors or problem-solving tasks; their relevance or application to measures of classroom deportment or reduced physical aggression seems more dubious.

Selection of Rewards or Reinforcers

Parallel differences in procedure also appear with respect to the rewards or reinforcers employed in these two sorts of studies. In the applied literature, the demonstrable effectiveness and empirical definition of reinforcers to be employed represents a sine qua non for proceeding with one's investigation. Confronted with data suggesting a lack of impact (or a negative effect) of a particular reward procedure designed to serve as a reinforcer, researchers in this tradition are unlikely to continue the program without altering their procedures. Instead, rewards and contingencies are modified until control over the relevant behavior is achieved. To the extent that the problem is cast primarily as a practical or engineering problem, failures of reward programs to achieve control do not represent a problem of great interest. Discussions of such "failures" (Kazdin, 1973a) or even active attempts at "counter-control" (Mahoney, 1974), therefore, typically appear only as footnotes in the report of eventually successful behavior-change programs.

Among researchers concerned with the potential costs of rewards, the situation is predictably different. Here the relative effectiveness of a given reward procedure in a particular context is a central theoretical issue. Reward procedures employed in these studies are typically chosen because of their resemblance to procedures proven effective as reinforcers in other contexts; and one issue under investigation is whether the particular context of administration leads the reward procedure to have different effects or significant costs (cf. Condry, 1977; McGraw, Chapter 3). Demonstrations that rewards that serve as reinforcers under many conditions (e.g., money for college students, or marshmallows for young children) fail to produce reinforcement effects or produce detrimental effects in particular contexts are designed to highlight the fact that the effects of rewards depend upon the manner and context in which they are delivered.

Experimental Design

Related to the issue of choice of reinforcement or reward is the issue of experimental design. Applied programs, as indicated earlier, have tended to employ intrasubject experimental designs, in which the effects of manipulations introduced at different times on response frequencies are evaluated with a single sample or subject. Rarely do these studies include control conditions against which experimental effects may be evaluated; instead, experimental effects are typically evaluated with respect to behavior in prior phases of the experiment. One consequence of this methodological tradition is that it is usually impossible to evaluate separately the effects of different components of a particular program or to draw conclusions concerning the effects of the "reinforcement procedure" per se on subjects' behavior. The results of these programs typically reflect the total influence of the procedure itself and the incentive it provides for appropriate conduct, the exercise of a much broader system of power and influence that forms the context for the introduction of such a program, the explicit definition of appropriate conduct, and the instructions and social approval that accompany the delivery of tangible rewards. Likewise, the effects of the reinforcement procedure are typically inseparable from the effects of the changes in behavior produced by the program, the potential effects of changes in the natural social environment that may accompany changes in conduct, and/or the effects of the acquisition of increased social or academic skills that may result from engagement in the targeted behavior.

From a practical point of view, given the commonality of these elements across the situations in which one might introduce such programs, these "confoundings" are natural and of less interest than the absolute effects produced by the program as a whole. From the shared theoretical perspective of this book's contributors, however, these issues become central; and this intrasubject methodology contrasts sharply with the use of between-subject designs and control-group procedures characterizing virtually all of the research outlined in this volume. To the extent that one is concerned with the effects of reward procedures per se, it is critical to control experimentally for theoretically extraneous influences such as increased engagement in the target activity, changes in the social contingencies encountered by the subject, or explicit instructions and definitions of desirable behavior. These studies explicitly assume that an individual's behavior will be affected by a host of such factors and that the effects of a particular reward system can only be evaluated with reference to the behavior of other subjects induced to behave in an identical fashion without the use of the reward system. The concern, ultimately, is less a definition of the conditions under which a particular procedure will be sufficient to produce some absolute effect on behavior than it is a description of the conditions under which procedures will be relatively more or less likely to produce positive or negative effects.

Dependent Measures

Although the foregoing considerations reveal a number of significant differences in approach between the two positions, the fundamental difference in orientation is nowhere more apparent than in the choice of dependent measures. This choice is made quite differently, depending on an investigator's acceptance or rejection of the distinction between intrinsic and extrinsic motivation.

Within the operant tradition, the concept of "intrinsically motivated" behavior, with its apparent reference to internal states of the organism, has no utility. In terms of a strict functional analysis, behaviors labeled as intrinsically motivated are simply those for which the appropriate external controlling stimuli have not yet been identified (Sidman, 1960). By contrast, within the framework developed in this volume, a crucial distinction is drawn between those measures of behavior obtained in situations where there is clear instrumental value in performing the target behavior (e.g., in order to obtain some extrinsic social or material reward) and those measures obtained in situations where such extrinsic constraints on behavior have been minimized. In the former case, behavior is assumed to be the result both of the expected instrumental value of the behavior in producing extrinsic rewards and the expected value of the behavior per se.

Only in the latter situation, where behavior reflects the anticipated value of simply engaging in the behavior itself, can one draw inferences concerning a subject's intrinsic interest in the activity (Lepper & Greene, Chapter 6).

Measures obtained in token economy programs to assess generalization or persistence of behavior change, though superficially relevant to the issues raised in this volume, are thus unlikely to provide a basis for conclusions concerning the effects of such procedures on intrinsic motivation. Quite apart from the possible measurement problems resulting from the selection of subjects for initially low baseline levels of the target behavior, there is generally little reason a priori to expect a withdrawal phase to be sensitive to a decrease in intrinsic interest, because withdrawal periods in these studies rarely represent an actual return to the preexperimental baseline conditions. Instead, as Kazdin (1973b) notes, token reinforcement programs typically involve a great deal more than the simple contingent distribution of tokens and back-up reinforcers. In virtually all token programs conducted in natural settings, for example, considerable energy is invested in training personnel (e.g., teachers, ward attendants, administrators, etc.) to observe the behavior of the target population systematically and to make their social approval contingent on the same behaviors the token economy attempts to modify. Often, specific verbal instructions are also provided to subjects, clearly conveying the values and the expectations of these personnel in positions of authority. Rarely when a token program is withdrawn are the effects of this training likely to be eliminated along with the program (Kazdin, 1973b). Often, teachers are specifically instructed to continue systematic social reinforcement for target behaviors in a fashion not present during baseline observations, or they are encouraged to substitute naturally available reinforcers for the withdrawn tokens in order to maintain gains in appropriate behavior (e.g., Jones & Kazdin, 1975; O'Leary, in press; O'Leary, Becker, Evans, & Saudargas, 1969). Finally, the potential continuing instrumentality of target behaviors (even when it is clear that specific token reinforcement will no longer be forthcoming) is likely to be emphasized by the continued presence of observers, record keeping, and the like (cf. Surratt, Ulrich, & Hawkins, 1969).

Similar complications also appear in much of the literature concerning the generalization of behavior change produced by token programs to other situations in which token reinforcement is not delivered. Consider, for example, the literature on the generalization of effects of token programs in schools from special classes or particular parts of the day to other classes or parts of the day. Again it seems likely that teacher instruction and training in the use of contingent social approval will alter the teachers' behavior even during periods when token reinforcement is not available. Understandably, if a treatment program has been successful in its primary goal of producing clinically significant gains in appropriate behavior, teachers or other personnel associated with the project may quite reasonably have a "vested" interest in maintaining these gains in other settings. This seems particularly likely, for example, in studies where generalization is assessed during brief periods of nonreinforcement interspersed between periods in which a token program is in effect (e.g., Drabman et al., 1973; Turkewitz et al., 1975). Significantly, the most impressive evidence for generalization of treatment gains to date comes from programs in which explicit extrinsic incentives (though different from those employed in the initial token program) are also made available in the new situation in which "generalization" is measured (e.g., Walker & Buckley, 1972). Such programmed generalization has obvious clinical significance. Performance under such conditions, however, hardly speaks to the theoretical issue of intrinsic interest.

These procedures contrast sharply with those employed by investigators seeking to examine the possible detrimental effects of reward procedures. To permit inferences concerning the effects of particular procedures on intrinsic interest, these investigators have attempted to insure that subsequent behavioral measures are obtained in situations in which subjects: (a) expect that their behavior will have no significant instrumental value apart from the value of task engagement itself; and (b) believe themselves free of surveillance and able to choose from a number of different alternatives. We take it to be significant, therefore, that the few programs showing some detrimental effects of relatively long-term token programs have obtained measures of subsequent behavior in which the continued instrumentality of that behavior has been minimized. This has been accomplished either by observing generalization in different situations in which personnel administering the token program are not present (Johnson et al., 1976; Meichenbaum et al., 1968) or by observing persistence in a setting in which the personnel present during the subsequent measurement phase have no vested interest in maintaining behavior changes produced during treatment (Colvin, 1971; Greene et al., 1976).

Duration and Withdrawal of Programs

Two other differences that generally characterize research in these divergent traditions seem worthy of note. First, research on token economies has generally involved relatively long-term field experiments, whereas research reported in this volume has tended to concentrate on shorter term laboratory investigations. It should be apparent that the extended use of a reward system may be important for subjects to acquire sufficient skills, self-assurance, or feedback from the natural environment for changes in behavior to become less dependent upon the immediate presence of the reinforcement program.

Second, and perhaps more significantly, investigations in these two traditions have differed in the manner in which reinforcement programs are withdrawn. In the token economy literature, a majority of the more recent investigations have included attempts to withdraw the reinforcement program gradually so that subjects will become successively less reliant on the expectation of immediate reward to maintain their behavior. Such "fading" procedures may play a significant role in attempts to produce generalization or persistence of the effects of token programs (Jones & Kazdin, 1975; O'Leary, in press; Turkewitz et al., 1975). Though increased persistence following a gradual withdrawal of rewards would be consistent with both a functional analysis and a more cognitive approach, the consequences of such procedures on measures of intrinsic interest have not yet been experimentally investigated.

DISCUSSION

Investigators concerned with the application of reinforcement principles to applied settings and those concerned with the potential costs of reward procedures often appear to be addressing similar issues. We have argued in the previous sections, however, that this apparent similarity actually masks a number of fundamental differences in purpose and theoretical presuppositions. Researchers in these two traditions have employed partially overlapping techniques in quite different fashions, have asked related but significantly different questions, and therefore have frequently arrived at seemingly contradictory results.

Precisely because these apparently contradictory results have been obtained in very different contexts, it is difficult to draw comparisons across areas on the basis of existing data. In most cases, the differences in approach and procedures dictated by these initially divergent paradigms have yielded results that are simply noncomparable. Although each literature is characterized by a considerable degree of internal consistency, extrapolation beyond the particular contexts in which each paradigm has received support depends upon assumptions and speculations that cannot be directly verified from the data at hand.

Consider perhaps the most fundamental difference between these two approaches, i.e., the nature of the dependent measures employed. The general approach offered in this volume suggests that data reflective of intrinsic interest in an activity may be obtained only in contexts where salient extrinsic contingencies relevant to one's engagement in the activity are lacking. Lepper, Sagotsky, and Greene (1977a; see Chapter 6), for example, found precisely opposite effects following a token reinforcement procedure depending on the dependent measure employed. The contrast between these two measures of subsequent behavior is significant, because the measures differ in their relevance to the construct of intrinsic interest. When interest was examined in a setting where subjects perceived their choices to be unconstrained and unobserved, prior contingent reinforcement produced detrimental effects. When these same children's behavior was observed in a setting where subjects expected no tangible reward but knew their choices to be observed and could expect social approval contingent upon those choices, prior contingent reinforcement produced positive effects.[1]

---

[1] To the extent that competing paradigms dictate different criteria for evaluating the significance of a particular finding, comparisons between procedures within a given study will be far more informative than further attempts to draw conclusions from experiments conducted in different settings for different purposes. Further progress in reconciliation would therefore be greatly facilitated by the collection of data in settings that would allow either kind of effect to be observed (Greene et al., 1976; Krantz, 1971; Mahoney, 1976).

This comparison, within a single experiment, provides clear evidence of the potential significance of traditional differences in procedures employed in these two literatures. Neither this study nor any related investigation, however, can provide a simple algorithm for deciding in every particular instance whether a measure of subsequent behavior will reflect intrinsic interest per se or, instead, some combination of intrinsic interest and perceived situational demands. At the extremes, one may be fairly confident in asserting that subsequent behavior assessed in the presence of explicit attempts to maintain behavior change would have little relevance to issues of intrinsic motivation or, conversely, that behavior in some totally different and unrelated situation would have considerable relevance. Between these poles, however, lie a variety of contexts in which it is difficult to make this judgment without specific information concerning the subjects' perceptions of the particular setting.[2]

Thus, in our view, it is premature to attempt to draw firm conclusions regarding the factors most critical to the different results obtained in these two areas of research. Clearly, the present literature seems far from sufficient to eliminate concerns that the use of overly powerful reward systems in applied settings may prove counterproductive outside of the setting in which rewards are made available. Broad assertions that deleterious effects of rewards do not occur in applied settings when empirically defined reinforcers are employed or following the use of long-term programs appear overstated on the basis of available data. On the whole, data from the token economy literature simply do not address the issue of intrinsic motivation and do not provide sufficient data to evaluate the comparative effects of programs involving the systematic use of rewards with comparable control conditions. The appearance of detrimental effects following the use of relatively long-term and demonstrably effective programs, when subsequent behavior has been observed in the absence of further social or material contingencies (Colvin, 1971; Greene et al., 1976; Johnson et al., 1976; Meichenbaum et al., 1968), further indicates that continued circumspection is warranted.

Conversely, the present literature on token economies seems equally unsupportive of the assertion that token economies, as employed in current research, will necessarily or frequently produce detrimental effects of the sort observed in the laboratory. Possibly, given appropriate measures and appropriate comparisons, such effects may prove more common than they presently appear. At the moment, however, we do not find evidence to support such a claim. Rather, we continue to find "nothing in the present line of reasoning or the present data to suggest that contracting to engage in an activity for an extrinsic reward will always, or even usually, result in a decrement in intrinsic interest in the activity" (Lepper, Greene, & Nisbett, 1973, p. 136). On the contrary, the appearance of both positive and negative effects of reward programs will depend upon the

---

[2]Attempts to ascertain directly subjects' perceptions of the context in which subsequent behavior is to be assessed may provide part of the answer (cf. Lepper & Greene, 1976). Because this sort of question is necessarily intrusive, however, this strategy also has obvious limitations.

specific manner and context of their application to particular problems, subjects, and situations.

Trends Toward Convergence

Thus far we have sought to draw a sharp contrast between two divergent approaches to the study of rewards. We have stressed the commonalities within each approach and have necessarily minimized differences among investigators and changes that have occurred over time within each of the traditions. At this point, however, we wish to step back and examine the extent to which these historically understandable differences might be reconciled in a more comprehensive model of human motivation.

In our view, a tentative basis for such a reconciliation is emerging in recent shifts in emphasis within both research traditions. In each area, an initial concern with the simple demonstration of beneficial or of detrimental effects seems to be giving way to a broader concern with the cognitive processes and attentional mechanisms that may underlie these effects and the conditions under which each of these effects will be likely to occur. In stressing the role of cognitive processes in mediating the reciprocal interaction between the subject and his or her environment, these trends reflect a basic restructuring of traditional questions. The search for models that capture the active, constructive, selective, and directive features of cognitive processes is apparent not only within the growing "cognitive" social learning or "cognitive" behavior modification movement (e.g., Bandura, 1974, 1977a, 1977b; Lazarus, 1977; Mahoney, 1974, 1977; Meichenbaum, 1977; Mischel, 1973) but also in recent developments in cognitive social psychology (e.g., Carroll & Payne, 1976; Fischhoff, 1976; Kruglanski, Hamel, Maides, & Schwartz, in press; Ross, 1977) and in cognitive approaches to more general motivational issues (Dember, 1974; Neisser, 1976; Weiner, 1972).

"Self-control" processes and "intrinsic" motivation.   Within the token economy literature, for example, the shift from a focal concern with demonstrations of functional control to a concern with the conditions that promote maintenance and/or generalization of treatment effects represents a significant transformation. On a procedural level, this concern has led to a markedly decreased reliance on single-group, intrasubject designs and a corresponding increase in comparative studies that assess the effects of treatment procedures relative to control conditions and to other possible treatment variations. On a theoretical level, this concern has been accompanied by an increased focus on the potential benefits of self-control or self-management techniques in which the "subjects" of a treatment program play a significant role in the construction, administration, and maintenance of that program. The use of techniques involving self-monitoring, self-imposed performance standards, and the self-administration of rewards and contingencies in applied settings has multiplied explosively within the last several years (Bandura, 1976; Mahoney, 1977; O'Leary, in press).

In the present context, the possibility for reconciliation of approaches offered by these recent trends lies primarily in the potential relationships between self-control processes and self-management skills, as discussed in the behavioral literature, and intrinsic motivation and self-directed learning, as discussed in the present volume. Though the precise translation of constructs between these frameworks represents a nontrivial problem, the general compatibility of these two positions seems reasonably clear. To the extent that a cognitive, social-learning analysis allows the possibility of the self as agent in the definition of contingencies, the imposition of goals and standards, and the definition and administration of rewards, it is possible to speak of issues of maintenance and generalization of behavior change in terms other than those involving only a description of the external environment. Clearly, this framework has proved amenable to discussions of processes involving perceived competence and control (Bandura, 1977b; Seligman, 1975), attributions concerning the causes of one's actions and outcomes (Mischel, 1973; Rotter, 1966), and the expected value of particular courses of action in the presence or absence of salient extrinsic contingencies (e.g., Bandura, 1977a; Mahoney, 1977; Mischel, 1973).

The interpolation of self-management procedures between the introduction and the eventual withdrawal of an externally imposed contingency system in order to achieve greater maintenance or generalization of behavior change (e.g., Brownell et al., 1977; Drabman et al., 1973; Turkewitz et al., 1975; Weiner & Dubanoski, 1975), for example, seems consistent with many of the theoretical formulations offered in this volume (Condry & Chambers, Chapter 4; Deci & Porac, Chapter 7; Lepper & Greene, Chapter 6). The apparent success of such techniques in producing increased persistence of behavior change, moreover, is notably paralleled by the finding that self-determined reward procedures may eliminate the detrimental effects of equivalent externally imposed procedures (Lepper, Sagotsky, & Greene, 1977b). Whether an analysis of these data in terms of the particular mechanisms considered in this volume will ultimately prove of use, of course, remains an open issue. Nevertheless, such findings illustrate the possible general compatibility of these initially divergent approaches.

Empirical parallels.   Relevant to this contention are several further empirical parallels that have emerged in the results within these two areas. Increasingly, it is becoming clear that the optimal conditions for producing persistent or generalized behavior change in applied settings are generally those least likely to yield detrimental effects in the laboratory. In a typical demonstration of the detrimental effects of reward, subjects are selected for their initial interest in the target activity, functionally "superfluous" rewards are offered to subjects contingent simply upon engagement in the activity, and subsequent behavior is observed in some distinctly different situation such that "withdrawal" of reward is abrupt rather than gradual. In fact, existing data suggest that a number of these characteristics are probably important preconditions for the demonstration of detrimental effects. For example, detrimental effects are less likely to occur when the activity is of low rather than high initial interest (Calder & Staw, 1975b; Upton, 1973), when the reward is made contingent upon success at the activity rather than on simple task engagement (Karniol & Ross, 1977), or when rewards are self-determined rather than externally imposed (Lepper et al., 1977b). Other characteristics such as the abrupt "withdrawal" of rewards have not been explored experimentally but would be predicted to increase the likelihood of detrimental effects compared to a more gradual "fading" procedure.

In a typical token economy, of course, reinforcement programs are applied to subject populations for whom the targeted behavior holds little inherent value; and frequently these programs are instituted in situations where other less powerful and less salient techniques of control have failed to produce behavior change. Within these constraints, however, recent reviews (Kazdin, 1975a; Kopel & Arkowitz, 1975; O'Leary, in press) have suggested that token programs will be most likely to produce persistent and general behavior change to the extent that the program: (a) provides subjects with reinforcement contingent upon successful performance; (b) is directed toward increasing the frequency of behavior patterns that may lead to the acquisition of new skills or responses that will be naturally reinforcing to subjects outside of the token program; (c) involves the gradual withdrawal of the token and back-up reinforcers; and (d) includes training of subjects in self-management or self-control techniques.[3] The parallels between these conclusions and those cited above with respect to *relative* predictions seem evident.

Boundary Conditions and Extrapolations

Taken together, these variables begin to define some of the boundary conditions that will determine the relative costs or benefits likely to accrue from the use of systematic reinforcement procedures. Differences of opinion appear likely, however, when one attempts to predict the absolute effects of a particular reinforcement program under conditions that overlap partially with the contexts in which beneficial effects and in which detrimental effects have been demonstrated. Unfortunately, it is precisely this issue of extrapolation to unexplored contexts that is likely to prove intractable to unequivocal, a priori analysis.

Again, the extreme cases should be reasonably clear. We doubt that any informed proponent of the approach forwarded in this book would gainsay, for example, the use of a systematic reinforcement program designed to reinforce back-ward patients for exhibiting responsible behavior patterns currently

---

[3]We are excluding from this discussion strategies that involve the explicit programming of the environment in which maintenance or generalization is measured (cf. Walker & Buckley, 1972), because this approach constitutes an escalation of, rather than an answer to, the underlying *conceptual* difficulty.

nonexistent in their hospital behavior (Ayllon & Azrin, 1965) or to induce chronic school dropouts to complete structured learning programs that may lead to their acquisition of basic reading skills (Cohen, 1968). Nor would thoughtful proponents of token economies typically recommend the use of elaborate payment systems to reinforce children for engaging in art activities or educational games that they already pursue with vigor and enthusiasm (O'Leary, Poulos, & Devine, 1972).

Questions arise, however, when the appropriate paradigm to which a given situation should be assimilated is not obvious. Should one institute a program, for instance, in which average school children are paid for successful completion of each homework assignment or are offered tokens for sitting quietly through each class period? In the absence of directly relevant data, the answer must depend on one's presuppositions and values. In fact, if the children in a particular class vary in their initial values, interests, and abilities, our own view is that an identical program will be likely to have very different costs and benefits for different individuals (Lepper & Dafoe, in press).

Of course, it is a natural tendency for one to extrapolate broadly from a particular paradigm to a general theory of behavior (e.g., Kuhn, 1970; Mahoney, 1976). Krantz (1971) has characterized this tendency as "conceptual imperialism" and has described the manner in which such extrapolation may lead investigators to a point where alternative viewpoints become literally "invisible." We believe that this predilection is a significant part of the history of the "hidden" costs of reward. Of course, this tendency is symmetric; therefore, we wish to emphasize our own view that a focus on these hidden costs should not be allowed to obscure the contexts in which rewards do have obvious and significant benefits.

A "Contextualist" Approach

This conclusion—that there are limits to the generality of any particular approach—has appeared throughout the present chapter as a set of interrelated, metatheoretical assumptions concerning the multiplicity of determinants, goals, and perspectives deemed relevant to the study of rewards and their effects. Thus, our argument may be viewed most generally as an appeal for a "contextualist" approach to the study of motivational processes and the effects of rewards on behavior (cf. Jenkins, 1974; Mischel, 1977). We have argued that both beneficial and detrimental effects of rewards are influenced by a variety of conceptually distinct factors; likewise, we have suggested that the study of such processes may be legitimately pursued with quite different theoretical or practical goals in mind. Consequently, there should be a number of perspectives on the study of rewards, each of which may prove useful, within particular contexts, in increasing our knowledge of the potential costs and benefits of reward programs.

In particular, it seems to us that a better understanding of how rewards affect behavior requires acknowledgment of the fact that the use of tangible rewards invariably occurs in a broader context of social exchange and control. This fact implies that the same activity will be differentially affected by the same reward as a function of how both the activity and the reward are construed (Kruglanski, Chapter 5; Lepper & Greene, Chapter 6; cf. Bandura, 1977b, pp. 200–202). In the case of activities, for example, solving a set of puzzles may be presented (or perceived) as a game ("I thought you might like to play with some puzzles."), a chore ("It's time to clean up your room and straighten up those puzzles."), or a test ("I'd like you to do these puzzles to evaluate your spatial discrimination skills."). In the case of reward, the same inducement may be presented (or perceived) as a bribe, as a bonus, or as fair remuneration depending on the extent to which the context makes salient such elements as the legitimacy of the reward, norms of equity, feedback about competence, and the degree to which the target of the inducement has been made "an offer he can't refuse," (cf. Folger, Rosenfield, & Hays, 1978). It is not at all clear how best to approach the study of "how both the activity and the reward are construed"; nor, indeed, is it clear that there is or should be a single "best" approach. But any viable theory of reward must be able to account for the kinds of broader contextual factors that lead investigators and subjects alike to interpret a particular episode in terms of one or another among the set of potentially appropriate "scripts" or schemata (Abelson, 1976; Rumelhart & Ortony, 1977).

The same point may be illustrated from a different perspective. Token economies typically presuppose a context in which reinforcement is under the control of an agent in a position of power or authority over the subject(s) of the program (Feshbach, 1976; Kazdin, 1976). In such contexts, it generally holds that the more salient, explicit, and powerful the agent makes the contingencies, the more effective the program will be (Kazdin, 1975a). Should it be assumed that this principle will apply across all other sorts of contexts?

Consider, for example, a reversal of the usual therapist-client, parent-child, or teacher-student relationship, in which a child is taught to use reinforcement principles to control a teacher's behavior. We know that the *subtle* use of contingent social approval by the child can be quite effective in this sort of a relationship in achieving changes in the teacher's behavior (Gray, Graubard, & Rosenberg, 1974.[4] But it does not follow that teaching the child to institute a more explicit system of tangible rewards would prove even more effective. On the

---

[4]Interestingly, the teacher–subjects whose behavior was modified in the course of these programs typically viewed the children running the program rather than themselves as having changed significantly. Of similar demonstrable effectiveness in this respect are techniques in which parents and children (or other parties of unequal power) mutually agree to participate in explicit, but reciprocal, behavioral-control "contracts" that require negotiated concessions on the part of both parties (e.g., Patterson, 1975).

contrary, we would expect the teacher's reaction to such a system to express the notion that the child's behavior was in violation of the rules typically implicit in the structure of teacher-student relationships. More generally, we would expect the same procedures to have different effects when they are consistent with mutually accepted constructions of a social context than when they depart noticeably from what people expect or are willing to tolerate. To the extent that contextual variables "interact" with reward procedures in these and other ways, one cannot assume the sort of generality for principles of reinforcement that a noncontextualist approach takes for granted. As Mischel (1977) has put the argument, in a more positive vein:

> The need to qualify generalizations about human behavior complicates life for the social scientist, but it does not prevent us from studying human affairs scientifically; it only dictates a respect for the complexity of the enterprise and alerts one to the dangers of oversimplifying the nature and causes of human behavior. [p. 247]

One of these dangers is that the hidden costs of reward will continue to be overlooked.

ACKNOWLEDGMENTS

Preparation of this chapter was supported in part by Research Grants MH-24134 from the National Institute of Mental Health and HD-MH-09814 from the National Institute of Child Health and Human Development. Development of the ideas presented in this paper was also facilitated by an Andrew Mellon Foundation Fellowship to the senior author. The authors wish to express their appreciation to Teresa Amabile, Janet Dafoe, and Lee Ross for their helpful comments and criticisms of an earlier version of this chapter.

REFERENCES

Abelson, R. P. Script processing in attitude formation and decision-making. In J. S. Carroll & J. W. Payne (Eds.), *Cognition and social behavior*. Hillsdale, N.J.: Lawrence Erlbaum Associates, 1976.

Ayllon, T., & Azrin, N. H. The measurement and reinforcement of behavior of psychotics. *Journal of the Experimental Analysis of Behavior,* 1965, *8*, 357–383.

Ayllon, T., & Azrin, N. *The token economy*. Englewood Cliffs, N.J.: Prentice–Hall, 1968.

Baer, D. M., Wolf, M. M., & Risley, T. R. Some current dimensions of applied behavior analysis. *Journal of Applied Behavior Analysis,* 1968, *1*, 91–97.

Bandura, A. Behavior theory and the models of man. *American Psychologist,* 1974, *29*, 859–869.

Bandura, A. Self-reinforcement: Theoretical and methodological considerations. *Behaviorism,* 1976, *4*, 135–155.

Bandura, A. *Social learning theory,* Englewood Cliffs, N.J.: Prentice-Hall, 1977. (a)

Bandura, A. Self-efficacy: Toward a unifying theory of behavioral change. *Psychological Review,* 1977, *84*, 191–215. (b)

Barrish, H. H., Saunders, M., & Wolf, M. M. Good behavior game: Effects of individual contingencies for group consequences on disruptive behavior in a classroom. *Journal of Applied Behavior Analysis*, 1969, *2*, 119–124.

Becker, W. C. *Parents are teachers*. Champaign, Illinois: Research Press, 1971.

Bem, D. J. Self-perception theory. In L. Berkowitz (Ed.), *Advances in experimental social psychology* (Vol. 6). New York: Academic Press, 1972.

Berlyne, D. E. *Conflict arousal and curiosity*. New York: McGraw–Hill, 1960.

Betancourt, F. W., & Zeiler, M. D. The choices and preferences of nursery school children. *Journal of Applied Behavior Analysis*, 1971, *4*, 299–304.

Birnbrauer, J. S., & Lawler, J. Token reinforcement for learning. *Mental Retardation*, 1964, *2*, 275–279.

Bornstein, P. H., & Hamilton, S. B. Comment: Token rewards and straw men. *American Psychologist*, 1975, *31*, 780–781.

Brehm, J. W. *A theory of psychological reactance*. New York: Academic Press, 1966.

Brownell, K., Colletti, G., Ersner–Hershfield, R., Hershfield, S. M., & Wilson, G. T. Self-control in school children: Stringency and leniency in self-determined and externally-imposed performance standards. *Behavior Therapy*, 1977, *8*, 442–455.

Burchard, J. D., & Tyler, V. O. The modification of delinquent behavior through operant conditioning. *Behavior Research and Therapy*, 1965, *2*, 245–250.

Bushell, D., Wrobel, P., & Michaelis, M. Applying ''group'' contingencies to the classroom study behavior of preschool children. *Journal of Applied Behavior Analysis*, 1968, *1*, 55–62.

Calder, B. J., & Staw, B. M. Interaction of intrinsic and extrinsic motivation: Some methodological notes. *Journal of Personality and Social Psychology*, 1975, *31*, 76–80. (a)

Calder, B. J., & Staw, B. M. Self-perception of intrinsic and extrinsic motivation. *Journal of Personality and Social Psychology*, 1975, *31*, 599–605. (b)

Carroll, J. S., & Payne, J. W. (Eds.). *Cognition and social behavior*. Hillsdale, N.J.: Lawrence Erlbaum Associates, 1976.

Cohen, H. L. Educational therapy: The design of learning environments. In J. H. Shlien (Ed.). *Research in psychotherapy*. Washington, D.C.: American Psychological Association, 1968.

Colvin, R. H. Imposed extrinsic reward in an elementary school setting: Effects on free-operant rates and choices. (Doctoral dissertation, Southern Illinois University, 1971). *Dissertation Abstracts International*. 1972, *32*, 5034–A.

Condry; J. Enemies of exploration: Self-initiated versus other-initiated learning. *Journal of Personality and Social Psychology*, 1977, *35*, 459–477.

Cronbach, L. J. The two disciplines of scientific psychology. *American Psychologist*, 1957, *12*, 671–684.

deCharms, R. *Personal causation*. New York: Academic Press, 1968.

Deci, E. L. Notes on the theory and metatheory of intrinsic motivation. *Organizational Behavior and Human Performance*, 1975, *15*, 130–145.

Dember, W. N. Motivation and the cognitive revolution. *American Psychologist*, 1974, *29*, 161–168.

Drabman, R. S., Spitalnik, R., & O'Leary, K. D. Teaching self-control to disruptive children. *Journal of Abnormal Psychology*, 1973, *82*, 10–16.

Feingold, B. D., & Mahoney, M. J. Reinforcement effects on intrinsic interest: Undermining the overjustification hypothesis. *Behavior Therapy*, 1975, *6*, 367–377.

Feshbach, S. The use of behavior modification procedures: A comment on Stolz et al. *American Psychologist*, 1976, *31*, 538–541.

Fischhoff, B. Attribution theory and judgment under uncertainty. In J. H. Harvey, W. J. Ickes, & R. F. Kidd (Eds.), *New directions in attribution research* (Vol. 1). Hillsdale, N.J.: Lawrence Erlbaum Associates, 1976.

Folger, R., Rosenfield, D., & Hays, R. P. Equity and intrinsic motivation: The role of choice. *Journal of Personality and Social Psychology*, 1978, in press.

Ford, J. D., & Foster, S. L. Comment: Extrinsic incentives and token-based programs (a re-evaluation). *American Psychologist*, 1976, *31*, 87–90.

Gray, F., Graubard, P. S., & Rosenberg, H. Little brother is changing you. *Psychology Today*, March 1974, 42–46.

Greene, D. Comment on Feingold and Mahoney's "Reinforcement effects on intrinsic interest: Undermining the overjustification hypothesis." *Behavior Therapy*, 1975, *6*, 712–714.

Greene, D., Sternberg, B., & Lepper, M. R. Overjustification in a token economy. *Journal of Personality and Social Psychology*, 1976, *34*, 1219–1234.

Heider, F. *The psychology of interpersonal relations.* New York: Wiley, 1958.

Hoppe, R. B. Comment: "Token" learning programs. *American Psychologist*, 1975, *31*, 781–782.

Hovland, C. I., Janis, I. L., & Kelley, H. H. *Communication and persuasion.* New Haven: Yale University Press, 1953.

Hunt, J. McV. *Intelligence and experience.* New York: Ronald Press, 1961.

Hunt, J. McV. Intrinsic motivation and its role in psychological development. *Nebraska Symposium on Motivation* (Vol. 13). Lincoln: University of Nebraska Press, 1965.

Jenkins, J. J. Remember that old theory of memory? Well, forget it! *American Psychologist*, 1974, *29*, 785–795.

Johnson, S. M., Bolstad, O. D., & Lobitz, G. K. Generalization and contrast phenomena in behavior modification with children. In E. J. Marsh, L. C. Handy, & L. A. Hamerlynck (Eds.), *Behavior modification and families.* New York: Bruner/Mazel, 1976.

Jones, R. T., & Kazdin, A. E. Programming response maintenance after withdrawing token reinforcement. *Behavior Therapy*, 1975, *6*, 153–164.

Karniol, R., & Ross, M. The effect of performance-relevant and performance-irrelevant rewards on children's intrinsic motivation. *Child Development*, 1977, *48*, 482–487.

Kazdin, A. E. The failure of some patients to respond to token programs. *Journal of Behavior Therapy and Experimental Psychiatry*, 1973, *4*, 7–14. (a)

Kazdin, A. E. Methodological and assessment considerations in evaluating reinforcement programs in applied settings. *Journal of Applied Behavior Analysis*, 1973, *6*, 517–531. (b)

Kazdin, A. E. Recent advances in token economy research. In M. Hersen, R. M. Eisler, & P. M. Miller (Eds), *Progress in behavior modification* (Vol. 1). New York: Academic Press, 1975. (a)

Kazdin, A. E. *Behavior modification in applied settings.* Homewood, Illinois: The Dorsey Press, 1975. (b)

Kazdin, A. E. The rich rewards of rewards. *Psychology Today*, November 1976, pp. 98, 101–102, 105, 114.

Kazdin, A. E., & Bootzin, R. R. The token economy: An evaluative review. *Journal of Applied Behavior Analysis*, 1972, *5*, 343–372.

Kazdin, A. E., & Polster, R. Intermittent token reinforcement and response maintenance in extinction. *Behavior Therapy*, 1973, *4*, 386–391.

Kelley, H. H. The processes of causal attribution. *American Psychologist*, 1973, *28*, 107–128.

Kelman, H. C. Compliance, identification, and internalization: Three processes of opinion change. *Journal of Conflict Resolution*, 1958, *2*, 51–60.

Kelman, H. C. Processes of attitude change. *Public Opinion Quarterly*, 1961, *25*, 57–78.

Kent, R. N., & O'Leary, K. D. A controlled evaluation of behavior modification with conduct problem children. *Journal of Consulting and Clinical Psychology*, 1976, *44*, 586–596.

Koch, S. Behavior as "intrinsically" regulated: Work notes towards a pre-theory of phenomena called "motivational." In M. R. Jones (Ed.), *Nebraska Symposium on Motivation* (Vol. 4). Lincoln: University of Nebraska Press, 1956.

Kopel, S. A., & Arkowitz, H. The role of attribution and self-perception in behavior change: Implications for behavior therapy. *Genetic Psychology Monographs*, 1975, *92*, 175–212.

Krantz, D. L., The separate worlds of operant and non-operant psychology, *Journal of Applied Behavior Analysis*, 1971, *4*, 61–70.

Kruglanski, A. W., Hamel, I. A., Maides, S. A., & Schwartz, J. M. Attribution theory as a special case of lay epistemology. In J. H. Harvey, W. J. Ickes, & R. F. Kidd (Eds.), *New directions in attribution research* (Vol. 2). Hillsdale, N.J.: Lawrence Erlbaum Associates, in press.

Krumboltz, J. D., & Krumboltz, H. B. *Changing children's behavior.* Englewood Cliffs, N.J.: Prentice–Hall, Inc., 1972.

Kuhn, T. S. *The structure of scientific revolutions.* (Second Edition) Chicago: University of Chicago Press, 1970.

Lazarus, A. A. Has behavior therapy outlived its usefulness? *American Psychologist, 1977, 32,* 550–554.

Lepper, M. R. Dissonance, self perception, and honesty in children. *Journal of Personality and Social Psychology, 1973, 25,* 65–74.

Lepper, M. R., & Dafoe, J. Incentives, constraints, and motivation in the classroom: An attributional analysis. In I. Frieze, D. Bar-Tal, & J. Carroll (Eds.), *Attribution theory: Applications to social problems.* San Francisco: Jossey-Bass, in press.

Lepper, M. R., & Greene, D. On understanding "overjustification": A reply to Reiss and Sushinsky. *Journal of Personality and Social Psychology, 1976, 33,* 25–35.

Lepper, M. R., Greene, D., & Nisbett, R. E. Undermining children's intrinsic interest with extrinsic rewards: A test of the overjustification hypothesis. *Journal of Personality and Social Psychology, 1973, 23,* 239–137.

Lepper, M. R., Sagotsky, G., & Greene, D. Overjustification effects following multiple-trial reinforcement procedures: Experimental evidence concerning the assessment of intrinsic interest. Unpublished manuscript, Stanford University, 1977. (a)

Lepper, M. R., Sagotsky, G., & Greene, D. Effects of choice and self-imposed vs. externally-imposed contingencies on children's subsequent intrinsic motivation. In preparation, Stanford University, 1977. (b)

Levine, F. M., & Fasnacht, G. Token rewards may lead to token learning. *American Psychologist, 1974, 29,* 816–820.

Levine, F., & Fasnacht, G. Comment: Extrinsic incentives and token-based programs (a re-evaluation). *American Psychologist, 1976, 31,* 90–92.

Lewin, K., Lippett, R., & White, R. Patterns of aggressive behavior in experimentally created "social climates." *Journal of Social Psychology, 1939, 10,* 271–299.

London, P. The end of ideology in behavior modification. *American Psychologist, 1972, 27,* 913–920.

Mahoney, M. J. *Cognition and behavior modification.* Cambridge: Ballinger Publishing Company, 1974.

Mahoney, M. J. *Scientist as subject: The psychological imperative.* Cambridge: Ballinger Publishing Co., 1976.

Mahoney, M. J. Reflections on the cognitive-learning trend in psychotherapy. *American Psychologist, 1977, 32,* 5–13.

McLaughlin, T. F., & Malaby, J. Intrinsic reinforcers in a classroom token economy. *Journal of Applied Behavior Analysis, 1972, 5,* 263–270.

Medland, M. B., & Stachnik, T. J. Good-behavior game: A replication and systematic analysis. *Journal of Applied Behavior Analysis, 1972, 5,* 45–51.

Meichenbaum, D. H. *Cognitive-behavior modification.* New York: Plenum Press, 1977.

Meichenbaum, D. H., Bowers, K. S., & Ross, R. R. Modification of classroom behavior of institutionalized female adolescent offenders. *Behavior Research and Therapy,* 1968, *6,* 343–353.

Mischel, W. Towards a cognitive social learning reconceptualization of personality. *Psychological Review, 1973, 80,* 252–283.

Mischel, W. On the future of personality measurement. *American Psychologist, 1977, 4,* 246–254.

Neisser, U. *Cognition and reality.* San Francisco: W. H. Freeman, 1976.

O'Leary, K. D. Token reinforcement programs in the classroom. In T. Brigham & C. Catania (Eds.),

The analysis of behavior: Social and educational processes. New York: Irvington–Naiburg/ Wiley, in press.

O'Leary, K. D., & Becker, W. C. Behavior modification of an adjustment class: A token reinforcement program. *Exceptional Children,* 1967, *33,* 639–642.

O'Leary, K. D., Becker, W. C., Evans, M. B., & Saudargas, R. A. A token reinforcement program in a public school: A replication and systematic analysis. *Journal of Applied Behavior Analysis,* 1969, *2,* 3–13.

O'Leary, K. D., & Drabman, R. Token reinforcement programs in the classroom: A review. *Psychological Bulletin,* 1971, *75,* 379–398.

O'Leary, K. D., Drabman, R. S., & Kass, R. E. Maintenance of appropriate behavior in a token program. *Journal of Abnormal Child Psychology,* 1973, *1,* 127–138.

O'Leary, K. D., Poulos, R. W., & Devine, V. T. Tangible reinforcers: Bonuses or bribes? *Journal of Consulting and Clinical Psychology,* 1972, *38,* 1–8.

Patterson, G. R. *Families: Applications of social learning to family life.* Champaign, Illinois: Research Press, 1975.

Reiss, S., & Sushinsky, L. W. Overjustification, competing responses, and the acquisition of intrinsic interest. *Journal of Personality and Social Psychology,* 1975, *31,* 1116–1125. (a)

Reiss, S., & Sushinsky, L. W. Comment: Undermining *extrinsic* interest. *American Psychologist,* 1975, *31,* 782–783. (b)

Rosenbaum, A., O'Leary, K. D., & Jacob, R. G. Behavioral intervention with hyperactive children: Group consequences as a supplement to individual contingencies. *Behavior Therapy,* 1975, *6,* 315–323.

Rosenhan, D. Some origins of concern for others. In P. A. Mussen, J. Langer, & M. Covington (Eds.), *Trends and issues in development psychology.* New York: Holt, Rinehart & Winston, 1969.

Ross, L. The intuitive psychologist and his shortcomings: Distortions in the attribution process. In L. Berkowitz (Eds.), *Advances in experimental social psychology* (Vol. 10). New York: Academic Press, 1977.

Ross, R., Meichenbaum, D., & Bowers, K. A brief summary of a case history of a correctional institution: Innovative treatment programs for delinquents. Unpublished manuscript, University of Waterloo, 1974.

Rotter, J. B. Generalized expectancies for internal versus external control of reinforcement. *Psychological Monographs,* 1966, *80* (Whole No. 609).

Rumelhart, D. W., & Ortony, A. The representation of knowledge in memory. In R. C. Anderson, R. J. Spiro, & W. E. Montague (Eds.), *Schooling and the acquisition of knowledge.* Hillsdale, N.J.: Lawrence Erlbaum Associates, 1977.

Scott, W. E. The effects of extrinsic rewards on "intrinsic motivation": A critique. *Organizational Behavior and Human Performance,* 1975, *15,* 117–129.

Sears, R. R., Whiting, J. W. M., Nowlis, V., & Sears, P. S. Some childrearing antecedents of aggression and dependency in young children. *Genetic Psychology Monographs,* 1953, *47,* 135–234.

Seligman, M. E. P. *Helplessness.* San Francisco: W.H. Freeman and Co., 1975.

Sidman, M. *Tactics of scientific research.* New York: Basic Books, 1960.

Surratt, P. R., Ulrich, R. E., & Hawkins, R. P. An elementary student as a behavioral engineer. *Journal of Applied Behavior Analysis,* 1969, *2,* 85–92.

Turkewitz, H., O'Leary, K. D., & Ironsmith, M. Producing generalization of appropriate behavior through self-control. *Journal of Consulting and Clinical Psychology,* 1975, *43,* 577–583.

Upton, W. E. Altruism, attribution, and intrinsic motivation in the recruitment of blood donors. (Doctoral dissertation, Cornell University, 1973). *Dissertation Abstracts International,* 1974, *34,* 6260–B.

Walker, H. M., & Buckley, N. K. Programming generalization and maintenance of treatment effects across time and across settings. *Journal of Applied Behavior Analysis,* 1972, *5,* 209–224.

Weiner, B. *Theories of motivation: From mechanism to cognition.* Chicago: Markham, 1972.

Weiner, H. R., & Dubanoski, R. A. Resistance to extinction as a function of self or externally determined schedules of reinforcement. *Journal of Personality and Social Psychology,* 1975, *31,* 905–910.

White, R. W. Motivation reconsidered: The concept of competence. *Psychological Review,* 1959, *66,* 297–333.

Winett, R. A., & Winkler, R. C. Current behavior modification in the classroom: Be still, be quiet, be docile. *Journal of Applied Behavior Analysis,* 1972, *5,* 499–504.

Woodworth, R. S. *Dynamics of behavior.* New York: Holt, 1958.

Zifferblatt, S. M. *Improving study and homework behaviors.* Champaign, Illinois: Research Press Company, 1970.

Author Index

Numbers in *italics* refer to the pages on which the complete references are listed.

Subject Index